THE SKINNY ABOUT
BEST BOYS, DOLLIES,
GREEN ROOMS, LEADS,
and other MEDIA LINGO

THE SKINNY ABOUT BEST BOYS, DOLLIES, GREEN ROOMS, LEADS, and other MEDIA LINGO

[THE LANGUAGE OF THE MEDIA]

by Richard Weiner

EDITED BY CHARLES M. LEVINE

RANDOM HOUSE REFERENCE

NEW YORK   TORONTO   LONDON   SYDNEY   AUCKLAND

Portions of this book originally appeared in *Webster's New World Dictionary of Media and Communications* (1996); permission granted by John Wiley & Sons, Inc.; and the author's columns in *Tactics* (permission granted by the Public Relations Society of America), and *The Editorial Eye* (permission granted by EEI Press).

Please address inquiries about electronic licensing of any products for use on a network, in software, or on CD-ROM to the Subsidiary Rights Department, Random House Information Group, fax 212-572-6003.

This book is available at special discounts for bulk purchases for sales promotions or premiums. Special editions, including personalized covers, excerpts of existing books, and corporate imprints, can be created in large quantities for special needs. For more information, write to Random House, Inc., Special Markets/Premium Sales, 1745 Broadway, MD 6-2, New York, NY 10019 or e-mail *specialmarkets@randomhouse.com*.

Library of Congress Cataloging-in-Publication Data is available.

Visit the Random House Reference Web site: *www.randomwords.com*

Design by Nora Rosansky

ISBN-13: 978-0-375-72147-2
ISBN-10: 0-375-72147-9

Printed in the United States of America

10 9 8 7 6 5 4 3 2 1

CONTENTS

Essays

INTRODUCTION

*W*e are all exposed to a dazzling array of slang and technical terms used by people who work in the media. Even five-year-olds know such words as *billboard, commercial, DVD, DJ, fast forward, iPod, theme song,* and *videotape.*

When we go to the movies, we see in the film credits mentions of *best boy, cinematographer, clapper/loader, dolly grip, Foley editor,* and *gaffer.* Broadcasters on TV may mention a *bird, bite, crawl, cue, feed, green room, standupper,* and *teleprompter.* Interviews of journalists and writers (the *Today Show* has a producer who *books* only authors) often include *beat, blurb, dateline, freelancer, masthead,* and *scoop.* When we go to a theater, we may see the *catwalk, flats, flies, Fresnel lights, gobo, props,* and *scrim,* but we won't see the *wings.*

Media include numerous communications channels: notably books, film, the Internet, magazines, newspapers, radio, television, and theater. People in advertising, journalism, public relations, and telecommunications must know the jargon of their media fields and of related fields such as photography, printing, and show business.

The skinny in this book is not for dieters, but for the more than one million students in mass communications and allied fields, and the millions more who are aspirants, novices, and aficionados. Most important, it is for all of us who live in this multimedia era, particularly word buffs, writers, and fans who delight in the behind-the-scenes jargon of disc jockeys and TV programs about media, such as *Entertainment Tonight* and *Curb Your Enthusiasm*, or magazines such as *People, Star, Us,* and *OK!*

Skinny is slang for inside information, the actual facts, confidential news, or gossip, as in, "What's the skinny on…?" The word, which probably refers to "getting down to the bare skin," has been used by sports reporters and others for more than seventy years.

Lingo means jargon or the specialized language of a field, ranging from gangsters to academics. In an attempt to keep this book wieldy (the opposite of *unwieldy*), I omitted computer jargon, with a few exceptions. Several excellent dictionaries are devoted to computerese, so my goal had been to define bits (as in a "bit part in a play") and bites (as in *sound bites*), not digital bytes. The lingo in this book is American, used around the world, plus a few British terms.

Almost everyone still sees and hears what today is called the *mainstream media*—like newsprint, film, and TV, which predate the digital age. Much of the jargon of film, newspapers, and other major media is used in their digital counterparts. Teenagers spend hours everyday on e-mail and cell phones, but they also watch lots of TV, go to the movies, listen to radio, and enjoy other traditional media. Podcasting, online broadcasting via iPods and similar devices, has become so popular that most consider it mainstream. And, the jargon of the radio, television, and recording industries still is used in podcasting.

This book is a roadmap to help you find your way through the daily labyrinth of media lingo. Now when you listen to a radio program, watch a TV show, or leave a theater, you'll no longer have to guess about some of the jargon. Our fast-changing communications environment (called *media ecology*) includes whirling from one medium to another. Our culture insists that we keep up with slang language.

To further inform you, almost all of the full names in the chapters are followed by the person's life dates: year of birth and, if no longer living, the year of death: standard dictionary style. If still living, b. means born.

I wrote *Webster's New World Dictionary of Media and Communications* (first edition, 1990, second edition, 1996; I acquired the rights from then-current publisher, John Wiley & Sons). That was the starting point of this book, plus several years of collecting books and articles; and hundreds of Internet searches, e-mails, and phone conversations with librarians and others.

There are 27 chapters. You can read them in any order. Here are a few highlights.

- Theatrical terms, including *catwalk*, *flies*, *gobo*, *house seats*, *wings*, and other parts of a theater.

- Film credits, including initials after a name, such as ASC (American Society of Cinematographers), or titles, such as ADR editors (automatic dialogue replacement). The film chapter includes *focus puller* and other job titles that appear in British films; the required sequence of the credits in a film or in an ad; and film language, such as *Roll it*! *Action*! *Makeup*! *Cut*! *That's a wrap*! and *Take five*! One of my favorite jobs is the *Foley editor*. DVDs of films often have commentaries by the director and others who use lingo.

- Broadcasting lingo, including the call letters of stations and why a few are three while most are four letters. How Clear Channel Communications (the nation's largest owner of radio stations) got its name. The names of the broadcast networks and more than forty cable channels. You may be a viewer of A&E, CNBC, C-Span, FX, MSNBC, and QVC, but not know their full names. Plus Peacock Network, Tiffany Network, The Eye, and other nicknames.

- Journalism terms, including *beat*, *dateline*, *dead-line* (from a Civil War prison), *extra*, *jump*, *mast-head* (some journalists and PR people use the term incorrectly), *pennysaver*, *reefer*, and *rewrite*.

- Sports lingo, inspired by baseball, basketball, football, golf, hockey, and other sports terms that are used off the sports pages. You'll hit a *grand slam* if you know the origin of *birdie*, *hat trick*, *Hail Mary*, and *par*.

A bar bet: Which word has more pages devoted to it than any other in the *Oxford English Dictionary* (or as lexicographers and librarians call it, the OED)? The answer is *set*, a common word in film, photography, printing, television, and other media.

Take, a word that rivals *set* for most space in standard dictionaries, is a multimedia term: film (a scene or shot); journalism (a version, as of an article); show business (total amount of money taken in an event); theater (a re-action; a double take is two reactions); and TV (a direction to move from one camera or source to another). *Cut* also is a multimedia term: journalism (a photo or artwork); recording (one song on a record or CD); and TV (instruction to end a scene).

Well, I hope that you'll now dip into this smorgasbord and enjoy it as much as I enjoyed preparing it. I've always been a media buff. I still have some of my compositions (as short stories were called in elementary school). I got my first byline as editor of the annual magazine at James Madison High School in Brooklyn, New York. I was a movie reviewer at the University of Wisconsin *Daily Cardinal,* and then was a science reporter at station WISC in Madison, Wisconsin. One of my programs, the first to broadcast a description of an actual childbirth, was distributed by Capitol Records. I was a public relations consultant in New York for many years, first at Ruder & Finn, then at my own firm (Richard Weiner, Inc., launched the Cabbage Patch Kids, which became part of our language), and then at Porter Novelli.

I wrote more than twenty public relations and media reference books, including *Professional's Guide to Public Relations Services* (Prentice-Hall for the first editions, and then Amacom) and *Webster's New World Dictionary of Media and Communications.* For many years, I wrote my books at home, at night and early in the morning. My daughters, Jessica and Stephanie, became accustomed to seeing me working in blue pajamas.

I received the Gold Anvil from the Public Relations Society of America, the highest award to an individual in the public relations field. For many years, I have written a column about media jargon in *Tactics*, the monthly publication of the Society, and some of the material in this book is excerpted from these columns. (Reprinted with permission from the Public Relations Society of America, *www.prsa.org*).

I also write a column about media jargon in *The Editorial Eye*, a publication for writers and editors published by EEI Press. (Excerpts from these columns are reprinted with the permission of EEI Press, Alexandria, Virginia, *www.eeicom.com*).

Finally, the obligatory section of acknowledgments, which in this case is really a pleasure. I appreciate the helpfulness of the telephone reference librarians, particularly in New York and Miami. My search engine is Google and I have used it hundreds of times.

Charles Levine is a multitalented person who has been my partner in this project as both my literary agent and personal editor. Jena Pincott and Rahel Lerner were my in-house editors and champions of this project at Random House, and Julia Penelope was the talented copyeditor. Zena Bernstein is my longtime assistant in production. My marriage partner, Florence (I call her Chick) Weiner, also a book author, provided advice, encouragement, and love. To all, thank you!

Technical details about this book. The punctuation and other style is mostly in accord with the *Chicago Manual of Style* (University of Chicago Press). Key media terms have been set in italics when first discussed or explained; and related terms within double quotation marks. The text is ITC Century Light, the sidebars are NewsGothic, the chapter titles are Bellamie, and the index is ITC Century Light. The italicized and related terms are listed in the index.

I hope that this book will have a second edition so that I can make corrections and updates. I invite you to send criticisms and comments, and perhaps compliments, to me c/o Random House Reference, Random House, Inc., 1745 Broadway, New York, NY 10019.

Now, the last word from this wordwise logophile: If I had to choose my favorite words, the list would include *dingbat*, *MacGuffin* (hint: Alfred Hitchcock used it in his films), *royalty*, *George Spelvin*, and *spinach demand*.

ADVERTISING: HAVE YOU SEEN THE COMMERCIAL ABOUT...?

THESE days, advertising is ubiquitous. We live in a world awash in ads. They confront us in elevators and restrooms; on top of taxicabs; and even overhead on banners towed by planes, or plastered on lumbering dirigibles, or sketched in the clouds by skywriters. Print, broadcast, and other media, including the Internet, carry advertisements promoting products, services, political candidates, and issues, or just information. Many consumers enjoy and appreciate advertising, particularly commercials that are zany or have special effects akin to major theatrical films. Slogans such as "the pause that refreshes" and "a Kodak moment" have become part of our language, along with advertising icons like the Marlboro Man. In fact, advertising is so commonplace that the word is also now used to mean "to make known," "call attention to," or "announce." An estimated $140 billion is spent annually on advertising in major media in the United States.

Advertisers buy *time* in broadcast media and *space* in print and other media. An in-house *advertising department* or an outside *advertising agency* creates the ads. Advertising ranges from "soft-sell" to "hard-sell." The former, sometimes called "institutional" or "image" advertising, is designed to create goodwill for a company or organization, whereas the latter aggressively promotes a product or other entity. An ad agency generally receives a 15 percent commission of the gross amount charged by the media, though many agencies now work for a fee in addition to or instead of a commission. The purchase order sent from the advertiser or its agency to the media is an *insertion order*.

Advertising lingo includes hundreds of specialized terms; some are so common that they crop up in everyday language. Children know that a *commercial* is a message paid for by a company or other sponsor for broadcasting on radio or TV. A *thirty* is a 30-second commercial, written as *:30*. A *straight commercial* is broadcast during an interruption in the programming (a *commercial break*), whereas an *integrated commercial* is delivered by the talent within a program, as by a disc jockey or announcer. A *commercial pod* is a group of radio or TV advertisements, generally bunched together in a two-minute segment, or "pod."

Public radio and TV stations, sometimes called "noncommercial," now air credits that include brief commercials from supporting companies, foundations, individuals, and other contributors.

Advertising even comes right to our door. *Direct marketing* distributes, promotes, and sells via one or more media directly linking the seller and buyer to elicit a direct response. A "direct marketer" can be a catalog company, manufacturer, or retailer. Direct marketers generally use a variety of techniques, such as door-to-door selling, media inserts, mail order, and telemarketing. Direct marketing has expanded and diversified in recent years, and many department stores and other retailers now sell via catalogs and other direct-marketing techniques.

A *lift letter*, a small memo in a direct mail solicitation, usually has an attention-getting line, such as "A once-in-a-lifetime offer," to encourage, or lift, the reader and to increase, or lift, the response—for a double lift—not to be confused with a *ding letter*, a downer or rejection. *Junk mail* is direct-mail advertising and other unsolicited material. Many customers use it as a derogatory term; however, advertising writers abhor the usage. Direct marketers also like to enclose a short, punchy message in a *Johnson box*, a rectangular outline (usually drawn with a series of asterisks). In 1941, Frank Johnson (1912-2001), a direct mail copywriter, created the box that informs the reader about the letter.

Well-known door-to-door, or in-home companies, such as Amway, Avon, and Tupperware, have expanded direct selling with armies of highly motivated, self-employed representatives.

"Mail order" is an old-fashioned term, as it now includes catalogs that are mailed or inserted in newspapers or promoted on radio and television; while the products can be ordered by phone (usually via a toll-free 800 number) or on the Internet, and, less frequently, by mail. *Mail order houses*, such as Lands' End (have you noticed the apostrophe comes after the *s*?), are highly respected; whereas *telemarketers*, who solicit via telephone, often are considered annoying, especially at dinnertime.

Out-of-home advertising, formerly called "outdoor advertising," is found everywhere—on billboards, car cards, posters, streets, buildings, shelters, and terminals. *Transit advertising* appears inside or outside buses, subway trains, and other vehicles.

A *billboard* (a "bill" is a public notice) consists of a panel or sign for the display of advertising on highways or in other public places; and also means the advertisement itself. Originally called a "show-board," it explains the name of *Billboard*, the renowned trade publication of the music and entertainment industries. A *baby billboard* is a car card, mounted inside or outside a bus, train, or other vehicle. A *billboard pass* is a free ticket to a show, given to a retailer or other person in return for displaying a poster in a store or other venue.

A *one-sheet* poster consists of a single sheet, 28 or 30 inches wide and 42 or 46 inches high, commonly used in movie theaters and on subway and railroad platforms. Larger sizes are called "two-sheet," "four-sheet," "eight-sheet" (about 5 feet high and 11 feet wide, a popular junior-size for an out-of-home advertising poster panel), and "30-sheet" (the standard outdoor advertising poster, about 23 feet wide and 10 feet high). Posters originally consisted of several separate sheets, but now they usually have a small number of larger sheets. Vinyl posters now are more common than paper.

In broadcasting, a *billboard* conveys the opening or closing credits, or announces a forthcoming program or segment, as on a news or interview program; or carries an announcement (perhaps unpaid) related to a sponsor or advertiser, such as, "This portion of the program is brought to you by . . ."

An *advertising specialty*, a handy or decorative item used to promote a company or product, is generally low in cost and given away free, like a cap, calendar, T-shirt, key chain, matchbook, pen, or other common or novel item. The name, logo (symbol), or message of the advertiser or donor is usually imprinted on an advertising specialty. The medium itself is called "specialty advertising."

A *premium* is an item of value offered free or at a re-duced price as an incentive to purchase a product or ser-vice. You've seen them inside of, or affixed to, boxes and promoted in direct mail and other advertising. An "ad-vance premium" is given before a purchase is made, in the hope of inducing a purchase. A "referral premium" is a product or other incentive provided to someone who refers a new customer.

Major job titles in advertising include account execu-tive, art director, copywriter, and creative director. An *ac-count executive* (AE), or account exec, at an ad agency or other firm maintains contact with the client, does the basic work, and coordinates with everyone at the agency who is working on the advertisement or promotion, as-sisted by an *assistant account executive* and managed by an *account group supervisor*. An *art director* creates or supervises creation of the graphics, photography, and other art. The *copywriter* creates or supervises the writ-ing. A *creative director* develops the advertising and marketing concepts, as distinguished from accounting, production, and other so-called noncreative people.

The two largest companies that own advertising agencies are the Omnicom Group and WPP Group. The Omnicom name comes from *omni*, which means "all," and *com*, short for "communications." Headquartered in New York, Omnicom owns BBDO; DDB (the initials come from the legendary agency, Doyle, Dane & Bernbach); TBWA; and other companies, including four major public relations firms, Brodeur, Fleishman-Hillard, Ketchum, and Porter Novelli. (Full disclosure department: My company, Richard Weiner, Inc., merged with Porter Novelli, Inc., in 1986.)

The WPP Group, headquartered in London, is the second largest. The name is derived from Wire and Plastic Products, a British manufacturer of wire shopping baskets. WPP owns Grey Advertising; Ogilvy & Mather; JWT (formerly J. Walter Thompson, one of America's first advertising agencies, started in 1864); and Y&R (formerly Young & Rubicam); and other companies, including three major public relations firms, Burson-Marsteller, Hill & Knowlton, and Ogilvy.

Back to advertising jargon. A manufacturer or wholesaler may pay an *advertising allowance* to a retailer for advertising (placed by the retailer) of the product. The fee may be deducted from the amount the retailer pays for the merchandise rather than paid directly to the retailer. It's also called a "promotion allowance" or "merchandise allowance." *Cooperative advertising*, or *co-op*, is the sharing of the cost of an ad between a manufacturer, publisher, or other supplier and its retailer. Common examples are supermarket ads and circulars.

An *advertising banner* is a headline, usually in a newspaper or magazine, under which advertisements are grouped by category, such as "Antique Dealers" or "Country Inns." A bannered advertising page has one or more categories of related ads. *Advertising pages* indicate the number of pages of advertisements in a publication for a single issue or over a period of time, such as one year. Adding together fractions of pages, the total number represents the entire advertising content (the portion of a publication devoted to advertising), expressed as pages or as the total number of lines ("linage") or as a percentage of the contents. *A/E* denotes this ratio of advertising to editorial (news and other nonadvertising) in a publication.

An *advertorial*, an advertisement written in an editorial style, can occupy a page or less, or several pages, for example, as a supplement (in a newspaper or magazine) with ad copy that resembles articles. An *infomercial* in an audio or video segment provides advertising (a commercial) with information. You've seen these promotions for such items as cooking equipment, exercise devices, and self-help workshops. They often are packed in hour-long programs, with frequent listings of 800 numbers, usually on cable channels but also on broadcast stations.

Advertisers rely heavily on *market research* to study the demands or desires of consumers, or other segments of the public, in relation to actual or potential products and services. Perhaps you've participated in a *focus group*: a small number of people selected to discuss a topic or product to reveal their attitudes and opinions. The client observes from an adjacent room, behind a mirror that is reflective on one side and transparent on the other. It's called a "one-way" or "two-way mirror," which can be confusing. The point is that the observers can see the participants but the participants can't see the observers. These mirrors also are used in police stations, as when a victim or witness tries to identify a person in a lineup.

ACNielson, the world's largest market research company, headquartered in Schaumburg, Illinois (near Chicago), was formed in 1934 by Arthur C. Nielsen (1897–1980). Note the unusual spelling of the company name, without periods or spaces. More important is what the company does: audit products in stores (about 170,000!), using on-site observations and scanning data from cash registers, to report to manufacturers and retailers on retail inventories, brand distribution, retail prices, product displays, and other aspects of sales performance and market share (percentage of sales, in dollars or units, of a brand in a category of products or services).

ACNielsen was acquired in 2001 by Dutch conglomerate VNU (Verenigde Nederlandse Uitgeversbedrijven, or United Dutch Publishing Companies), which also owns other market research companies, business publications, Nielsen Media Research (described in "Broadcasting"), and manages trade shows. Another Nielsen company tracks box office receipts at movie theaters.

In 1995, VNU acquired Standard Rate & Data Service, Inc. (SRDS), a unique publisher of reference books of advertising rates. Headquartered in Haarlem, The Netherlands, VNU operates in more than one hundred countries.

Advertisers like to work primarily with *mass media*, such as newspapers, magazines, radio, and TV stations, that reach large audiences, in contrast to newsletters and other media that are more specialized. A *mass magazine* targets a general audience, as distinct from a *class magazine* aimed at a more specialized audience. Other magazines include a special-interest magazine, a trade publication that deals with specific industries, a business publication, and a professional journal.

Advertisers purchase broadcast time based on various criteria, particularly *rating points*, the size of a radio or TV audience. *Accumulated audience* consists of the total number of individuals reached by a broadcast or publication over a specified period of time. It's also called "cume" or "reach," and represents the net unduplicated audience. *Reach and frequency* (R&F or R/F) are the total impressions (reach) and how often they are published or broadcast (frequency).

For example, consider a weekly TV program watched by ten million people: Fifty percent of the audience watches it twice during a four-week period, while 50 percent watches it only once. Thus, its cume or reach during a four-week period is ten million times two (totaling twenty million) plus ten million times one, so that the cumulative audience is thirty million.

Spot advertising is time purchased on an individual basis, different from a purchase on a multistation network or other national venue. The "first spot" opens a show, the "last spot" closes it, and a "wild spot" appears during station breaks (between programs). *Break position* is a commercial broadcast between programs (at the break) instead of within a program. It's usually a local commercial and also is called an "adjacency." *Spot buyers* buy time on local stations, as indicated on a "spot schedule."

Local spot advertising is so extensive that local station advertising in general is called "spot radio" or "spot TV." A sixty-second radio spot can cost anywhere from a few dollars to several hundred dollars, or more, depending on the station, time of day, and volume contract discount. A thirty-second TV spot can cost several thousand dollars. A network commercial can cost one hundred thousand dollars or more (for one commercial!) for the time plus the production cost.

Upfront is the time in the spring when advertisers negotiate network commercial time prior to the start of the fall season. Advertising bought during the fall season is called the "scatter market" (it's scattered, as compared to a single buy).

The popularity of TV programs is indicated by their *rating points*, as determined by Nielsen Media Research, which provides meters to a sample of households (Nielsen homes). Viewers are familiar with these figures, as they are published in newspapers and magazines. A *rating* is a percent of the TV households or persons watching a specific program or station. One rating point translates to more than one million homes. *Share* represents the number of viewers as a percentage of households or homes with TV sets in use at the time. A popular prime-time program on a broadcast network could have a "rating/share" of 15.4/23, which means about 16.9 million households watched the program (based on one rating point representing about 1.1 million households) or 23 percent of the households with TV sets in use at that time. The top-rated program each year usually is the Super Bowl, with a rating of more than forty.

Radio audiences are measured by Arbitron (formerly American Research Bureau).

Advertisers and their agencies are focused on their target audiences, and the demographics of different programs and channels vary considerably. For example, the *cost-per-thousand* (CPM; the roman numeral for one thousand is M) for a 30-second spot on late-night programs oriented to young men (eighteen to thirty-four years old) could be about seventy dollars on broadcast TV and about fifty dollars on cable TV.

In print media, the cost is calculated by column inches, with discounts for total size of the ad, total volume in a year, and other factors, such as national rate (higher than local, retail rate) and section of the publication. One column inch in *The New York Times* costs about seven hundred dollars (gross; the net rate is 15 percent less, after deducting the agency commission), but the cost range is considerable; entertainment ads cost much less than ads in the main news section. At *Time* magazine, the card rate for a one-time, black-and-white, full-page ad is about $130,000. Some media sell at discounted ("off-the-card") rates.

DMA (Designated Market Area) is a Nielsen Media Research term for a group of counties in which a TV station obtains the greatest portion of its audience. The "DMA Rating" is the percentage of homes within the area viewing an individual station during a particular time period.

Advertising, marketing, and public relations people often set up campaigns in specific DMAs. Of the 210 DMAs in the United States, 001 comprises New York City, Long Island, and several counties north of New York City and in northern New Jersey; while DMA 210 covers the entire state of Montana.

If you are job or house hunting, peruse the *classified advertisements* (or "classifieds" for short) in newspapers. These brief listings usually contain all text set in single columns. Larger ads, usually with art, are *display advertisements*. A *tombstone ad*, common in business sections of newspapers, is an all-text ad announcing a stock offering or other information that meets legal requirements. It's generally dull looking and lifeless; hence the name. A *blind ad*, such as a classified ad with a box number, is unsigned.

Business-to-business advertising (B-to-B, or B2B) is advertising of a business product or service to a business audience. *Consumer advertising* is intended for the general public.

Advertisers use hundreds of slang and technical terms in their work with artists, media, photographers, printers, researchers, and others. Some of this lingo is discussed elsewhere in this book, but here are a few of my favorites.

Wonder Bread describes an ad or other work that is bland. The first Wonder Bread was baked in Indianapolis in 1925. "White bread" and "vanilla" are other synonyms for bland.

To *massage* is to revise and revitalize an ad. Similarly, to *punch up* is to add vigor. A *logo*, or logotype, is a unique name, signature, symbol, or trademark that identifies the advertiser. A logo originally was a word or name set as a single piece of type or on a single metal plate. A *bulletin*, a very large outdoor advertisement, can be painted ("paint bulletin") or on paper ("pasted bulletin"). A prime location, or *100 percent location*, is the best possible site for an outdoor advertisement.

Branded entertainment is the insertion of a product such as a Starbucks thermos or a bottle of Coca Cola (with its name visible) or other item, such as a poster, within a film or TV program, so that it does not appear to be advertising. The technique is not new (public relations people call it "product placement"), but it has proliferated during the last few years so that advertising agencies and other companies pay the TV networks or film producers for the product promotion, rather than trying to sneak in the mention or showing of a product by working with the scriptwriter, producer, prop manager, or other personnel. Sometimes product placements have backfired, such as a Swiss Army knife used in a violent act. But these days, the sponsor of branded entertainment can be certain of a favorable result, particularly in a multimillion dollar promotion. In theaters, *Playbill* credits usually list the sources of products, including the names of companies that specialize in product placement.

Advertising helps in *branding* or "brand building." A *brand*—a specific product within a product category—is indicated by its brand name, the usually unique and distinctive name of a product, the word part of a trademark, or sometimes the name of the manufacturer. The term "brand" comes from an old English word that literally meant burn—and you know about the branding of cattle or other animals. Advertisers don't use branding irons.

In print media, advertisers know that a top-of-the-page position gets higher readership than a bottom-of-the-page; and right-side pages are preferable to left-side ones (though this is not so in all cultures; for example in Japan, the left side carries more weight). For decades, a two-column ad in the upper right corner of page three of *The New York Times* has been placed by Tiffany & Co., the jewelry retailer. It appears every day and is called the "Tiffany position."

A *gutter* is the blank space between facing pages in a publication. *Bleed ads*, or "gutter bleed," go to the outside edges of the pages and also fill the gutter. However, the "gutter position," next to the inside margin, such as a one-column ad next to the gutter, is less desirable than an outside position in the outermost column.

A *reading notice* is an all-text advertisement in a newspaper, typeset to look like an editorial. It generally is labeled "advertisement" to prevent deception. A *reader*, or *reader ad*, is a brief text advertisement. Take a look at page one of *The New York Times* and you often will see these two- or three-line ads skirting the bottom of the page. Because of their high readership, they carry a high price tag. A two-line reader ad in the *Times* costs about twelve hundred dollars. An expensive way to say, "Happy Birthday!"

USA Today sells ads across the bottom of page one of each section and in the right-hand ears (upper boxes) of all fronts except the first section. Outside of the United States, ads are common on page one of newspapers.

Advertising people sometimes are called, pejoratively, "hidden persuaders" or "hucksters." *Hidden persuasion* is the attempt to change or influence public opinion by unidentified means or sources. The term was coined by the American author Vance Packard (1914–96). A *huckster* uses aggressive, devious, or haggling methods to promote or sell. It's an old word, from the Middle Dutch (twelfth- to fifteenth-century) *hokester*, to haggle. Clark Gable (1901–60) starred in *The Hucksters* in 1947.

Broadcasters sometimes refer to commercials as "messages," as in "We'll be right back after these messages." Advertisers claim that advertising increases sales, which enables manufacturers and retailers to charge lower prices. So the next time you are in a movie theater that has a twenty-minute block of commercials and trailers before the feature film starts, you might feel entitled to buy yourself a super-sized popcorn and Coke.

ANIMALS: THE MEDIA LINGO ZOO

OUR close relation with animals is evidenced both by an-thropomorphism—attributing human characteristics (like feelings and thoughts) to animals—and its opposite, zoomorphism, attributing animal characteristics to peo-ple. Our language is replete with such animal compar-isons, and media lingo follows the herd.

Let's start at A, or alligator: When a *gaffer* (an electri-cian) asks for an *alligator*, he will be handed a metal spring-clamp with serrated jaws. The same item is used to attach lights and other items to a bar or other support, and is also called a "bear trap" or "alligator grip," or more prop-erly, a "gaffer grip."

Birds fly in many media. For example, a *bird* is a com-munications satellite. *Birding* is slang for a radio and TV transmission via satellite. The news value of a potential story for satellite transmission is called its *birdability*. To "lose the bird" is to suffer an interruption in transmission. In theater, *bird* is slang for an unfavorable reception by an audience, as in "getting or giving the bird." The expression comes from the birdlike whistle of unruly spectators, par-ticularly those sitting up in the balcony or bleachers. A less disturbing interruption, *birdie,* is a tweeting noise due to malfunctioning sound equipment.

A rather common bird, the *pigeon*, in theater, film, and television, denotes a riser or portable platform used to elevate a camera, other equipment, or a performer. It is bigger than a "pancake" (a small platform about 2 inches high), but smaller than an "apple box" (about 8 inches high). Among salespeople, a *bluebird* is an unexpected, easy sale. In show biz, a *canary* is slang for an unidenti-fied noise.

Small insects or bugs are found everywhere, including

in the media. Starting with printing, a *bug* is the little oval mark, shaped like a bug, usually found at the bottom of a page, indicating that a booklet or other printed matter was produced by a union printer. It's also a labor union insignia placed in the credits of a motion picture and, more generally, a small, frequently used piece of art. The insignia, or bug, of the International Typographical Union appears on the dateline at the top of page one of some newspapers.

To most of us, a *bug* is a malfunction, defect, error, or difficulty that occurs in a computer or other system. To "debug" is to remove the error or malfunctioning device. The first computer bug allegedly was an actual moth that produced a hardware failure in the early days of computers during the forties. Other general meanings of *bug* are an "enthusiast, devotee, or buff"; and also a "hidden microphone or eavesdropping device."

Bug-eye is an extreme wide-angle lens of a camera. A virus or microorganism is also called a "bug," and from this comes the expression "caught the bug" or "bitten by the showbiz bug" (or some other enthusiastic interest). Another common bug (in this case an arachnid, not an insect), the spider, describes several devices used in the media.

A *spider box* (or *function box*), a small, portable receptacle for several electrical outlets, such as for lighting units, is commonly used in film, theater, TV, and exhibitions. A *spider dolly* is a camera mount with projecting legs on wheels. It is also called a "spyder." A *crow foot* and *spider* are metal braces on which a camera tripod is mounted. On the other hand (or, possibly, other foot), the metal brackets that fit into slots to form the support or feet of a point-of-sale display or other device are called "crow's feet." Before the advent of computer graphics, artists used a *crow quill*, a type of sharp pen point, akin to the stem (quill) of a crow's feather, for line drawings.

Aspiring actors are familiar with the *cattle call*, an audition for minor roles, for which a stampede of applicants is likely. A *cowlick*, a term for an unruly tuft of hair, also is slang for a hasty or cheap process, particularly a poorly varnished book jacket. A "sacred cow," derived from the veneration of cows by Hindus, is a person immune from criticism; or individuals or subjects favored by the media.

In theaters and studios, a *catwalk* suspended overhead provides access to lighting and other equipment via a narrow, elevated walkway or platform; also called "rigging" or "scaffolding." To view a catwalk in action, see the movie or play *The Phantom of the Opera*.

In the *crab* method of moving a TV or film camera on a pedestal, all the wheels are steered simultaneously to move sideways (for *crab shots*), particularly in small areas. The instructions are "crab left" (or "truck left") or "crab right" (or "truck right"). Someday, cars will be able to crab left or right into tight parking spaces.

A *dog*, in general, means an unattractive person or an inferior product or performance. In theatrical slang, a "dog" is a small town; and a "doghouse" a small theater. To try it out "on the dog" is to preview a play in a small city, and if things don't go well ("go to the dogs"), you may have "performed a dog show at a doghouse in a dog town." (In which case, you might end up "in the doghouse," panned by fans and critics alike.) *Bow-wow* is slang for a failure or something unattractive, like a poor scene or clumsy act. To "put on the dog" is to make an ostentatious display. To a radio broadcaster, a *doghouse* is a small building with transmission equipment at the base of a radio transmitter. Elsewhere in the lingo kennel, during the *dog watch* at a newspaper or other medium, a skeleton staff remains on duty to maintain operations after the last edition or local program is completed.

Dogear, a turned-down corner of a leaf of paper, arises when a page is folded back in such a way that it will not trim during bookbinding. *Doggerel* is trivial, loosely constructed, generally humorous verse. *Dogleg* is a line that is bent intentionally to point to an object: The line begins horizontally, then curves or doglegs toward the item, perhaps terminating in an arrowhead. In many parts of the country, to "dogleg right (or left)" is a common road direction.

In the nineteenth century, a small circus consisted mostly of trained dogs and ponies, a ringmaster, a band, and perhaps a few performers. In vaudeville, too, a trained dog and pony were a common act. Hence, the *dog-and-pony show*, which lives on today as a presentation or description of results, usually involving several individuals, using audiovisual and show-business techniques, sometimes referred to more prosaically as "show-and-tell."

Now let's look at the aquatic world, starting with an *aquarium*, film slang for the glass-enclosed room for mixing sound. In a television studio, observers, such as sponsors and VIPs, sit in a special booth called a *fishbowl*. A *fishpole* rod, generally made of aluminum or bamboo, holds a microphone attached at the end, and is also called a "fishing rod" or "fishpole boom." To *fishout* is to lower the microphone on the pole. A *fisheye* or wide-angle lens (also called a *bugeye*) covers a view of about 180 degrees, producing a distorted circular image, as if peering out of a fishbowl.

Also on the water are ducks. In publishing, *duck* refers to a cotton or linen cloth, somewhat like canvas, that sometimes is used in bookbinding. In broadcasting, a *duck circuit* automatically fades or reduces the volume of music or other background sounds to enable a voice to be heard (called a "voice-over ducker"). The English refer to quotation marks that consist of straight lines instead of curves as *duckfoot quotes*. The French call them *guillemets*.

The insect appearing in the greatest number of media terms is the fly, often in reference to rapid movement. For example, in newspaper plants, a *fly* is the point at which printed and folded newspapers enter a conveyor or are removed from the press. The procedure, formerly done manually by a person called a "flyboy," now is done by a machine that is also called a "fly."

In a theater, to *fly* is to suspend or move scenery or other items above the visible performance area, or stage, into a high area called the "flies" or "fly loft." A *fly plot* diagrams the lighting and other equipment attached to the flies. Along the *fly gallery*—the narrow platform (or *fly-walk*) located on a side wall of a stage—the lines or ropes to the scenery are attached to a beam or rail on the fly-gallery floor, called the "pin-rail." The fly gallery is also called the "flies" or "operating gallery." In theaters with more than one fly gallery, the lower or lowest one is also called the "fly-floor." In modern theaters, the scenery usually is controlled electrically rather than manually.

A *fly bill* or *fly sheet* is a pamphlet, particularly an advertising circular distributed free (and usually called a "flier" or "flyer"). Advertising salespeople sometimes also refer to a form used to quickly record orders (particularly over the phone) as a "fly sheet." A *fly fold* is a sheet folded once; also called a "four-panel fold." In printing, the *fly title* is a half-title of a book (the title without the subtitle or author's name) that may appear on the right side of the leaf preceding the page with the full title; it is also called a "bastard title," "pretitle," or "half-title page." *Fly-leaf* is a blank page that is part of a printed signature (a section), such as the front or back pages of a book, usually the free half of an *endpaper* (a folded sheet of paper pasted to the inside of the front or back cover). It's also called "end paper," "endleaf," "endsheet," or "lining paper."

A *flyaway pack* is a portable container with satellite communications equipment that can be set up at a remote location for TV transmission. *Fly-in* is a computer graphics technique commonly used in television for moving a title or other item quickly onto the screen, as if it were flying in. Moving off-screen is a *fly-out*.

A *flying paster*, common in high-speed newspaper presses, automatically splices a new roll of paper onto the one being used without stopping the press. It is also called an "automatic paster" or "autopaster." A *flying spot scanner* converts film into a format suitable for TV transmission, such as videotape, and consists of a cathode-ray tube that sends light (a "flying spot") through each film frame onto a photocell that records and converts each frame into the new format.

Let's move onto other animals. A *cub* is a novice, like a cub scout; and, in journalism, an inexperienced reporter. *Elephant doors* are, unsurprisingly, large doors leading to a TV studio or other place. Bullish words in the media include *bullpen* (a large room), *bullseye* (an attention-getting poster), and *bullhorn* (a portable electronic amplifier). A *fox message*, a standardized text used as a test, includes all the letters and numbers and some of the punctuation marks on a keyboard, and is derived from the phrase, "The quick brown fox jumped over the lazy dog's back, 1234567890." Another typing test is "etaoin shrdlu"—containing all five vowels and the seven most common consonants.

A popular feature in *The New Yorker*—insiders call it *GOAT*, an acronym for "Goings On About Town"—appears in the front of the magazine and lists films, plays, and other activities during the coming week. *Goatskin*, leather made from the skin of goats, is used in bookbinding and is commonly called "morocco" after the country where many fine goatskins originate. Goatskins for bookbinding also come from South Africa ("Cape morocco leather"), Nigeria ("Niger leather"), and elsewhere.

In the precomputer era, a *horse* on a film-editing table dispensed film, particularly film leaders. A *horse opera*, in a film or broadcast, dramatizes the American West or, more generally, emphasizes fighting and chases. In a theater, the *horseshoe* is a U-shaped area usually encircling part of the area above the orchestra; also called the "dress circle." In *horseshoe staging*, a live performance projects out into the audience so that part of the audience sits on each side of the front of the stage. The audience configuration thus is shaped like a U or a horseshoe. A "horseshoe arrangement" in a restaurant or meeting room places tables in a U-shape with chairs around the outside and sometimes also on the inside. *Horsey* artwork or type is too large or poorly proportioned for the layout.

Had enough verbal horsing around? Then, let's skip to the diminutive mouse, which in show biz, can only mean Mickey Mouse, the icon of the Walt Disney Company that first appeared in animated films in 1928. Even children who have never seen a real mouse know about Mickey. In addition to the most famous of the Disney characters, a *mouse* is the small hand-operated computer device that controls movement of the cursor and the selection of functions (by clicking the mouse) on the video screen of a computer. Incidentally, everyone has seen *mouse type*, which is very small type.

Piggyback refers to the shipment of goods in containers, as in trucks, ships, or planes. It also describes the presentation in sequence of two commercials by the same sponsor, enabling the sponsor to purchase them as a single unit. A commercial used in a piggyback configuration is called a "split commercial." A self-adhesive *piggyback label* attached to a mailing piece can be pulled off and affixed to an order form or reply card.

Pigskin, a strong, grained leather made from the skin of pigs, like goatskin, sometimes is used to bind books. A *pigtail* end of a cable has bare wires without a jack or other connector. In theaters, a "pigtail" is a short piece of electric cable or wire that hangs or protrudes from a lighting instrument or other source; also called a "lead" (pronounced LEED) or, in the United Kingdom, a "tail."

A *polecat*, a small support for lamps used in studio photography, named after the small weasel-like animal of the same name, often has collapsible, or telescopic, sections of tubes that can be extended to fit between two walls or between the floor and ceiling.

Do you remember *rabbit ears*? Before cable, every television set had a two-pronged antenna attached to it that looked somewhat like rabbit ears. In fact, not everyone today subscribes to cable or satellite TV and rabbit ears still are around.

Back to the aquatic world for a colorful term: *red herring*, a preliminary prospectus for the proposed financing of company or government project, so called because of a warning notice prominently placed on the cover page, generally printed in red ink, stating that some of the information may be changed before the final prospectus. A *red herring* also is a character or device in a fictional work, such as a mystery, designed to mislead or confuse; also called a "false plant." The origin is from the practice of nineteenth-century bandits who rubbed a herring across their trail to divert the bloodhounds.

A *seal* is an initial, design, or other device used as a mark of authenticity, placed on an envelope, letter, or document. It also refers to a stamp or other device used for making the impression. Seals were originally used by nobility or government officials and now are used more popularly; common types include Christmas seals or other ornamental stamps. In graphic design, a *seal* is simply a name or several words rendered in a cohesive form.

A "seal of approval" is a symbol granted by a publication, such as *Good Housekeeping*, for use in advertising, stating that the advertised product has been tested and found satisfactory.

Before the media ark closes, here's an uncommon animal term, the *yak*, slang for excessive or idle chatter. Sometimes called "yakkety-yak," it also means a loud laugh or a joke that evokes a laugh. The spelling also is "yock" or "yuk." I could continue yakking about other animal terms, but by now, you may have had enough of the lingo zoo. I don't want to get your goat.

AWARDS: THE ENVELOPE, PLEASE

ALMOST everyone knows that two of the most prestigious awards are the Nobel and Pulitzer. Named after Alfred Nobel (1833–96), the annual *Nobel Prizes* are awarded in Stockholm in six categories, most notably world peace and the sciences, but also in literature. The *Pulitzer Prizes*, named after St. Louis newspaper publisher Joseph Pulitzer (1847–1911), are annual awards in journalism, literature, and the arts that are presented through the Graduate School of Journalism of Columbia University in New York City.

Among the many academies explicitly associated with the media, the best known to the general public probably is the Academy of Motion Picture Arts and Sciences, an organization in Beverly Hills, California, of film producers, performers, and technicians. Usually referred to simply as "the Academy," it publishes the *Academy Players Directory*, a listing of actors and actresses with photos and credits, commonly used for casting. The Academy presents those famous annual awards commonly called the "Oscars," and establishes various standards for the film industry including Academy leader. You probably have seen the *Academy leader*: an eight-second numbered strip of film that precedes the first picture frame in a reel of film.

The Oscar name is so well known that it's sometimes used as a synonym for achievement in other fields. One story of the origin of the name for these golden statuettes relates how the executive secretary of the Academy thought the first figurines resembled his uncle Oscar in Texas. Another tells how Bette Davis (1908–89) named the figurine for her first husband, bandleader Harmon Oscar Nelson, after she won the award for best actress in

1935 (for the movie *Dangerous*). Still another attribution is to Margaret Herrick, a librarian at the Academy, who said in 1931 that it looked like her uncle Oscar.

The two major academies in television cause a bit of confusion, even in the media. The first, the Academy of Television Arts and Sciences, formed in 1976 in North Hollywood, gives awards for prime-time programs. The second, the National Academy of Television Arts and Sciences, formed in 1955 and headquartered in New York, presents local awards and also national awards for daytime programming and other categories. The awards of both academies are called *Emmy*. If you knew that, you deserve an award.

Now about the derivation of *Emmy*. The original name, in 1949, was *Immy*, after the image-orthicon tube used in television, but the name changed as a result of a typographical error. The award is a small statue of a woman with wings, representing one of the Muses.

The *Peabody Award*, established in 1940 and awarded annually by the University of Georgia School of Journalism, in Athens, is for public service in radio and television. It's named after George Foster Peabody (1852–1938), a banker who graduated from the University of Georgia.

TV viewers also are familiar with the Grammy and Tony awards. The *Grammys* (not "Grammies") are presented by the National Academy of Recording Arts and Sciences, an association of the recording industry with headquarters in Burbank, California.

The etymology of this award is from "Gramophone," an early version of a record player invented by Emile Berliner (1851–1928) that replaced the wax cylinders of Thomas Edison (1847–1931) with flat, reproducible records, called "Berliner discs." For many years, the British referred to a phonograph as a "gramophone."

The *Tonys* (not "Tonies") are annual awards presented to theatrical performers and others. Created in

1947 by the American Theater Wing and now presented by the American Theater Wing along with the League of American Theaters and Producers, the *Tony Award* is named after Antoinette Perry (1888–1946), who was the executive director of the American Theater Wing. Her nickname was Toni, but to avoid confusion with the similarly named hair product, the name of the award was changed to Tony with a *y*. The Tony does not mean tony (or toney), which is high-toned, luxurious, or stylish.

Another prize that confuses even the media is the *National Book Awards*, presented for literary excellence by the National Book Foundation, a nonprofit organization based in New York City. The awards, presented for many years (1950–79) by the Association of American Publishers, were originally called the National Book Awards, then changed to the American Book Awards, but are now back to National. More curiously, many people, even in the book industry, still don't know that the awards are no longer presented by the Association of American Publishers.

However, here's where it really gets confusing. There still are other awards called the *American Book Awards*, presented to authors by the Before Columbus Foundation, located, surprisingly, on the coast the explorer never reached, in Oakland, California. The foundation promotes contemporary multicultural literature and, as its name connotes, the idea that American literature evolved before European, Asian, and later ethnic groups came to North America.

The *Newbery Medal*, an annual award for excellence in children's book publishing, is presented by the American Library Association in Chicago and named after John Newbery (1713–67), a British publisher. Note the unusual spelling, which has led to countless misspellings since the award was first presented in 1921. Newbery's own famous book was *Little Goody Two-Shoes* (1765). The American Library Association also annually presents to an outstanding children's book illustrator the *Caldecott Medal*, named after Randolph Caldecott (1846–86), a British-born illustrator.

The *Kelly Award*, for a notable advertising campaign in a magazine, is presented by the Magazine Publishers of America (MPA) in New York City. It's named after Steven E. Kelly (1909–78), who was publisher of *Sports Illustrated* and president of the MPA. The National Magazine Awards are presented to magazines by the American Society of Magazine Editors (ASME) in New York City. The ASME annual awards—replicas of a sculpture by Alexander Calder (1898–1976)—are administered by the Columbia University Graduate School of Journalism and informally called the "Calder" awards. Somewhat resembling an elephant, the award is also sometimes called an *Ellie*.

The Recording Industry Association of America, in Washington, D.C., presents *Gold Awards* (half-million copies of an album, single record, or CD), *Platinum Awards* (one million copies), and *Diamond Awards* (ten million copies or more).

Many awards are golden, including the *Gold Quill*, presented by the International Association of Business Communicators of San Francisco; and the *Golden Globe Awards* (commonly called the "Golden Globes"), presented by the Hollywood Foreign Press Association. The one that I prize most is the *Gold Anvil*, presented annually by the Public Relations Society of America (PRSA), headquartered in New York City, to a top practitioner and also a top educator in PR. I was the 1990 recipient.

BODY PARTS: FROM HEAD TO FOOT

BODY parts—head, nose, eyes, ears, hand, spine, and foot—have a variety of nonanatomical meanings in the media, particularly as slang for parts of a publication.

Let's start with a *heads up*, an advance warning, about some head terms that generally refer to the top of a publication. A *head rule* is a horizontal line across the top of the page of a newspaper or other publication, with the page number and date above it. A *header* indicates the beginning of a section or a computer file, usually with a number and title, and in word processing, *header* is the equivalent of *running head*, the line repeated at the top of each page to identify the section or chapter.

A *headline* at the top of a page or article gives the title or description that serves as a synopsis to attract attention. *Subheads* sometimes are inserted within the text. A *head slug* is a ruled line below the headline or to separate it from text or other headlines (more about this in "Journalism").

The white space above the first line of a book or other publication is called the *head margin*. A *headnote* contains a brief introduction or summary placed beneath a title or headline. Newspaper and magazine editors often use the slang *hed*; for example, a *hed sked* catalogs all the types of headlines regularly used by a publication. A *headwriter* specializes in writing headlines, or can be the chief writer in a group of writers, as for a TV program. In theater and other performing arts, a *headliner* is a featured performer or leading attraction. A *head shot*, or *mug shot*, is a photograph of a person's head. In a dictionary, the *headword*, or *entry word*, is the principal word usually prominently set in bold type, which is defined and explained.

Now, let's look down the head at parts of the face. *Nose* can mean to have an instinctive talent, as a "nose for news." Reporters and others are instructed to *nose around*, or to investigate and pry; or to *count noses*, to estimate the number of people, as in a crowd.

"Ear" and "eye" are two of the most ubiquitous head terms found in media lingo. In journalism, *ears* flank the title as boxes in the left and right top corners of a publication (generally a newspaper). Incidentally, the title logo or nameplate on page one of a newspaper is called the *flag*, though many public relations, media, and other people call it the masthead. Common usage changes, but the original and primary meaning of *masthead* is an area of a publication that indicates its name, details of ownership, and other information, and usually appears on the editorial or contents pages, not atop page one.

Newspaper "ears" (sometimes called "earplugs") carry weather reports ("weather ear") or other messages, including advertising, particularly outside the United States. At *USA Today, forehead* refers to the space between the ear and the center logo (the "nameplate").

In typography, an "ear" is an appendage, a corner, or a short stroke, such as sometimes found extending from the letter *g*. In music, *ear* means the ability to recognize, appreciate, and reproduce slight differences in sound. To "have a good ear" is to be proficient in this ability; to "have a tin ear" is to be tone-deaf and, by extension, can mean verbal or social insensitivity or general obtuseness. To "play (it) by ear" is to play a musical instrument without sheet music or, in general, to improvise in any particular situation.

There's more to impress your audiologist or physician. An *ear shot* captures a close-up of a person in profile. *Earphones*, akin to miniature loudspeakers, that reproduce sound and are worn over the ears, are more commonly called *headphones* or a *headset*. Clicking on an *earcon* symbol on a computer screen initiates a digital sound or soundtrack.

An *ear prompter*, a tiny ear plug connected to a small audio recorder, enables a performer to hear a recorded script while onstage or on camera. A delightful term for Muzak or other innocuous music is *ear candy* (which might have inspired *eye candy*, an attractive but superficial person).

Moving on to media ophthalmology, an eye is the recognizable symbol of CBS-TV. Media coaches recommend that speakers on TV programs use *eye bounce*, in which the eyes do not move horizontally. Instead, the speaker first looks down and then to the side, to avoid looking glazed or shifty-eyed. *Eye contact*, looking a person in the eyes, requires looking directly into the camera. By recording *eye movements*, an "eye camera" in advertising research measures relative amounts of visual stimulation, helping marketers determine what is eye-catching and effective in ads or promotions.

Eye light projects a small light or special illumination on a person to produce extra reflection from the eyes, teeth, or other features; it's also called a "kicker" or "catchlight." Graphic designers and others like to *eyeball* (closely examine visually) a layout or other work instead of doing it mechanically or electronically. *Eyebrow*, a brief overline above a newspaper headline, photograph, or art, is also called a "kicker," particularly in the tabloids; while in the United Kingdom it's called a "strap." *Eye-level* positions a camera for a straight shot of a standing person. The exact height varies, of course, but is generally about 5 feet from the floor to the camera lens opening.

Eyeline is the direction in which the eyes are looking. In TV, a "cheated eyeline" occurs when a performer turns somewhat toward the camera and does not look directly at a subject, such as another performer. "Clear the eyeline" cues the removal of any people who are in the actor's line of vision, other than other performers who are supposed to be in the scene.

A display device mounted on a person's head, with

stereo display screens and headphones, called an "eye-phone," enables head movements to simulate virtual reality. An *eyepiece* is the lens nearest the viewer's eye, such as the lens of a camera viewfinder. A director of photography in film production determines lighting contrasts with an eyepiece.

The *eyewitness news* format on TV features on-the-scene reporters, often broadcasting live. *The Editorial Eye*, a monthly newsletter for editors and writers, is published by EEI Communications in Alexandria, Virginia.

Looking at the ears and eyes brings us to a great word for media mavens: *face*. "Face" has numerous meanings, including the surface of a piece of type as well as its style (hence, *typeface*); appearance or look, as of a publication; and a surface, particularly the front surface, as of an outdoor advertising structure to which an advertisement is affixed.

In a book or other publication, the *face margin* space lies between the text and the end of the open side, opposite the binding; it's also called an "outside margin," "thumb margin," or "trim margin." The "inside margin" near the binding, without any intention of being demeaning, is generally referred to as the *gutter* or "gutter margin."

In *facing editorial page*, an advertiser instructs a publication to place an advertisement adjacent to a non-advertising, or editorial page, also called "facing editorial matter" or "facing text." "Facing first editorial page" refers to placement on the page before the first text or editorial page of the magazine or other publication; "facing last editorial page," to the page after the last text or editorial page.

An amusing term is *face time*, the amount of time that the head of a TV newscaster or other person appears on-screen. Anchors (who read the news and introduce news segments) love to get lots of face time; their program directors usually do not, preferring to avoid the limelight by staying behind the scenes. "Face time" also is slang for a person meeting with another person, in contrast to communicating on the phone or via e-mail.

Supermarket shoppers and marketing people know about *facings*, the number of units of a product visible on a shelf in a supermarket or other retail store. "Four-facing" placement has more visibility and probably will sell more units than "two-facing" placement. To "face up" is to arrange products on the shelf or in a display in an orderly manner, that is, with the face, or front, of the product turned toward the customer. A "rack jobber" (the wholesaler's representative who keeps the sales racks stocked and replenished) often tries to keep her products face out, particularly with books, whose front covers can be obscured by a competitor's, or unseen if shelved sideways, "spine out." (In these cases, "losing face" results not only in embarrassment but in lost sales as shoppers notice and buy the better displayed goods.)

Next time you're in a bookstore, look for a person surreptitiously readjusting books that are aligned vertically (with a "spine-out" display) to give them full-cover facings (a "face-out" display). Chances are the culprit rearranging the books is the author or a family member or maybe even the editor or publisher!

You see *facing identification marks* almost every day, though you may not know the name for the series of vertical parallel lines required by postal regulations on business reply cards and envelopes. These bars are used by the U.S. Postal Service for machine identification of the mailer.

Faced mail saves postage costs by arranging envelopes and other mailing pieces with all addresses and stamps facing the same way. "Facer-cancelers" automatically cancel the stamps. Before going through the canceling machine, letters are gathered and faced (arranged in the same direction) on a "facing table" or "pickup table".

In outdoor advertising, a billboard (called a *facing*) is characterized by the direction it faces, as in "south" facing; or by the group of billboards it adjoins, such as a "double" or "triple" facing.

Now, let's get under the skin. Media can be a bloody business. In advertising, journalism, and printing, the *bleed* portion of an illustration or text, generally an advertisement, exceeds the standard text area of a publication's page, running to the edge of the paper and leaving no margin. Advertisements produced in this manner, called *bleed ads*, often get assessed an additional *bleed charge*.

In journalism and public relations, "bleeding" produces more dramatic effects in magazines, brochures, and other printed matter by trimming or eliminating the margin or white space. *Bleed pages* can be "full" bleed (on all four sides) or "partial" bleed (on one, two, or three sides). *Bleed* also can refer to unintentional running or spreading of ink, such as to "bleed a page," also called *feathering*.

Bleed through occurs on a page or sheet on which underlying printed material can be seen, such as a wet outdoor advertising poster on which an underlying poster is visible; or printing on one side of a sheet that is visible on the other side (commonly called *strike-through* or *show-through*). In outdoor advertising, a *bleed-face poster* or bulletin has no frame molding or margin, so the design area extends to its edges.

In television, *bleed* refers to a small amount of space at the edges of a shot to compensate for any unwanted trimming or cropping of the picture as it may appear on the home screen. In radio, a *bleeder* is audio from an unwanted source.

Anyone who feels queasy about the amount of blood in media lingo may require *handholding*, strong personal support and reassurance. *Handwaving* is the use of insubstantial words or actions that are intended to convince or impress. *Handwringing* is excessive display of concern or distress. Resounding applause is called a *big hand*. A *heavy hand* means acting clumsily, while a *fine hand* is deft. *Hands-on* suggests direct participation; *hand delivery*, personal delivery, as by messenger. *Hand-carry* is an instruction to personally deliver an item, such as a confidential memo.

A *handoff* is a transfer, such as the shifting of responsibility from one person to another; or from one ground station to another, a common procedure in aircraft control and transmitters for cell phones. To a sportswriter or fan, a "handoff" is an offensive maneuver in which a quarterback or other player hands the ball directly to a running teammate. On the other hand (I couldn't resist), *hands-off* refers to not interfering or intervening.

If you live in a city, you probably have passed walls (particularly of deserted buildings) on which the notice, "Post No Bills," was affixed. You may know what that means, but do you know what those "bills" are? The term is short for *handbills*, once popular in the nineteenth century when printed notices and advertisements were distributed by hand. Handbills were also used as posters to promote circuses and shows, and usually were surreptitiously affixed on walls, lampposts, and other public places. Chances are that you've seen the people who post these bills—called *billposters* or, more commonly, *snipers*. A *snipe* means a sheet with a retailer's name, the place and time of a show, or other information, pasted across the bottom of an outdoor poster or other item.

In public relations, one of the most common items is called a *handout,* a news release or other item distributed, or handed out, to the media or others.

The icon of a hand [☞] is common in the virtual world as well—on computer screens and in many publications—usually depicted with a pointed finger, and also called an *index*. In publishing, *handselling* involves a person in a bookstore recommending a book to a customer. A *handbook,* often small enough to be carried in the hand, is a concise manual with instructions or reference material. It also can denote a book in which a bookie records bets, such as those made on horse races.

In theater, an *outcue* is the last few words of a part, signaling the next performer; in the United Kingdom, it is logically called a *handback*. Young members of the audience are sometimes called *hand-holders*, from the idea that children hold hands with each other.

Thumbs up is an expression of approval; *thumbs down*, of disapproval. *Two thumbs up* means a top rating, an expression and gesture popularized by well-known film critics Roger Ebert (b. 1942) and Gene Siskel (1946–99), succeeded by Richard Roper (b. 1959).

Let's go back (no pun intended) to the *spine*, in this case, the backbone of a publication that connects the front and back covers: In a book, the *spine* is the part of the binding that encloses the inner edges of the pages and usually bears the title (the *spine title*), author's name, and publisher. The spine of a magazine does the same. Incidentally, the opposite of "spine" is *fore-edge*, the front edge of a book. The *fore-edge margin* is the outer margin of a page. In television, the *spine* is the basic plot or story line (the backbone) of a dramatic series.

Back is a common term in the media, including *back light* (behind the subject or focused on the foreground), *back lot* (exterior area of a movie studio), and *backstage* (behind the stage of a theater). A *backgrounder* is a briefing session or document. *Deep background* is information provided, as by a government official, on the condition that the source not be identified. A *background story* is an article with the history of the circumstances or events preceding the current story.

Backstory in film, TV, and theater, is the events in the characters' lives that preceded the story, as in earlier episodes of a series. In journalism, *back story* (two words) is a review of the events or people involved in one or more articles, such as introductory comments by the editor or an appendix of sources in a fashion feature.

A myriad of footsy words also appear in the media. *Foot* is the bottom end of a printed piece. In the United Kingdom, it's called a "tail." A *footer* is text at the bottom of a page, containing a page number or footnote, often called a "running foot" when it appears at the bottom of each page. An "even footer" appears only on even-numbered (left-hand) pages; an "odd footer" only on odd-numbered (right-hand) pages. A *footnote* (abbreviated "fn") gives a reference, explanation, or a comment that appears at the bottom of a page, an article, or a book. Footnotes are indicated in the text by a *footnote callout*, a small raised number (superscript) or other symbol, such as an asterisk (*) or dagger (†).

Technical papers and nonfiction books are replete with footnotes. In an annual report or legal document, the footnotes may occupy a full page or more. *Footnote capability* is the ability of a computer system to identify footnote callouts and footnotes and handle the process of footnoting. An "automatic footnote tie-in" is a computer-programming device that links a footnote to specific text so that, if the text segment is moved, the footnote moves with it. If the notes appear at the end of each chapter, or all together at the back of the book, they are called, appropriately, *endnotes* or *chapter notes*.

In telecommunications, a *footprint* denotes the area on Earth in which the signal of a specific satellite can be received. A *footprint map* shows contour data of satellites with various signal strengths. In film and television, *footroom* measures the distance between a performer's feet and the bottom of the picture. The camera operator tries to include this area so that the feet are not cut off in a tight shot.

A portion or length of a film or tape is called *footage*, such as daily footage or news footage. The *footage counter* indicates the amount of film or tape already used or remaining in a camera, recorder, or projector. Film length is expressed in the number of *feet* plus frames (instead of inches). One foot of 35mm film is 16 frames. At the regular speed of 24 frames per second, one foot (16 frames) plus 8 frames pass through the camera per second.

Of course, we know that ordinarily a foot equals 12 inches. Therefore, in films, the standard unit of illumination, a *foot candle*, is defined as the amount of light thrown onto a surface 12 inches from one candle or its equivalent.

One of the most common words heard in show business is *footlights*, often shortened to simply *foots*, a row of lights along the front of a stage. The word often refers to the theatrical field in general. Newspaper columns about theatrical news sometimes are headed "Across the Footlights" or simply "Footlights." Performers occasionally are called *footlighters*. A *footlight spot* is a small spotlight (a light with a directed beam) that is usually in a recessed area, the *footlight trough*, or *well*, at the front of the stage.

Toenails is printer's slang for parentheses.

Close to the foot are shoes and socks. *Softshoe* is a nearly noiseless type of tap dancing done without metal taps on the shoes. *Sock* is theatrical slang meaning "very successful," as with a *sock show*; also called a "socker" or "socko." A *sock line* is a punch line or climax of a joke or scene. To *sock it* is to emphasize or "punch" a part of a script, layout, or other item.

To *shoehorn* is to squeeze copy or visuals into an advertisement or other work. *Shoestring* means inexpensive, as with a "shoestring production" or *shoestringer*.

Some terms are obvious even if you've never seen them before. When a TV reporter or an interviewer strolls inside a home, or anywhere else, and chats with a celebrity or other person, each carrying a lapel mike, it's called a *walking shot*.

Walk-along radio refers to people on the move who listen to radio sets, such as the Sony Walkman, while walking or working. This is a hard-to-measure audience and is different from car-radio and home-radio listeners. With the proliferation of cell phones, it's relevant to note that the *walkie-talkie* (a small portable radio transmitter and receiver) has been around for decades.

Here's one more before you walk away. In theater, a *walker* is a nonplaying musician paid in accordance with a labor union contract that requires a minimum number of musicians for each theater. It used to be that the excess musician could sign in before a performance and then walk away. Now the walker has to be available as a replacement for one of the playing musicians.

Bigfoot is slang for VIP (very important person), such as a "media bigfoot." *Net bigfeet* are well-known reporters, anchors, and other celebrities at the broadcast and cable networks.

Feel free to quote any of these phrases at your next meeting. The lingo here is not *eyes only* (confidential and not to be reproduced).

BOOKS: READING BETWEEN THE LINES

"I cannot live without books," Thomas Jefferson (1743–1826) wrote in an 1815 letter to fellow Founding Father John Adams (1735–1826). I agree, and assume that you feel the same, though you may not be so devoted as to be a *bookworm* or *bookish* (a person devoted to reading and studying). When drama critics or others use "bookish" to describe a play or other work that is literary, it may be a criticism that it is too intellectual.

A *book* contains a set of written or printed pages, usually bound together, similar to what you are reading now. A book can be many other things and bookish terms abound in various media. For example, *book* means a libretto or text, without the music, of a play or other work. A *libretto*, Italian for small book, is written by a librettist. In journalism, a *book* is a collection of articles from various sources, such as different reporters and wire services, about the same event. The term often refers to a magazine. For example, a "woman's book" is a magazine with primary appeal to women. A portfolio of a person's work, particularly in advertising, is called a *book*. Similarly, a summary of a performer's past performances is also called a *book*. In advertising, a broadcast audience ratings report is referred to as a *book*.

In radio or TV, a *bookend commercial* is split, usually 30 seconds before one or more other commercials and 30 seconds after. A *bookend ad* is an advertisement that is split, with half on one side of a page or facing pages in a publication, the other half on the other side, and editorial matter between the two. In the United Kingdom, "bookend" also is slang for the first and last episodes in a TV drama series. A radio or TV commercial with an area left open in the middle for insertion of a local dealer tie-in or other material is called a "doughnut" (as it has a time slot or "hole" in the middle).

In theater, a script is called the "book." It's also short for *promptbook*, the text of a play or other work, held by a prompter who is *on the book* (follows the script). A performer *on book* still needs the script; a performer *off book* no longer needs the script. To *sit on book* is to prompt the performers, as in a rehearsal. *Books down* in a rehearsal directs performers to work without their scripts. A *book show* is a musical with a plot (a book). A *book number* is a dance or musical selection (a number) that relates to the plot (book) of a musical comedy or other production.

To a stagehand, a *book* refers to two pieces of scenery (*flats*) hinged so that they can be folded for storage; also called a "two-fold" or "booked flat." A "book ceiling," or two-leaf ceiling, involves two pieces of scenery hinged together to form the top, or ceiling, of a stage setting. A "book wing" consists of several (usually four) sections of scenery attached to a spindle so that each section, or flat, can show a different scene when the device is turned. Akin to the pages of a book, it is used particularly in the United Kingdom.

As a verb, *to book* means to hire, such as an entertainer, or to make arrangements, such as to book a trip or, in public relations, to set up an interview. In the United Kingdom, if you want to buy a theater ticket you "book a seat." A *booked-up show* is sold out. The person who books guests on a radio or TV program is a *booker* (not a bookie).

A *booking*, an engagement, such as for a lecture or performance, often scheduled by a *booking agent*, goes in the *schedule book*. At some magazines, the *associate editor/bookings* arranges for models to be *booked*, or hired, for photo shoots.

Advance sales, particularly of theatrical productions, are also called "bookings." A *booking office* or *booking agency* makes arrangements for engaging (booking) performers. A *booking memo* or sheet is an agreement with a performer sent to the appropriate labor union.

Various *book* terms also show up in more general discourse, such as "bookmaker" or "bookie," a person who takes bets (*makes book*); "bookkeeper," a person who maintains financial records; and "bookwork," the studying of textbooks, in contrast to practical work.

To "take a page" from someone's work is to copy or emulate. To "throw the book" at someone is to charge or find someone guilty of every possible violation. To "be on the same page" with someone is to be in agreement. (To "push the envelope," a term that originated with aviators, is to be innovative and exceed the limits.)

These days, about 185,000 books are printed in English annually in the United States (and the number keeps growing), including *trade books* (general interest books sold in bookstores and other retail outlets, as well as online or via mail order or telephone), textbooks, directories, and other specialized books. An *audio book* is a recorded reading of a book or other work. About 3 percent of the books sold in the United States are on tape cassettes or CDs.

A *stepladder* is a tall display stand with the front covers of a book facing out. You've seen this as you enter a bookstore, which is why publishers pay for this valuable space.

Let's focus more on book publishing and the parts of a book, starting on the outside. "Book cloth" or "binding cloth," which covers a book or other publication, is generally made of cotton in various weights and weaves, finished (fitted or coated) with starch, pyroxylin, or plastic. The number of threads per inch and their tensile strength determines the quality or grade of the cloth. *Bookbinding* gathers and holds together the pages in books, booklets, and other publications. Often done by a specialist, a "bookbinder," at a *bindery*, who uses various types of binders and binding machines, the process can utilize glue, staples, and stitching to attach pages to the cover.

"You can't judge a book by its cover," a time-worn proverb, warns that outward appearances may not be a reliable indication of a person's true character. However, in the book business, the covers or jackets (see below) are essential elements in selling and can serve much the same role as an advertisement for the book.

The *spine* connects the front and back covers and conceals the back or bound edge attached to it. The spine usually bears the book's title and the name of the author and publisher. *Book paper* is a general term for both coated (glossy) and uncoated papers used in books and other printed material, and usually comes in 25-inch x 38-inch sheets or on rolls.

A *book jacket* consists of detachable protective paper placed around a hardback (a book bound in cloth, cardboard, or leather; not a paperback). Attached by flaps folded over the edges of a cover, it is also called a "dust cover," "dust jacket," "jacket," or "wrapper." Generally, the *front flap* carries a description of the book while the *back flap* has biographical information about the author or other promotional material (all called *flap copy*).

Dust wrapper (d.w.) generally refers to a protective wrapping on a rare book. Dust jackets originated in the United Kingdom in the 1830s in the form of papers slipped around books to keep off dust and soot.

[A BOOK'S LAYOUT]

A book's layout—internal arrangement of paged elements—usually follows this traditional sequence:

Front Matter

half title or bastard title
(first recto, or right-hand, page)

card page (first verso,
or left-hand, page)

title page (next recto)

copyright (verso)

dedication

foreword

preface

acknowledgments

table of contents (recto)

list of illustrations

list of figures

introduction (recto)

Text

part (or section) title

chapter title

chapter text

Back Matter

appendixes

notes

glossary

bibliography

index

colophon

The order and number of elements varies, according to the book and publisher. For example, the *card page* or *book card* is a page opposite the title page on which appears a list of books by the same author or publisher, and may appear elsewhere.

A *paperback* or softcover book is bound in heavy paper cardboard instead of cloth or leather (as a *hardcover*). Smaller paperbacks that fit into conventional rack sizes found almost everywhere are called *mass-market paperbacks*; while *trade paperbacks* are generally larger and have more expensive softcovers. A "paperback original" is a work not previously published as a hardcover; a "paperback reprint," on the other hand, is a book that has appeared previously in another, usually hardcover, format.

Front matter is the material that precedes the main text, such as the introduction, preface, and the title page. Also called "preliminaries," "preliminary matter," or "forematter," these pages generally are numbered with Roman numerals (i, ii, iii, iv, etc.), or sometimes not numbered; whereas the main body of the book, the text, is numbered with Arabic numerals (1, 2, 3, etc.). Many publishing terms have British origins, such as *frontispiece*, which is an illustration facing the title page.

Back matter comprises the appendix, a bibliography, glossary, index, notes, and other material following the main text, continuing with Arabic page numbers.

Copyright (usually abbreviated as © or *cop.*) refers to the exclusive legal rights of artists, authors, composers, publishers, and others to the contents of a publication, broadcast, or other piece of work, so that it is protected from plagiarism or imitation, or any use without the copyright holder's permission.

In the United States, copyright is granted to the copyright holder (owner) by the Copyright Office of the Library of Congress. In books, the copyright notice generally appears on the copyright page, right behind the title page: the copyright symbol ©, followed by the year (copyright date), and the name of the author or copyright holder. The word also can be used as a verb. In the United Kingdom, copyright, or statutory, copies of books are sent to the British Museum in London.

The copyright page also lists the *International Standard Book Number*. Commonly called the *ISBN* (pronounced IZ-bin for short), it is a numerical system for identifying books and their publishers. Publishers are identified by their assigned prefix.

Cataloging in Publication is a procedure by which the Library of Congress issues a reference number to a publisher for a book prior to its printing. If it were not for this procedure, the first printing of a book would lack a library catalog card number.

A *preface* (pref.) is a usually succinct preliminary description by an author before the first chapter of the material in the book. It generally starts on a recto, or right-hand page. A *foreword* (not spelled "forward") differs from a preface in that it is usually written by someone other than the author who generally endorses the importance of the book and its creator.

In an *acknowledgment*, the author recognizes or thanks sources or other help, usually on a separate acknowledgment page. It's different from the *dedication page*, which usually says "to my wife," "significant other," or other persons.

In the publishing business, a *TOC* (sometimes pronounced TOCK) is a table of contents, which lists all the main parts of the book, in the order in which they appear.

In an *introduction*, the author generally states his or her intentions and prepares the reader for the work. A preliminary section that is part of the front matter, an introduction is different from a preface and may be longer, providing the background of the subject and perhaps a summary of the key points in the book. The introduction may be written by someone other than the author, often an authority on the subject.

The *index*, appearing at the end of the book, lists alphabetically names or subjects and the pages on which they can be found. The plural is "indexes" or "indices."

A *colophon* inscription at the beginning or end of a book usually contains information about its production. The word comes from the Greek *kolophon*, finishing touch. The term more generally has come to designate the imprint of a publisher, though this usage is technically incorrect.

An *appendix* is a collection of supplementary material; the plural is "appendixes" or "appendices."

An *afterword* provides an update or other perspective on the subject since the text was written. Also called an *epilogue* (or "epil"), the afterword may be a critical or interpretive commentary by someone other than the author. A play sometimes has an epilogue, a short speech or poem spoken to the audience by one of the performers after the last act.

Bibliophiles, book editors, and printers use lots of other terms specific to their crafts. For example, *perfect binding* affixes the pages of a book or other publication to the spine by using glue instead of stitches or staples; a book manufactured this way is "perfect bound." For quite some time, the main method of binding books has been "Smyth sewing," in which printed and folded sheets are sewn down the middle before a backing is affixed, so that even the pages of a thick book open flat. A continuous thread links each signature, or section of pages, with the next. A Smyth-sewn book thus differs from a "side-sewn" or "perfect-bound" one. Named after David M. Smyth (1833–1907), who invented the first thread sewing machine for books in 1856, today the process can be done on several types of machines; and the word sometimes is not capitalized.

The most important part of a book, of course, is the *main text* between the front and back matter, which is the heart and soul of the author's creation, be it a great adventure story or a household repair manual. To make more room for the text, in fact, these days many of the elements, particularly in the front matter, are now being combined or omitted.

You may even find your favorite comic book character in the main text of today's books. Comics—a magazine with a series of captioned drawings, often an adventure story and not necessarily humorous—are enormously popular today and have evolved into longer works called *graphic novels*. A fictional work narrated mostly in sequential panels akin to a comic book, graphic novels have become popular even with adults. Graphic novels from Japan, called "manga," are all the rage.

A *pop-up* is a piece of paper or cardboard that is "die cut" and folded or pasted so that part of it assumes a vertical position (pops up) when opened or unfolded. Many children's books are delightful pop-up books. Incidentally, the die that is used for cutting has a male side with the pattern or shape and a female side that receives the pressure and provides resistance on the other side of the material.

A book author generally is paid an *advance* prior to publication. As in other fields that provide commissions to salespeople, it's an advance payment to be deducted from *royalties* (called an "advance on, or against, royalties"). Royalties, also common in music and other fields, are calculated as a percentage of actual sales. The origin is from the days when kings and queens (royalty) owned the land and received payments from tenants. Then mineral producers (especially of gold and silver) paid fees to landowners; and from this evolved payments for the use of patents and published or recorded material. In publishing, royalty payments usually are made semiannually, reported on a "royalty statement."

A *vanity press* is a publisher of books printed at the author's expense, such as for conceit (vanity), pleasure, posterity, or other purposes. For many years, some authors self-published their books by working directly with printers. It's now possible to work with an online publisher who will print books when they are ordered (called "print-on-demand" companies).

Book publishers are listed, along with considerable data about publishing, in *Literary Market Place*, published by Information Today, Inc. (www.literarymarket-place.com). I can't resist noting that Random House, publisher of this book, is the world's largest English-language general-interest book publisher, and a division of Bertelsmann, described in the chapter, "Media."

Other common *book* terms include "book club" (an organization that sends selected books to its members, usually on a set schedule and at discount prices); "reading group" (also sometimes called a "book club"), a group of people who meet regularly to discuss commonly read books); "book awards" (see the chapter, "Awards"); "book rate" (a special postal rate, now called "media mail"); and *book packager* (a person or company that creates a manuscript and arranges for its publication).

A *bookragger* is a book reviewer who usually is very negative. If a reviewer refers to a book as a "tome," it usually means that it's a heavy or dense work; though a *tome* is simply one of the books in a work of several volumes, usually scholarly. As for me, I prefer to think of this book as my magnum opus, Latin for great work.

Last but not least, an embarrassment to publishers and authors are *errata*, errors and corrections inserted on a separate sheet, printed at the end of a book or other publication, or published in a subsequent issue or edition. The singular is *erratum*, from the Latin *errere*, to err.

So let's end with more upbeat terms. "For the book" or "one for the books" means extraordinary, as meriting inclusion in a book of record achievements. "By the book" is strictly according to the rules. "Like a book" means thoroughly or completely, as in "I know the media like a book."

BROADCASTING: NOT JUST FOR COUCH POTATOES

MOST people spend more time watching TV than any other medium. Radio also takes large chunks of our time, particularly in cars. Terms such as *anchor, commercial,* and *sound bite* have become a part of our everyday language. Television sometimes is called the "small screen," as compared to the "big screen" of the movies.

We even have a term, "couch potato," for someone who spends little or no time exercising and instead sits on a chair or couch watching many hours of television. Whether you are a couch potato or the opposite (a casual viewer?), the following lingo may help you to enjoy and appreciate both television and radio media.

In the United States, there are about 5,300 AM radio stations and about 7,700 FM radio stations.

AM (*amplitude modulation*) radio, first popularized in the twenties, uses medium-range radio signals (with frequencies of 535 kilohertz to 1.7 megahertz) that can travel the earth's surface. FM (*frequency modulation*), first popularized in the sixties, uses higher frequency radio signals (88 to 108 megahertz) that can travel only as far as the horizon. An FM station has a smaller geographic range, but is received with less static or interference.

Broadcasting stations are licensed by the Federal Communications Commission (FCC or F.C.C), which was formed as an independent agency in 1934. Before then, it was called the Federal Radio Commission (1927–33) and from 1912 to 1927 it was part of the U.S. Department of Commerce. I was once a radio broadcaster (at station WISC in Madison, Wisconsin) and am fascinated with the *call letters* of stations—the unique combination of letters that identify each radio station. (The more general term is *call sign* for any unique combination of letters and numbers identifying an operator, office, activity, vehicle, or station for use in communications.)

Most radio stations have four letters, most randomly assigned by the FCC, but some are initials with stories behind them. For example, WABC and KABC, and WCBS and KCBS, refer to their respective network owners. WEVD in New York was named after socialist Eugene V. Debs (1855–1926). WFLA is located in Tampa, Florida; KCOL-AM in Fort Collins, Colorado; and KCAL in San Bernardino, California.

You can spot a pioneer radio station because it has only three letters. WHA, the oldest noncommercial radio station in the United States, started broadcasting in 1921 at the University of Wisconsin in Madison. Most of the three-letter stations are on the AM dial and broadcast at fifty thousand watts (50 kW), the maximum power permitted by the FCC.

Call letters of Canadian radio and television stations start with a C; Mexican stations with an X. In the United States, call letters of stations east of the Mississippi River start with W; west of the Mississippi, with a K.

There are a few notable exceptions. KYW, America's seventh radio station, started in Chicago in 1921, moved to Philadelphia in 1934, to Cleveland in 1956, and returned to Philadelphia in 1965, when it became the country's second all-news radio station, with the slogan, "All News, All The Time." WINS in New York was the first all-news radio station, starting in late 1964. Both stations are now owned by Infinity Broadcasting Corporation. KDKA, which has the longest continuous record of operation, started in Pittsburgh in 1920. KQV also started in Pittsburgh in 1920. KFI started in Los Angeles in 1922, when FI were the initials of "Farm Information." Now it's an all-talk station and FI refers to "For Information."

Several three-letter stations east of the Mississippi start with the letter W, including WBZ, Boston (1921);

WOR, New York (1922); and WJR, Detroit (1922). The number within parentheses is the year the station started. WGY, the first radio station in New York, started in 1922. The W stood for Wireless; the G for General Electric, its first owner; and the Y for Schenectady, its first location. It's now in Albany, so the Y is still apt.

Many public radio and TV stations operate on university campuses but reach sizable audiences off-campus. Examples are KUSC-FM (University of Southern California), WBUR (Boston University Radio), and WTUL-FM (Tulane University in New Orleans).

WIP, the first radio station in Philadelphia, started in 1922, originally was owned by the Gimbel Brothers Department Store, and its slogan was "Wireless In Philadelphia." Now owned by Infinity Broadcasting Corporation, it's called "SportsRadio 610."

There are seven radio stations in the United States that start with the call letter X, all in San Diego, near Mexico. XLTN-FM is owned by the Imagen Group, a Mexican company, while the other six are owned by Clear Channel Communications: XHOE-FM, XHRM-FM, XHTS-FM, XHTV-FM, XTRA-FM, and XTRA-AM. Clear Channel also owns KGB-FM in San Diego.

Clear Channel Communications, Inc., headquartered in San Antonio, Texas, is the largest owner of radio stations in the United States, with about 1,200 stations, or about 9 percent of the approximately 13,000 stations in the country. (About 10,000 are commercial; the rest, noncommercial.) Clear Channel also owns TV stations and is a majority owner of outdoor advertising companies. In 1975 it acquired its first radio station, WOAI-AM, a fifty-thousand-watt station in San Antonio. Lowry Mays (b. 1935) started the company in 1974 and now is chairman; his son, Mark Mays (b. 1963), is CEO. The FCC defines a *clear-channel station* as an AM radio station that dominates its frequency by virtue of its power (usually fifty thousand watts) and its geographical protection (no other station can be assigned at its frequency for a specified, large geographical area, indicated by latitude and longitude).

Clear Channel Communications—what a great name for a radio broadcaster! Of the fifty-seven clear-channel stations licensed by the FCC in the United States, sixteen are owned by Clear Channel Communications. Here's the roster of their call letters and cities, listed alphabetically by state: KENI, Anchorage (AK); KFI, Los Angeles (CA); KFBK, Sacramento (CA); KOA, Denver (CO); WHO, Des Moines (IA); WHAS, Louisville (KY); KFAB, Omaha (NE); WGY, Albany (NY); WHAM, Rochester (NY); WLW, Cincinnati (OH); WSAI, Cincinnati (OH); KEX, Portland (OR); WLAC, Nashville (TN); WOAI, San Antonio (TX); WRVA, Richmond (VA); and WWVA, Wheeling (WV). You could call this the Clear Channel clear-channel lineup!

Among the public radio networks, the largest is National Public Radio (NPR) in Washington, D.C. Its most popular program, *Morning Edition*, is broadcast for four hours Monday to Friday, with a cumulative weekly audience of about thirteen million people.

American Public Media, in St. Paul, Minnesota, broadcasts *A Prairie Home Companion* to about 570 stations. The weekly program, hosted by author and raconteur Garrison Keillor (b. 1942), has an audience of more than four million listeners. (If you can find Lake Wobegon on your map of Minnesota, let the world know.)

Westwood One Companies, Inc., in New York, is the largest syndicator of radio programs, including *Imus In The Morning*, hosted by Don Imus (b. 1940).

Premiere Radio Networks, in Sherman Oaks, California (near Los Angeles), syndicates many popular radio programs, including the *Rush Limbaugh Show*, hosted by Rush Limbaugh (b. 1951). His full name is Rush Hudson Limbaugh III, and he started the call-in program in 1988 that now has a cumulative weekly audience of more than twenty million people, the country's best-known and most influential politically conservative talk show.

Listeners who call in regularly to Limbaugh are known as *dittoheads*: Callers often start their conversation by saying, "I like the show and listen every day," and to save time, subsequent callers start by saying, "Ditto." Originally a term used by critics of Rush Limbaugh, "dittohead" is now accepted as simply meaning "a regular listener."

The Voices of America (VOA) is a radio service operated in forty-four languages throughout the world (but not in the United States, as it is specifically for foreign audiences). The VOA formerly was part of the U.S. Information Agency (U.S.I.A.), which in 1999 was folded into the U.S. Department of State. At that time, the Voices of America (note that, once singular, it's now plural) became part of the Broadcasting Board of Governors, an independent agency reporting to the U.S. Congress.

The Corporation for Public Broadcasting, a nonprofit, nongovernmental agency, promotes and assists noncommercial radio and TV stations within the United States. Funded by the U.S. government and private sources, it is based in Washington, D.C. The Public Broadcasting Service (PBS) is an organization, in Alexandria, Virginia, of noncommercial TV stations that produces and distributes TV programs to its member stations.

A major recent development is the broadcasting of radio programs, the sound portion of TV programs, and, most important, more than one hundred commercial-free music channels, via satellite to audio receivers in cars (primarily) and elsewhere. The two companies leading this growth business are Sirius and XM. The immediate popularity of *satellite radio* has led to a new term, "land-based radio," to refer to the traditional AM and FM stations and networks broadcast from fixed towers.

Sirius Satellite Radio (the clever name comes from Sirius, the brightest star in the night sky) beams network radio and the audio portion of TV programs, sports programs (including the National Football League), Spanish-language channels, and its own star, Howard Stern

(b. 1954). XM Satellite Radio also provides network programs, sports programs (including Major League Baseball), and, of course, all types of music. The name XM is sort of a pun on AM and FM, or radio to the x-power (x is the mathematical symbol for an unknown).

A pioneer in radio was the Radio Corporation of America, formed in 1919 and headed by David Sarnoff (1891–1971). RCA formed the National Broadcasting Company in 1926, and the following year set up two networks, the Red Network (the larger) and the Blue Network. In 1943, the Blue Network became the American Broadcasting Company (ABC). RCA, which also made radio and TV sets, was acquired by the General Electric Company in 1986. The RCA building, at 30 Rockefeller Plaza in New York, is seen by viewers of the *Today Show* and tourists who take a tour of its studios. It's now called the GE Building.

Of the approximately ten thousand commercial radio stations in the United States, the most common format is country music. Next most common are the news, talk, business, and sports stations, followed by various types of music, including oldies and classic hits, rock, adult contemporary and standards, Top 40, plus Spanish, religious, and other formats.

Arbitron, Inc., measures the audience size of radio stations and provides reports for more than 2,200 counties in the United States, based on diaries maintained by listeners. The quarterly reports to subscribing stations are called "The Books." Formerly called American Research Bureau, Inc., Arbitron was known for its use of an automatic electronic meter device (called "Arbitron," a name loosely based on the original company name) attached to the TV sets of a sample of viewers; the TV service was terminated at the end of 1993.

Nielsen Media Research provides information about TV audiences, published in newspapers and magazines, so the term "Nielsen rating" is known by the general public (certainly, the media-savvy readers of this book). Nielsen Media Research obtains local and national TV program and station audience ratings, based on electronic meters (called "People Meters") attached to TV sets plus personal diaries maintained by the individuals in Nielsen homes, which are representative of the general population. Nielsen classifies a viewer as anyone over the age of two. A related company, Nielsen//NetRatings//, monitors the unique visitors to Web sites and "stickiness" of a Web site, as indicated by the time that an average visitor spends on a site, such as 5:15, or five hours and fifteen minutes on AOL.

The current standard time of a sixty-minute, prime-time network TV program is forty-four minutes of content interrupted by sixteen minutes of commercials and promotional spots. This number of commercials may be so astounding that maybe I should repeat it, but I won't. (In fact, some programs have even less content time.)

In the United States, there are about 1,700 broadcast TV stations, of which about 700 are VHF (*very high frequency*) TV stations. The VHF band is 54 to 200 megahertz, or channels two to thirteen. There are about one thousand UHF (*ultrahigh frequency*) TV stations, transmitting from 470 to 890 megahertz, with lower power and over a smaller area than VHF stations. However, cable system operators can assign stations to any channel so that, for example, a UHF public station can be on channel two and Showtime, a subscription cable service, can be on channel five.

The Big Four TV networks are ABC (American Broadcasting Company), CBS (Columbia Broadcasting System), FOX Broadcasting Company, and NBC (National Broadcasting Company). It used to be the Big Three, but FOX has gained considerably in recent years (FOX populi!). Note that FOX uses all-caps in order to have the same style as the other networks, but print media invariably spell it "Fox" as it is not an initialism but is named after William Fox (1879–1952), founder of the Fox Film Corporation. ABC is owned by the Walt Disney Company; CBS was owned by Viacom (it became a separate company in 2006); Fox by the News Corporation; and NBC, which in 2004 became NBC Universal Television, primarily by General Electric Company. NBC Universal, Inc., is partially owned by Vivendi Universal S.A., based in Paris. Vivendi is not a French word; the name was made up.

The Tiffany Network was the nickname of the CBS-TV network in the sixties and seventies, when its high-quality programs (particularly news) were likened to the prestigious Tiffany jewelry store. CBS also is called "Black Rock," a reference to its headquarters in a black-granite building on the corner of Fifth Avenue and 52nd Street in New York. The symbol of CBS-TV, called The Eye because of its oval shape, was designed in 1951 by William Golden (1911–59), creative director in the CBS-TV advertising and sales promotion department. The Peacock Network is the nickname of NBC-TV; a colorful peacock is its on-air symbol.

The other broadcast networks include Public Broadcasting Service (PBS); United Paramount Network (UPN); and The WB Television Network (WB), owned by Time Warner. The two Spanish networks are Univisión Network (the largest) and Telemundo (owned by NBC Universal).

To appeal to different viewers, by age or interest, some of the cable networks operate a family of channels under the same brand name, such as C-Span, Discovery, Fox, HBO, and Showtime. Nickelodeon provides children's programming fifteen hours a day and, for nine hours a day, adult programming, called *Nick at Nite*. Listings of TV programs from 6:30 p.m. to 1 a.m. on more than one hundred channels now appear in the metropolitan New York area editions of *The New York Times*.

Among America's one hundred and twelve million TV households (homes, apartments, or other dwelling units with one or more TV sets), about seventy-three million are subscribers to cable systems, and about twenty-two million are subscribers to satellite systems.

The most-watched program each year is the Super Bowl, which is seen by about eighty-six million viewers. About forty-three million individuals saw the final episode of *Friends* in 2004, and more than forty-one million people watch the Academy Awards show.

Nielsen Media Research provides extensive data to its subscribers—TV stations, advertising agencies, and others. The charts that are published in the media indicate the ratings (discussed in the chapter, "Advertising").TV rating points vary by time of year: higher in the winter and lower in the summer. A TV rating point currently translates to about 1.1 million households.

Broadcast TV programs have much higher audiences than cable shows, which typically average under one million viewers. Top-rated programs on cable channels, such as wrestling on Spike and *Law & Order* reruns on TNT, are seen by more than four million viewers. The number of subscribers to a cable channel is, in no way, to be equated with the number of viewers of that channel.

The exceptions are the premium channels (primarily HBO and Showtime), which generate big audiences for *The Sopranos* and other popular series.

A few programs are so well known that the media sometimes refer to them by their initials, such as DH (*Desperate Housewives*), ET (*Entertainment Tonight*), GMA (*Good Morning America*), and SNL (*Saturday Night Live*).

About one hundred million Americans watch prime-time television on a typical weekday night. Now's my time to sign off. It's no wonder that so many of us have become channel surfers. So, watch out for a big media kahuna.

[MAJOR CABLE COMPANIES]

*Here's a list of many of the major compa-
nies, including the premium services, with the
full names and initials of their channels. Their
initials or ID (in parentheses) generally appear in
the lower right corner of the screen. You may be
a viewer of C-Span and ESPN but not know the
meanings of their names. Well, here they are!*

- American Movie Classics (AMC)

- Animal Planet

- Arts & Entertainment Television Network (A&E)

- BBC America (British Broadcasting Corporation
  America, BBCA)

- Black Entertainment Television (BET)

- Bravo

- Cable News Network (CNN)

- Cartoon Network (CN or TOON)

- Christian Broadcasting Network (CBN)

- Consumer News and Business
  Channel (CNBC)

- Cable-Satellite Public Affairs Network
  (C-Span or C-SPAN)

- Cinemax

- Comedy Central (COM)

- Country Music Television (CMT)

- Courtroom Television Network (Court TV)

- Discovery Channel (DSC)

- The Disney Channel (Disney)

- E! Entertainment Television (E!)

- Entertainment & Sports
  Programming Network (ESPN)

- Food Network (FOOD)
- Fox News Channel (FOX)
- FX Networks (FX)
- Hallmark Channel (HALL)
- The History Channel (H)
- Home Box Office (HBO)
- Home & Garden Television (HGTV)
- Home Shopping Network (HSN)
- Independent Film Channel (IFC)
- The Learning Channel (TLC)
- Lifetime Television
- Microsoft National Broadcasting Company (MSNBC)
- Music TV (MTV)
- Nickelodeon
- Oxygen Network (oh!)
- Quality, Value and Convenience (QVC)
- Showtime Networks (Showtime)
- Spike TV (Spike)
- STARZ!
- The Travel Channel
- Turner Broadcasting System (TBS or tbs)
- Turner Classic Movies (TCM)
- Turner Network Television (TNT)
- TV Land
- USA Network (USA)
- Video Hits 1 (VH1)
- The Weather Channel (TWC)
- WE: Women's Entertainment (WE)

BROADCASTING ABCs:
ACROSS-THE-BOARD TO ZOOM

TALK show hosts, news anchors, and broadcasters frequently use the jargon of radio and TV on the air. We also hear broadcasting lingo on programs such as *Frasier*. Following, in alphabetical order, is an abridged collection of some of these terms.

Many broadcasting terms also are discussed in other chapters, particularly "Advertising," "Awards," and "Film."

Across-the-board is a program or commercial scheduled at the same time each day, generally Monday through Friday. It's also called "strip."

An *actuality* is a live or taped news report broadcast from the scene, containing the voice(s) of the newsmaker(s), as well as of the reporter.

Air is the medium for radio and TV broadcasting. A station or program, when broadcasting or being broadcast, is "on the air" or "airing." An "air check" is an audio or video transcription or recording, made from an actual broadcast, of a radio or TV commercial or program. "Air date" is the time of a broadcast. *Airplay* is the broadcast of a disc, record, or tape. One measurement of a hit recording is the number of airplays it receives.

An *anchor* ("anchorman" or "anchorwoman") is the key narrator of a newscast or other program. Two or more individuals sharing these functions are "co-anchors." A "local anchor" works at a local station; a "network anchor" at a network. Specialized newscasters include "sports anchor," "weather anchor," and "weekend anchor." A "field anchor" reports from a studio outside the studio headquarters. Don Hewitt (b. 1922), the longtime executive producer of *60 Minutes*, was one of the first to use "anchor" (in 1952) in a broadcast sense. The term was a sports reference to the fastest person on a relay team, the one who usually ran the last leg.

Arc is a miniseries within a regularly scheduled program, such as a "two-parter," "three-parter," or several episodes with the same plot. In general, *arc* denotes the path of the plot that continues from one segment or program to another. Some series, such as *Law & Order*, tell a complete story in a single program.

Auntie is a somewhat derogatory, though affectionate, colloquial term for the British Broadcasting Corporation (BBC). Brits refer to a television set as the *telly*.

Back announce is a recap or summary by a disc jockey or announcer of the recordings, tapes, or discs broadcast during the preceding period.

Beat is common in journalism, music, acting (a "brief pause"), film (the "heartbeat" or "theme"). In TV, a "beat" is a revealing moment, such as an outburst of emotion.

A *bite* is a short segment, such as a ten-second *sound bite* (frequently spelled "soundbite" in the media), that is colorful or pithy and is repeated on radio and TV news programs. A major excerpt from an interview, a very quotable sentence or two, is called the "news bite" or "bite-of-the-day." A "strong bite," the opposite of a "weak bite," is dramatic. To *pull a bite* is to find a usable short section in a longer tape.

To *bleep* is to delete sound, as in bleeping an expletive from a program.

A *boom* is a long movable stand, crane, arm, or pole for mounting and moving a microphone ("boom microphone") or camera in a film or TV production.

Breaking news is currently happening or impending news. It's also called a "breaking story." Even more of the moment is "late-breaking news."

To *bump* is to cancel a guest or segment. A second meaning of *bump* is a tape, photo, or graphic used to promote or tease a forthcoming segment of a program, usually with the words "coming up next." A *bump*, or *bumper*, also is a transitional device, such as fadeout music, or "We'll return after these messages," inserted between story action and a commercial.

A *button* is a strong musical or sound effect, such as the end of a commercial, or a bit of music between segments of a program; also called a "stinger."

A *call screener* receives phone calls from listeners to a talk show (a *call-in* program) and designates which ones to forward to the show host. It's a key job and the person usually is the show's producer or associate producer.

A *camera cue*, a red light or buzzer, indicates that a TV camera is shooting for transmission, live or taped. It's also called a "cue light," "tally light," or "warning light."

Television talk shows often post notices in the middle of a program to recruit participants for future shows; the announcement is called a *cart*, akin to a shopping cart.

Churn, the opening monologue of the host of a talk show, is designed to stimulate ("churn") the listeners so they do not switch to another station.

The Chyron Corporation is a major manufacturer of electronic image and character generators and TV graphics systems, particularly those commonly used by many TV stations and producers to create lettering and graphics. The systems are so common that the company name sometimes is used generically or as a verb (for example, to *chyron* an identification). An *electronic character generator* (ECG) is a typewriterlike machine that produces lettering for broadcasting on-screen. The instruction often is "font" (for a typeface) or "super" (superimposition).

Continuity refers to the quality of a script, giving the broadcaster a continuous flow of spoken words. A "continuity acceptance department" (or "continuity clearance department") reviews programming and advertising to eliminate unsubstantiated claims and illegal or objectionable material. "Continuity" also means the impression that events, scenes, and shots flow smoothly and naturally in proper sequence, without any inconsistent transitions ("continuity flaws").

The *control room* is the room in which the director, engineer, and others adjust sound and/or video. It's the command center from which the director and producer and their staffs run the broadcast.

A *cough button* is a switch used by a radio announcer to cut off the microphone during a cough or sneeze.

A *cover shot* is a wide or long-distance view, such as generally begins a sequence, to establish the location of a story. It's also additional coverage of an event to be used as a replacement or addition.

A *crawl* is information, such as a news bulletin, promotional message, telephone number, or cast credits, transmitted in a continuous flow across all or part of a TV screen (often the bottom). The crawl can be horizontal (across the top or bottom of the screen) or vertical (from the bottom, moving up) and is positioned in the crawl space, or *stripe*. Some cable news programs have several simultaneous crawls filling a large part of the screen.

Cross talk means live conversation between broadcasters, as between an anchor and an on-site reporter.

A *cue* signals in words or signs to initiate action, dialogue, effects, or other aspects of a production, such as an indication from a director to a performer or interview subject. Exact timing is *on cue*. Cues may be given with a "cue light," such as an "On The Air" sign or warning light. A *return cue* is a verbal or other signal to return to the studio from a remote broadcast, such as a sports event. To "cue ahead," or "cue up," is to move a tape to the next broadcast or edit point. An *incue* is the first few words, generally four, of a taped report or interview, written on a script to help the engineer identify the tape and use it. To *cue in* is to begin or initiate action, music, dialogue, or effect. An *end cue*, or "outcue," is the last few words, generally four, of a taped report or interview. It's an important guide to the engineer, producer, director, and newscaster that the item is over.

A *cue card* is a large card containing lines to be spoken by a performer, often held up off-camera on TV. It's also called a "flip card," "idiot card," or "idiot sheet." You've seen it on *The Late Show with David Letterman.*

Daypart is a programming segment of a broadcast schedule, such as, for radio, morning and afternoon *drive time* (when many listeners are in their cars commuting to or from work), and, for TV, morning, afternoon, prime, early, and late fringe. "Dayparting" is the scheduling of programs at specific parts of the day, targeted to specific audiences that are predominant during those times, for example, stay-at-home women during the afternoon.

Dead air is a broadcasting term for silence, perhaps resulting from a "dead mike" (inoperative microphone).

On deck is to be ready. An "on-deck camera" is a TV camera whose picture is currently not being transmitted though it is ready to become an on-air camera.

Delayed broadcast (D.B.) is the broadcast of a radio or TV program at a time later than its original transmission, a common procedure in the Pacific time zone.

A *dish* is a microwave transmitter or receiver with a concave (dishlike) reflector to concentrate and focus signals. A small dish can be attached to a microphone to pick up sound from a large area; a large dish can be set atop a tower or roof to transmit or pick up from a satellite. A communications satellite sometimes is called a "skydish" or "big dish" (in the sky). *Downlink* is the portion of a signal down to the receiving point. An *uplink* is the portion from the ground source up to the satellite.

A *dub* means a dupe, or duplicate; or an insert in an audiovisual medium. "Dub" is also used as a verb, as to *dub* something into the body of a radio or TV program or motion picture. Material to be dubbed may consist of a different language soundtrack or other editing.

DVD is a *d*igital *v*ideo and *d*isc, a disc on which images and sound are recorded for reproduction on a DVD player.

DVDs now are more commonly used in homes than videotapes, but TV stations still use videotapes.

An *ear prompter* is a tiny earplug connected to a small audio recorder, enabling a performer to hear a recorded script while onstage or on camera.

Electronic news gathering (ENG) is the use of an electronic, portable TV camera (a *minicam*) to videotape or broadcast news from outside the studio. *Electronic sports gathering* (ESG) uses cameras, mobile units, and other equipment to telecast a sports event.

A *feed* is a segment or an entire program sent from a "feed point" by radio or TV networks to local stations or by a local station to the network or other stations.

Feedback is loud noise, a squeal, or howl from a microphone or speaker caused by improper placement, circuit noise, or other problem.

A *fitting* is an adjustment, and a *TV fitting* is a type of rehearsal, generally of a forthcoming live news event such as a political convention, in which stand-ins are used to test camera angles and other technical details.

In a *five and under*, a performer has a maximum of five lines. A larger number requires a higher payment.

Flight is an advertising campaign, generally for radio or TV, that runs for a specific period, such as four weeks.

In a *follow shot*, the camera follows the action. It's also called a "following shot," "action shot," "moving shot," "running shot," or "tracking shot."

In a *freeze frame*, a single picture, or frame, is repeated or reprinted in sequence to give the effect of frozen, suspended, or stopped motion. Also called "hold frame" or "stop frame," the technique often is used at the end of a theatrical or TV film as a final scene that remains motionless for a short period. *Frame up* is a director's command to adjust the picture.

From the top is a show-business expression that means "from the beginning." The opposite is "from the bottom." The term originates from the days when each scene in a script started at the top of a page.

The abbreviation *f/x*, or *fx*, means "special effects," a term for visual illusions, now often computer-generated, and also an abbreviation for sound effects. The name of the cable TV channel FX, however, is based on its owner's name, the Fox Broadcasting Company.

Gain is an increase of signal power, particularly sound volume. The control that regulates the volume or another level is also called the "gain," as in "turn up the gain." To "ride the gain" is to monitor the control indicator. To "gain-up" is to increase the volume.

Go is a command to execute; such as "go theme," an instruction from the director to the audio-control operator or sound engineer to start the theme music. "Go to black" is to let the image fade out entirely. When *going off*, an actor or performer speaks while moving off-stage, off-camera, or off-mike.

On-air guests wait in an area called a *green room*. The origin is sometimes attributed to the wall color of rooms adjacent to studios at the National Broadcasting Company in New York and Los Angeles. Actually, the term predates television. The earliest such rooms probably were found in seventeenth-century Elizabethan theaters, where they were called "tiring rooms." Performers attired there, and the rooms sometimes contained green shrubbery. The color green is nonglaring and helps occupants to relax; though many of these rooms are not actually colored green. In the United Kingdom in the nineteenth century, "green-room gossip" meant theatrical shoptalk.

Happy talk, a format of some local programs, features light banter among an ensemble of newscasters.

Headlines are used in broadcast and other media, in addition to newspapers. For example, the lead item or indication of a forthcoming item on a broadcast may be referred to as a *headline*. The preliminary on-air indication sometimes is called a *billboard*.

A *headphone*, or *earphone*, is a radio or telephone receiver held in place to the ear or ears by a band over the head. It's commonly used by individuals at home and at work. In broadcasting, the headphones are called *cans*. An *insert earphone* fits in the ear and is commonly used by broadcasters.

A *holdover audience* is that portion of a television or radio audience of one program who tuned into the previous program on the same station. It's also called an "inherited" or "carry-over" audience.

An *interruptible feedback line* (IFB) is a telephone line for a producer or director to talk to a newscaster or an interviewer during a broadcast.

Interstitial programming is the placement of a short program between full-length programs. For example, HBO and other movie channels schedule shorter programs, often about thirty minutes long, between the full-length movies. These programs often feature "Behind-the-Scenes" (BTS) interviews and shots, made during the production of the film, and can highlight the technology or other unusual aspects of making the film.

A *jingle* is a musical commercial, usually sung, or a short verse or tune that is easily remembered.

A term that has achieved recent popularity is *jump the shark*, the moment a major TV series starts to decline. The phrase refers to *Happy Days*, a sitcom on ABC-TV from 1974 to 1984, that allegedly started to decline after the principal character, Fonzie, water-skied over a shark. (For more about this, log on to www.jumptheshark.com.)

Kilocycle (kc) means "one thousand cycles per second," or one thousand alterations of current or sound waves per second. The number of kilocycles determines a radio station's frequency, and thus its position on the dial.

A *kinescope*, or "kine" (pronounced KIN-ney), is a film of a transmitted television picture. Kinescopes have been replaced by videotapes and videodiscs. Originally, "kine-scope" was a synonym for picture tube.

A *lead-in* is an introduction, such as in a newscast preceding a report. The opposite, *lead-out*, is an announcement or segment after a commercial, news report, or program. A lead-in also can be a brief segment at the beginning of a sitcom or other TV program, with highlights of the previous program or programs in the series. A "lead-in program" precedes another on the same station or network. The audience carryover from one program to another can be extremely important.

Letterbox format is the ratio of width to height (the "aspect ratio") used in showing a film on TV, so that the film has the same relative dimensions as it did when shown in a theater. Films shown on a TV screen generally do not have their original aspect ratio. These days, most films appearing on TV and DVDs have been reformatted to avoid blank spaces above and below the picture. The term refers to the rectangular shape of a letterbox (mailbox).

Level is the degree of sound volume. A radio engineer or recording-studio technician may ask for "a level"—that is, request that the performers speak in order to determine a general setting of the volume controls.

Liner cards are large index cards for use by announcers and disc jockeys. The cards contain slogans, information about current promotions and upcoming programs, and other on-air remarks, messages, and chatter. The information generally now is displayed on computer screens.

Lineup is the arrangement of items in a newscast, or the order of elements and segments in any program.

A *listening shot* shows an interviewer listening. It's usually called a "reaction shot" or "cutaway shot."

Live on tape is a TV or radio program of an actual performance, recorded and broadcast subsequently and therefore not really live. A *liver* (pronounced LIE-ver) is a live report without accompanying tape or other material.

To *make local* is to insert a station identification in a

network program. To *make system* is to identify a network, such as the Columbia Broadcasting System.

Man-on-the-street (MOS) is an interview in which the opinions of the general public are sought.

A *microphone*, or *mike*, is a device for transmitting sound. A "mike boom" is a crane or arm that holds a microphone. A "mike box" is a unit connecting one microphone with others, as on a lectern or table at a press conference. A "sitting mike" is a table microphone. A "rifle mike" is a long, narrow, directional microphone that can be aimed like a rifle. An "open mike" is a live microphone. A "roving mike" is a hand-held microphone, cordless or on a long cord, used by talk show hosts, reporters, and others to move through a studio or other sites. A "lapel mike" is a small microphone clipped to a lapel, necktie, shirt, or elsewhere, or worn around the neck. A "gallows mike" is a gooseneck microphone hung from a support base. A "mike sock" is a cover, such as a foam rubber sleeve, that fits over a microphone to reduce external sounds.

A *minicam* is a small, self-contained portable TV camera for videotaping on-site news events. (Minicam is the brand name.) When linked to a mobile transmission unit ("minicam van"), the minicam can provide live coverage at relatively low cost.

A *mixer* is the unit that controls and blends audio and/or video signals; and also the technician who operates the unit (also called a "rerecording supervisor" or "chief recording mixer").

A *mobile unit* is a vehicle for originating broadcasts from on-the-spot locations, away from the studio, or for carrying equipment for on-location production; it's also called a "mobile production unit."

A *monitor* is a device for checking or regulating performance; for instance, an instrument that receives TV signals by direct wire rather than over the air, as in a TV studio or closed circuit, sometimes without the sound.

A *monologue,* or "monolog," is a long speech or soliloquy. In show business, a monologue is often a continuous series of jokes. The late-night TV shows of Jay Leno (b. 1950) and David Letterman (b. 1947) start with walk-on music and opening monologues.

A *moray* is a video disturbance caused by flashy jewelry, brightly colored apparel, or other sources. Commonly called a "moray pattern," it's perhaps named after a type of brightly colored eel called a "moray." More likely, it's from *moiré*, an irregular wavy finish on a fabric.

Morphing is a computer process that continuously transforms one photograph or image into another, commonly used in videos and film. A *morph* is the resulting image. The terms come from a shortening of *metamorphose* (the verb) or *metamorphosis* (the noun), denoting "change in form."

Natural sound consists of animal noises, sounds of weather conditions, and other actual sounds recorded for broadcast or other use, as contrasted with artificial sound or sound effects. The script notation is *natsot*, for *nat*ural sound *o*n *t*ape.

NEMO is a remote pickup, a broadcast not originated by the station transmitting it. Pronounced NEE-moh, the acronym stands for "not emanating from main office."

News, in its simplest sense, refers to fresh information. *Hard news* refers to reporting of current events, whereas *soft news* is more likely to be human-interest features or less current or less urgent news. A "news feature" is an elaboration on a news report. The "news department" of a radio or TV station or network, headed by a "news director," prepares and/or broadcasts news reports. A *news envelope* is a brief news segment, such as a 60-second news update on a local, network, or syndicated program, with its own local or national sponsor.

A *nodder* is a reaction shot of an interviewer in which he or she is nodding in agreement. The British call them "noddies."

O&O means "owned and operated," as with the stations in New York, Chicago, Los Angeles, and other major cities that are owned and operated by the networks.

Pan is a direction given to the person operating the film or TV camera, to move the camera slowly and evenly, vertically or horizontally, in a panorama (the source of the term). A *pan shot* also is called a "blue pan," "swish," "whipshot," or "wiz pan." The process of laterally moving the camera to photograph a wide view is called "panning."

Parting gifts are products or services announced during or at the end of TV talk or game shows, such as hotel accommodations and airline transportation for the guests on the program.

A *phoner* is a telephone interview or report on radio and television.

A *pilot* is a sample or prototype broadcast or other proposed project.

Play on, or "play-on," is a brief musical passage to introduce a performer; usually music associated with the performer. It's also music to begin a program or a performance. *Playoff* is music to end the performance.

A *playlist* is a schedule of music recordings on a radio or TV program.

Plot is a common noun and adjective, in books, film, television, and theater. The "plot line" is a summary of the narrative. A "subplot" is a sequence of story threads (they weave their way through the main plot) or strands. A dramatic TV series may have many threads, some continued from preceding programs. On the Internet, a "thread" is a series of comments, by different individuals, on the same subject on a discussion board, forum, or blog.

Point of view (POV) is a camera shot seen from or obtained from the position of a performer so that a viewer sees what the performer is seeing.

In broadcast advertising, a *pool*, or "commercial pool," is the full complement of radio or TV commercials that is available for broadcast at any one time. The development of commercials to be added to the pool is known as "pooling out" or "filling the pool"; each new commercial is a "pool partner."

Pool-out is the ending of a TV commercial, often ten seconds long, produced in several versions so that a basic thirty- or sixty-second commercial appears different.

A *pop* is an unscripted on-the-scene report, usually live, by a TV reporter. A *pop-off* is a sudden move, such as the quick removal of an object or the departure of a performer from the scene. A *pop-on* is the reverse: a sudden or quick entry. *Popping* is the explosive sounds microphones make with the volume turned high or a speaker who is too close.

Preempt is to replace a regularly scheduled program or commercial. A "preemptable" may be sold by a radio or a TV station at a reduced rate ("preemptable rate"); the program or commercial is subject to cancellation prior to broadcast if another advertiser pays a higher rate or if a pending news event replaces, or bumps, it.

A *preview light* is the green warning light on a TV camera, indicating that it is about to transmit, at which point, the light turns red.

A *preview monitor* (PV) is a TV screen used by the director to monitor and select a picture to be used from among shots by various cameras and other sources.

Prime time is the period with the greatest number of listeners or viewers. In television, prime time generally is from 8 to 11 p.m., Eastern Time. The transitional period immediately before or after prime time is called *fringe time*.

The *producer* is in charge of finance, personnel, and other aspects of the production. In broadcasting, the producer has more creative responsibilities and control than in the movie industry; it is the associate producer who is in charge of the business elements of production. A *field producer* works outside the headquarters studio, in the field, to prepare pieces for an upcoming broadcast. A *production assistant* (P.A.) aids a producer, director, or others involved in film or TV production.

The *program director* (PD or P.D.) is in charge of programming everything except the commercials and promotions. The program director reports to the station or network manager, usually called the *general manager*.

Promo, which is short for "promotion" (the short-form plural is "promos"), refers to the overall activity conducted by a radio or TV station, or any organization, designed to help sell a particular product or service. More specifically, the word refers to the preliminary announcement of a program, broadcast earlier in the day of the program or on the preceding day or days.

A *prompter* is a device to enable speakers and performers to read a script while looking at the audience or camera. The computer-generated copy is transmitted to one or more prompter/monitor readouts that are mounted on or off a TV camera. The prompter script can be superimposed over the lens of the TV camera so that it is visible to the speaker but not transmitted to the home viewer. *Prompter* is also another term for "teleprompter."

Pronouncer is the phonetic spelling of a word, particularly important in helping announcers pronounce foreign names. The Associated Press issues a pronunciation guide for broadcasters.

A *public access channel* is reserved by a cable company for community or other public service programs. It is generally available to nonprofit organizations and others. Public radio and public television are noncommercial stations, supported primarily by grants and contributions from listeners and viewers. The original TV term was "educational television." In recent years, corporate underwriters were given more air time, particularly on television, and their enhanced credits at the beginning and end of programs often resemble commercials, including some since 2003 as long as thirty seconds.

A *reality show* used to be a program that combined news and other techniques, such as discussion, dramatization, and entertainment. In recent years, the term refers to *survival-*

type programs, personal and home makeovers, and other programs with "real people" (not professional actors). A *scripted drama*, such as *Desperate Housewives*, is a dramatic program with professional scriptwriters and actors.

A *red light* is the warning light over a door of a studio indicating that it is in use; and also, as previously noted, a light (called a "camera cue" or "tally light") on a TV camera indicating that it is in use.

A *remote* is a broadcast from a place other than the station's studio, often transmitted from a remote truck or van.

A *reporter* is a person who gathers news and other journalistic material and writes or broadcasts it, the basic job in journalism. A *street reporter* works outside the studio and an "on-air reporter" is shown on camera, either from outside the studio or within it.

Repurposing is placement of a series by a network very soon (a few days) after the original broadcast. It's not the same as a "rerun," which usually is aired a few months, a year, or more after the original.

A *residual* is a payment to performers ("talent") in broadcast programs or commercials for its use beyond the original contract, according to a formula developed by AFTRA (American Federation of Television and Radio Artists) or another union.

A *return monitor* is a TV screen linked to a TV camera, so that an interviewee or broadcaster in one studio, for example, can see the interviewer or anchor in another studio. Ordinarily in such situations, the interviewee can hear only the interviewer.

Ripomatic is a TV commercial made by an advertising agency or other producer as a demonstration. It's made (ripped off) from parts of actual commercials but is not intended for broadcast use.

A *rosr* (pronounced ROSE-er) stands for a *r*adio *on-scene r*eport featuring a reporter's voice from a news scene, generally without background sound.

Rotation is the scheduling of commercials and other

materials. A music disc that is kept *in rotation* is broadcast frequently throughout the day on a radio station.

A *routing room* is a room in a TV station or network with a wall of monitors on which are shown live feeds of remote transmissions for routing to tape decks or for broadcast. You've seen this in newscasts.

A *rundown* is a summary or a schedule of scenes in a production or segments of a program. It's also called a "rundown sheet" or "timing sheet."

Running time is the time from the start to the end of a program, segment, or commercial, or the minutes it takes to show a movie.

A *satellite* is a relay station for audio and video transmission, orbiting in space or terrestrial. A "satellite station" is a radio or TV station used as a relay, broadcasting on the same or a different wavelength as the originating station. Almost all communications satellites are synchronous satellites that hover in the same place in the sky, 22,300 miles above the earth, in stationary orbit. A *satellite loop* is a sequence from a satellite, such as cloud movement in a TV weather report.

A *satellite news* (or *newsgathering*) *vehicle* (SNV) is a van or other vehicle with equipment for transmission via satellite to a radio or TV station, usually including tape-editing equipment. It's also called a *star truck*.

Scatter is the scheduling of commercials throughout a broadcast schedule rather than at specific times, such as rotating throughout the day or night or both. It's also called "scatter plan" or "scatter buying."

Shoot is a session at which performances are filmed or taped. One goes on or to a *shoot*, especially on location instead of in a studio. It's also to film, photograph, record, or tape such a session or any scene, or an instruction to start the camera. To "overshoot" is to shoot too much footage; to "undershoot" is to shoot too little.

A *shooter* is a photographer or field camera operator. A *shooting script* is a script for a film or TV production.

A *show runner* is a slang title for a key person at a television drama or sitcom who supervises all aspects of the production, including writing and casting. The official title usually is "executive producer."

A *simulcast* is a broadcast of a program at the same time on a television station and a radio station or on two radio stations, generally one AM and one FM, as well as on the Internet.

A *slot* is the location of a program, announcement, news item, interview, or commercial on a broadcast schedule. Communication satellites are positioned ("parked") in orbit in "slots" two or more degrees apart.

Slow down is a signal to slow down action or to talk more slowly. It is conveyed by a movement of one's hands, as in pulling taffy. *Speed up* is a signal to a performer to talk more rapidly. The nonverbal speed-up signal is both hands rotating in a circular motion.

A *slow* (or *light*) *news day* is a day with relatively little hard news or news of consequence. The opposite is *heavy news day* (not "fast news day").

A *soap opera* is a dramatic serial TV program, originally sponsored on radio mainly by Procter & Gamble and other soap companies. It's also called a "soap," "soaper," or "daytime drama" (because it originates during the day). A *telenovella* is a Spanish soap opera.

Sound is the programming format or orientation of a radio station. A *sound engineer* is responsible for the audio portion of a broadcast. The sound-effects person, generally called a "sound man" or "sound woman," is responsible for the "sound effects" (S.E. or SFX), which include sounds other than music and human voices.

A *spin-off* (or *spinoff*) is a show or other item derived from an existing or earlier work. The two current TV spin-off champs are *Law & Order*, which debuted on NBC in 1990, and *CSI*, which debuted on CBS in 2000.

A *sponsor* is a broadcast advertiser who pays for part or all of a program. The word now is used to indicate any broadcast advertiser, including a sponsor of an individual spot or commercial. "Sponsor identification" (S.I.) is the announcement at the beginning and/or end of a sponsored program or segment identifying one or more sponsors.

A *spotter* is a person who looks for something during a broadcast, such as an assistant to a sports announcer, who helps to identify the participants in a game.

Squeeze is slang for a visual inserted in a window on the screen, generally to the right of a newscaster, to identify the subject of a news report. It is more commonly called a *topic box*.

Standards and practices is a broadcasting network department that reviews programming and commercials with regard to morality and taste. At an individual station, this function generally is called *Continuity Acceptance*.

Standby is a person or thing ready for use as a substitute, usually on an emergency basis. *Standby weather* is a script used by an anchor or announcer when the prompter fails or the feed from the weather reporter fails.

A *stand-up* is an on-site TV report or interview, as compared to in-studio. A *standupper* is a report at the scene of an event with the TV camera focused on the reporter, who is standing up and not seated. In a "walking standupper," the reporter moves.

A *still store*, or "electronic still store" (ESS), is an electronic memory unit (storage or store) for retaining single "visuals," such as graphics and photos ("stills") used in newscasts. A still "store supervisor" is in charge of this function. "Stills" also is slang for the photographers of the print media, as when TV crews shout, "Down stills!," a request to still photographers at a media event to stoop down so that the TV cameras, generally behind them, can "catch the action."

A *storyboard* is a series of illustrations ("storyboard sketches") or layouts of scenes in a proposed TV commercial or other work, used as a guide prior to production. A "storyboarder" or "sketch artist" does "storyboarding."

Straight up is a signal, such as to an announcer, to start when the clock's second hand is at twelve.

A *superstation* is a local TV station transmitted via satellite to cable systems in many markets. The word was coined and copyrighted by WTBS-TV of Atlanta, Georgia.

Surfing is the rapid changing of TV channels with a remote control, akin to the sport of surfing (fast movement on water). It's also called "grazing."

A *sweep* is a period of the year when rating services measure station audiences. During sweep periods, or *sweeps*, networks and stations employ more sensational programming and audience contests and promotions. (Sweeps currently are four times a year, but the times and frequency may change.)

A *sweeper* (also called a *tag line*) is the station's motto, such as "Easy Listening." "Secondary sweepers," usually longer, are often used throughout the hour and may change. The sweepers are prepared by the "promotion department," which sometimes is called the "imaging department" (that promotes the station's personality—its image). "Promotional spots" are commercials that advertise a program, station, or network.

Switch is a direction to move or change, as from one camera or video source to another, or to change camera angles. The device ("video mixer") or person ("studio engineer") responsible for camera mixing or switching is called a "switch" or *switcher*.

Take it away is a broadcast-engineering cue, such as "Take it away New York," indicating a transition to a studio or location in New York.

A *talent coordinator* is a person who auditions and schedules performers and guests on TV talk shows, the equivalent of a casting director in films.

Talk set is conversation on a radio program between recordings. *Talkback* is a brief sequence at the end of a live remote news report in which the anchor asks one or more questions of the reporter. A *talking head* is a person shown merely speaking, usually presented in a dull or unimaginative way.

A *tape delay system*, used on call-in radio programs, tapes a phone call and delays it for a few seconds prior to broadcast, so that obscenities can be deleted or the call cut off prior to broadcast.

Radio and TV newscasters and others compile highlights of their broadcasts on a *Tape*, when auditioning for a job. It's the equivalent of the portfolio used by designers and copywriters in advertising.

TBA ("to be announced") is used in broadcasting schedules when the name of a program or other information is not available.

A *tease* is a bit of news preceding the newscast, an announcement of an upcoming story to whet interest, or a brief segment promoting an upcoming program. It's also called "teaser," "come-on-spot," or "hooker."

The *technical director* (T.D.) is the director of the technical facilities in a television studio. He or she generally sits next to the director in the control room and operates the switcher.

TelePrompTer is a trademarked visual prompting device for speakers and television performers that reproduces the current portion of the script in enlarged letters, originally made by a New York-based company no longer in business. Today, *teleprompter* has become a generic term for the device attached to the TV camera enabling performers to look into the camera while reading the projected script. It is also called a "teleprompt," and most frequently, "prompter."

A *tell story* is a news report read by a radio or TV announcer or reporter without accompanying tape or film.

A *tent-pole* is the time slot or position of a popular program that is preceded or followed by a weak one. In *hammocking*, a weak program is scheduled between two popular programs, which have the outside, or tent-pole, positions, in an attempt to bolster the weak program.

("Hammocking" refers to the way that a canvas hammock hangs between two supports.) The weak program is in the *saddle* position. A "tent-pole franchise" is a popular program that generates spin-offs. The term also is used in the film business to describe a film that becomes the centerpiece for toys and other products.

Tight on, or "close on," is an instruction to a television camera operator for a close shot of a specific person or object, as in "tight on (name of performer)."

Tilt is a direction to move a camera up or down; it's also called a "vertical pan."

TiVo is a service that can be programmed to record TV programs, music, and other material. TiVo, Inc., formed in 1997, started operating in 1999 and now is so popular that its name is used as a verb—to "*TiVo* a program." The name "TiVo" is coined; its initials do not refer to anything, nor is it an acronym.

Top is the beginning, as in "top of the script" or "top of the story." Thus, a tape starts "at the top" and ends "at the bottom."

Top forty is a radio-station format playing the forty most-popular recordings as determined by *Billboard* magazine or other trade sources. It's also called "contemporary hit radio."

A *topic box* is a visual inserted in a window (a box) on the screen, generally to the right of a newscaster, to identify the subject of a news report. It's also called a "box," "frame squeeze," or "theme identifier."

A *toss* is one or more words spoken by a newscaster that serves as a transition to a colleague, such as a reference to a forthcoming news report and/or the colleague's name. A "split story toss" is a reading of part of a news report by one newscaster followed by a continuation of the same story by another. On cable news channels, a common toss at the end of a program is for the talk show host or newscaster to introduce and promote the broadcaster who follows. It's also called a "throw" or "handoff."

A *two-way* is an on-air conversation, as an anchor with a reporter or a guest in a remote location.

Ultrahigh frequency (UHF) refers to limited-range wave bands for television channels that transmit with lower power and over a smaller area than *very high frequency* (VHF) stations (channels two to thirteen).

Up full is a direction for audio to be heard at full volume. *Up-and-over* is a direction to a sound engineer or music conductor to increase music or sound as speech fades or ends, the opposite of *down-and-under*. The direction *up-and-under* means to bring in music and then lower it below the dialogue or other sound.

A *V-chip* (the *V* stands for "violence") is a computerized device in a television set that automatically blocks the receipt of specific programs that are coded to indicate they contain violent segments. The V-chip is activated at the option of the viewer, and was designed primarily for parents who wanted to limit the amount of violence their children watched on television.

A *video news release* (VNR) is a news item or feature on videotape, sent free by a public relations source to television stations, sometimes with additional material (called "B-roll"). (More on this in the "Public Relations" chapter.)

Video-on-demand (VOD or V.O.D.) is a service on some cable systems that enables subscribers to order a videotape or disc from a list of films to be transmitted to them immediately.

Voice-over (VO) is the sound of an unseen narrator on a TV program or a reading by an announcer while a videotape is shown. "Voice-over credits" (V.O.C.) are audio identifications of sponsors, cast, or other credits, such as at the beginning or end of a TV program. The TV voice-over story, in which a newscaster reports while a tape is shown, is very common.

Wallpaper video is slang for generic, or stock, visuals, graphics, or other stills or tape that can be used as introductions or backgrounds, or that can be inserted in a window on the screen. They are commonly used in newscasts. However, the reverse term, *video wallpaper*, means a TV background that is dull.

A *wheel*, or *clock*, is a chart in the shape of a clock showing the segments for the news, traffic, weather, and other reports, programs, and commercials. A *news wheel* is a news program that is repeated with updates, as on an all-news radio station.

A *window* is a rectangular insert or other predefined area, as on a video screen. It's also a scheduled time slot on a satellite.

Wraparound is the introductory and concluding segments of a program or series, or the live portion before and after a taped segment. In a "wraparound" on TV news, a reporter at the scene or in the studio introduces a previously taped report and then provides additional information or an update.

To *zap* is the use of a remote-control device (a "zapper") to change stations, or to blip out commercials, as with a pause button.

A *zipper* is a bit of music or sound effect to signal a local radio or TV station to interrupt for identification, a commercial, or other break. Also, as noted in "Comic Relief," a *zipper* is an inconsequential or humorous final item on a newscast.

To *zoom* is to move the camera or change the lens, as from a long shot to a close-up (to "zoom in") or the opposite (to "zoom out").

Well, there you have it, the A to Z of radio and TV broadcasting.

COLORS: A MEDIA RAINBOW

WE live in a colorful and color-filled world, in every sense. Colors can signify characteristics or have special meanings, and these meanings often carry over into media lingo in interesting and sometimes confusing ways. For example, red is the universal signal to stop. However, a red light on a camera, called a *tally light,* indicates that the camera is on.

When you reveal your *true colors*, you show your real character. A novel with color contains vivid writing. Music with color has a particular strength (timbre). However, to *color a story* may mean to distort or exaggerate, or simply to add a variety of expressions so you have a colorful story to entertain others.

Unless you're *color-blind* (unable to distinguish shades of red or green), you are likely to be able to recognize a color and its connotation or its context. In recent years, print and TV media have maps of the United States with those states that are predominantly Democratic colored blue and Republican states red. The reasons are somewhat hazy (in the 1992 and 1996 presidential elections it was the reverse), but that's the current custom.

Green generally connotes anything new, fresh, immature, unprocessed, natural, inexpensive, or naïve. The best-known green quotation undoubtedly is the second line of the twenty-third Psalm, "He maketh me to lie down in green pastures."

In media jargon, *greenlighting* means the process of approving a project or proposal. To *greenlight* a story idea is welcome news to a film or television writer and literally signifies a go-ahead, as on a traffic light.

In film studios, the *greenery department* grows plants, trees, and other greenery and arranges them on the sets or locations. Film credits often indicate the *greensman*, who works in this department.

In theaters, performers can relax in the *greenroom* area near the stage before going onstage. TV viewers often hear an interview guest mention the pre-performance wait (often with catering) in the greenroom (discussed in "Broadcasting ABCs").

Directories often are referred to by the color of their covers. For example, the green-covered *Green Book* is titled *The Social List of Washington*, an annual directory of prominent individuals, located mostly in the nation's capital. Perhaps it should have a blue cover and be called the "Blue Book," because it's a listing of bluebloods. (Aristocrats in Spain and other countries probably were first called "bluebloods" because of the visibility of the veins in their fair skin.) In fact, local directories of socialites in such upscale areas as Southhampton, New York, do have blue colors and are called "Blue Books." Many directories, such as the *Standard Directory of Advertisers*, have red covers and are called "The Red Book."

Newspaper reporters used to wear hats inside their offices. Famous gossip columnist Walter Winchell (1897-1972) comes to mind. Copyeditors and proofreaders usually wore caps or visors, called *green eyeshades*, to prevent glare. In precomputer days, copyediting was done using a color pencil. To *green out* (the term still is used and originates from the use of a green pencil) means to edit tightly or to take out descriptive phrases or other text. Editors also used blue pencils and to *blue pencil* something had the same meaning. And, from the editor's use of a red pencil comes *redlining*, meaning to track changes in a word-processed document.

Green connotes fresh and vigorous, but also young, immature or not aged. *Greenbacks* usually denote U.S. paper money (printed green); while *green mail* denotes a financial maneuver in which one publicly traded company purchases the stock of another company in order to avoid being acquired by that second company. The word is a blend of *green* and *blackmail*.

"To be green" can mean gullible or jealous (*green-eyed* or *green with envy*). A *greenhorn* is an inexperienced or immature person. Immigrants unfamiliar with the language and culture of their new lands often were derogatively called "greenhorns." The word comes from the Middle English (twelfth- to sixteenth-century) *greene horn*, denoting a newly slaughtered animal.

"Evergreen" means foliage that remains green throughout the year, or more generally anything that remains fresh and enduring. A timeless newspaper article or other work that can be published at any time is called an *evergreen*. An *evergreen* book, show, or product can generate sales year after year.

Moving down the color scale, blue sometimes symbolizes sadness (the "blues"), aristocracy ("bluebloods"), military dress (Union soldiers in the Civil War were called the "Blues"), or indecency (a "blue movie").

Blue covers are used for various directories, as well as in high school and college classrooms for examination writing books. The precursor of today's paperbacks, *The Little Blue Book* series, consisted of small (3 ⅓ inch x 5 inch) publications, with flexible blue covers, launched in 1919 by E. Haldeman-Julius (1888–1951) in Girard, Kansas. These popular books were sold directly to the public via newspaper advertising. More than 300 million copies were sold during their creator's lifetime, originally for as little as five cents, and included novels, advice books, and books in just about every other category.

Architects and engineers still use *blueprints*, paper negatives exposed to light and developed to produce white lines against a blue background. In precomputer days, printers provided proofs in blue ink and the terms *blues* or *blueline* still are used in publishing, for proofs. In general, a "blueprint" means a detailed, broad plan. A similar term of recent popularity is *roadmap*, a set of guidelines that also can be broad-ranging and detailed.

In many telephone directories, listings of government agencies are printed on blue pages. In the film industry, a revised script is printed on blue pages, with subsequent revisions printed on pink, yellow, green, and goldenrod, in that order. (In this case, going all the way to the goldenrod may be arduous, instead of glamorous.)

Big Blue is the nickname of I.B.M. and stands for the company's official color, derived in turn from the color of its mainframe computers of the 1960s.

Radio stations that feature *rhythm and blues* ("R&B") music are now more generally called "urban contemporary." The *blues* is a melancholic style of music that evolved from African American spiritual songs.

Bluegrass is a type of country music featuring string instruments, particularly banjo, fiddle, and guitar, named after Bluegrass Country in central Kentucky, where lush bluegrass is grown.

In advertising, film, and other fields, to *blue sky* is to loosely or creatively express a view, such as an estimated budget. *Into the blue* is a far distance, but *out of the blue* means the unknown.

In the days when daily newspapers published many editions, a "blue-streak" or "red-streak" edition had a line of blue or red ink on the front page. It usually was a late edition, such as with sports scores. Now, to *talk a blue streak* means to talk rapidly and endlessly, usually exaggerative, an allusion to a lightning bolt.

Among salespeople, an unexpected easy sale is a *bluebird*. For the rest of us, the most common association is with Judy Garland (1922–69) singing in *The Wizard of Oz*: "Somewhere over the rainbow, bluebirds fly."

A *blue moon* is the second of two full moons in the same month. In the media and general slang, however, it's a relatively long period of time, as in *once in a blue moon*, a reference to the rare times when the moon appears bluish due to volcanic or other particles in the atmosphere.

Now to yellow, a symbol of money (gold) and slang for cowardly. Advertising people and others sometimes conduct creative meetings in rooms with vibrant yellow walls.

Yellow taxicabs are ubiquitous in New York and other cities and sometimes carry advertising atop or within. John D. Hertz (1879–1961), a Chicago car dealer who started the Yellow Cab Company in 1915 and franchised the name in other cities, is the same Hertz who, in 1924, started the car rental company.

A blinking yellow traffic light indicates caution. In general parlance, a "yellow light" can mean a decision to proceed with caution on a project. (To some impatient drivers, a yellow light often is a signal to speed up before the light turns red!)

*Yellowback*s were low-priced popular novels, bound in yellow board, that were popular in the nineteenth century. *Yellow Pages* (capitalized because it's a trademark) are classified telephone directories, arranged alphabetically within business categories and other classifications. The covers and pages usually are printed yellow, with the pages filled with advertisements and "enhanced listings" (in boldface or larger than the one-line free listings). Yellow Pages are now common online.

YMCK are the initials of yellow, magenta (purplish-red or blue-red), cyan (greenish-blue), and black, the sequence in which colors are applied on a printing press. Actually the K stands for "key color," the central color in a "color build" from which other colors are calculated. However, the key color almost always is black, which coincidentally ends with *k*. Take a look at your computer color printer, and you'll see six ink cartridges: black, cyan, light cyan, magenta, light magenta, and yellow.

PMS colors (from the Pantone Matching System) are a series of ink-matching guides, available in paper swatches and digitally, that identify hundreds of colors. Published by Pantone, Inc., the PMS colors and their reference numbers are essential to graphic artists and printers, as a standard for communicating color choices.

Red is the color of blood and a symbol of courage, as in *The Red Badge of Courage*, the novel about the Civil War written by Stephen Crane (1871–1900).

A red light or flashing red lights over the door of a television studio or entrance to a film set indicates that it is in use—and it's called the *red zone*. A different "red-light district" is an area with brothels, sex clubs, formerly indicated by a red light in the doorway or on a window.

Red tape, which describes delays due to excessive regulations, goes back to eighteenth-century England when red tape tied official documents.

A *red carpet* often is laid down at an entrance for important visitors, so to "roll out the red carpet" or "give red-carpet treatment" means to provide special attention. Red is associated with royalty and red carpets have been used for centuries.

The darkest (black) and lightest (white) ends of the spectrum also are filled with media terms. Black is dark so it often connotes evil, depression, gloominess, or disaster; for example, a "black day" in the stock market.

"Black-and-white" photos still are popular and black-and-white films and documentaries still are shown on television and in theaters. The symbol is *B&W* or *B/W*.

Pitch black or *pure black* means totally without light. *Television black* reflects a very small amount of light from the screen, about 3 percent reflectance. In British theaters, the forestage or apron is painted black to enhance lighting effects and is called the *black*.

In the precomputer era, the *Little Black Book* was a small directory of names and other data, particularly valued by publicists, lobbyists, and others with prized contacts. Today, it's the title of many directories and other books; Google gives more than 65 million listings that include the name!

In contrast, the *Black List* was a collection of individuals or organizations banned or disapproved of, during the forties and fifties, when Hollywood film studios and broadcast networks compiled these names, especially those suspected of being Communists. The term *blacklist*, still in general use today, dates from the early sixteenth century in England. Black books were official books, bound in black cloth, that sometimes listed names of people who were liable to punishment or censure. To *blackball* is to vote against or block the admission of a potential member, harking back to the eighteenth century when an adverse vote was indicated by placing a black ball in a ballot box.

Black comedy is humor that is morbid, macabre, or cynical; it is also called "black humor." This is not the same as "gallows humor," which is amused cynicism, as of a person jesting about a life-threatening situation or death.

Blackface is the dark makeup (sometimes it actually was burnt cork) worn by white performers in a minstrel show (a comic variety show) or vaudeville act. Perhaps the best-known blackface actor was Al Jolson (1886–1950), particularly in *The Jazz Singer*, one of the first (1927) movies with sound. (These days, blackface is considered an outgrowth of racial stereotyping.)

"Blackface" also means bold, heavy-faced type. A *black letter* is a heavy, ornate boldface type with angular serifs, commonly used in medieval books and scrolls. Black-letter typefaces are derived from thirteenth-century German writing and were commonly used until the thirties. Some German newspapers still use them for their nameplates. "Black letter" (or "blackletter") sometimes is called *gothic*, but modern black letter lacks serifs; and it is sometimes also called *textura* because its ornateness appears to weave a texture on the page, resulting in a black look from a large number of tightly spaced compact letters. Black-letter calligraphy still is used for a formal look on certificates and other documents. "Black ink" indicates profits, the opposite of red ink.

A "blackout" is a temporary loss of consciousness, the suppression of light, or in general, concealment, as in a *news blackout* created by censorship or technical problems; or *sports blackout*, in accordance with a contractual prohibition of telecasting in a specific area.

In theater, a "blackout" is a sudden, complete darkening to indicate the passage of time or the end of a scene or the play. In vaudeville, a comic sketch often ended with a blackout. A *blackout switch* is a master switch that controls all lights on a stage or set. A *false blackout* occurs within a scene but without any change of props or scenery. It usually indicates a passage of time.

"Black tie" on an invitation calls for formal wear. The performer best known for his black tie was Fred Astaire (1890–1987), the dancer whose films still are seen and appreciated by TV viewers. Black also is the color of mourning.

A *black box* is a device, particularly used with computers, with specified performance characteristics but with components or modes of operation unknown to the typical lay user: You don't need to know what's inside as long as you know what goes in (input), what comes out (output), and what it does. It's called black, regardless of its color, because black connotes mystery. The "black box" in an airplane records information that can be retrieved after an accident.

Black light is invisible ultraviolet or infrared rays, used for photographing in the dark or for special effects.

A *black mark* can indicate a problem or blemish, as a black mark on a record, such as for an arrest. *Black magic,* which involves evil spirits, also is called "black art," a mysterious or sinister technique.

"Black" is a skin color and the word still is used as a racial identifier, though it sometimes is replaced in the United States by the term African-American or Afro-American. The *Associated Press Stylebook* prefers the word "black" (lowercase).

"White," the opposite of black, refers to white or light-skinned people, also called "Caucasian," as a reference to European origin, though the actual area, the Caucasus, also includes parts of North Africa and India.

"White" symbolizes innocence, spirituality, purity, and virginity. Bridal gowns traditionally are white, and "white tie" and tails is the epitome of male formal wear. A "white flag" is a symbol of surrender. *Whiter than white* is morally beyond reproach. To *whitewash* is to use a solution of lime and water to whiten, or figuratively to conceal mistakes or faults. Terror may cause a face to blanch, become pale, or "turn white."

"White-collar" workers are employed in offices, in contrast to "blue-collar" laborers. White also is the traditional color of nurse's uniforms, doctor's jackets, naval uniforms, and tennis clothes.

White shoes once were fashionable attire among wealthy people, and traditional, conservative law firms or investment companies still may be called "white shoe."

White goods include household appliances, such as refrigerators and washing machines; and home furnishings, particularly linens, bed and bath items, including those not colored white. (In the liquor business, gin and vodka also are called "white goods.") *White sales* feature these items.

The *White House*, at 1600 Pennsylvania Avenue NW in Washington, D.C., is the official residence of the president and also the offices of the staff of the president and vice president. "White House" often is used in headlines and news articles as a substitute for the president or presidential office, a figure of speech called a *metonym*. Similarly, Whitehall, a street in London on which many government offices are located, is used as a reference to the British government.

A *white paper* is a report by a government, organization, or team of journalists that authoritatively provides information about an issue. A "white paper" also is printer's slang for a blank sheet of paper, regardless of color. The *white pages* is a volume or section of a telephone directory that lists individual subscribers.

White noise is acoustical or electrical noise with many frequencies of the same intensity. It sometimes is used in a psychotherapist's office or other place as a block-out to ensure that conversations are not heard outside the office.

White mail is correspondence from consumers sent in their own envelopes instead of in business reply envelopes or envelopes provided by the marketer.

An unprinted area on a page, called *white space*, can be part of a design ("active"), as in an advertisement; or outside the design ("passive"), such as a margin.

The *White Way* is a theatrical area, particularly the Broadway area in mid-Manhattan, with its lighted marquees and other lights. It's also called the "Great White Way" or "white-light" district. *White hot* is so intensely hot that it emits white light. An extremely popular performer may be dubbed "white hot" or more likely, "red hot."

One of the most-played songs is *White Christmas* by Irving Berlin (1888–1989), particularly as sung by Bing Crosby (1904–77) in the 1954 movie of the same name.

Now one last color: purple. *Purple prose* is an ornate or elaborate literary style. A *purple passage* in a novel or other work is vivid, akin to the color purple, though the designation can be derogatory and mean excessively ornate. More than two thousand years ago, Horace, the Greek poet, referred to a purple piece of cloth as an irrelevant, ornate insertion in a literary work.

The red lights are signaling to end. As to the etymology of *color*, it's simple. The Latin word actually was *color*.

COMIC RELIEF: HAVE YOU HEARD THE ONE ABOUT…?

NEWSPAPER editors and broadcasters used to call summertime the *silly season*, when hard news was slow, but trivialities, stunts, and other soft news were rampant. Nowadays, lighthearted or humorous features, called *brites*, enliven the media throughout the year. An attractive item, article, or photograph, called a *kicker*, such as a beach, a park, or other scene, often starts or *kicks off* a page, particularly page one of a periodical. In broadcasting, a humorous, zany, or inconsequential final item is called a *zipper*.

Though I have achieved some success as an author, a lexicographer, and a public relations consultant, my aspiration always has been stand-up comedy. (A performer does a stand-up, standing alone onstage.) No kidding. So, in that spirit, here is a selection of droll terms from *show biz* that can be useful (and perhaps amusing) to editors, writers, and others.

To *knock 'em* (or *lay 'em*) *in the aisles* during a comedy is to be so funny that the audience (figuratively) falls or rolls in the aisles laughing. This idea has carried over to the world of IM (instant messaging), where *ROFL* means "rolling on the floor laughing" and denotes wild enthusiasm.

Maybe IM will someday also embrace *batta-bing, batta-boom*, the drumroll sound calling attention to a joke, pratfall, or other funny action at a burlesque or vaudeville show. A drumroll is still used in comedy acts, and the expression "batta-bing batta-boom" even crops up in everyday conversation to enliven a punch line. (More about the drumroll in the next-to-last paragraph, which I was tempted to pretentiously call the "penultimate" one.)

Of course, even the best actors sometimes get a *bad laugh*—audience chuckles at a point in a play or other production not intended to be funny. No drumroll there.

In vaudeville, a *sidekick* was a person (a "straight man") who a comic kicked to get a laugh. In television, such as *The Tonight Show with Jay Leno* and the *Late Show with David Letterman,* the announcer or bandleader sometimes serves as a foil to the host. A *straight man* is a performer who "plays it straight," directly with no jokes or stunts.

A *punch line* is the humorous last line of a joke; it comes as a surprise, like a punch. The punchline is preceded by a *setup,* one or more lines about an event or situation, and sometimes is followed by another funny line, called a *topper.*

Banana is slang for a silly person, particularly a man (the penis is shaped like a banana). In burlesque and vaudeville, the "top banana" was the number-one comedic performer; next was the "second banana." *Bananas* is British slang for excessive or glitzy, a term commonly used today in British advertising and graphic arts. From burlesque and vaudeville, we also got *baldheaded row*, the first row in the orchestra, where older men sat close to the stage to better ogle the chorus girls and strippers. It's a rare but colorful term that still crops up today.

Boff is a gimmick, such as a device in a plot, to move along the action; also called a *plot plant* or *weenie. Boff*, from English before the sixteenth century, meant to hit. A "boff" or *boffola* is also a loud laugh, or a joke that provokes laughter. However, *boffo* means "box-office hit" (and is derived from *box office*). A *smash hit* is really big. (A *sleeper* is a dormant film or other work that awakens and achieves unexpected success.) The opposite of "boffo" is a *bomb*, a major failure of a film, play, or other work. In the United Kingdom, however, to *go a bomb* is to have a big success, so it all depends on where you're "bombing."

The *Borscht Belt*, or *Borscht Circuit*, was a group of resort hotels in the Catskill Mountains (north of New York City) that featured comedic and other entertainment, primarily from the thirties through the sixties. The hotels catered to Jewish guests and the menu included borscht (Russian beet soup), hence the name. Jerry Lewis (b. 1926) and other prominent comedians and singers started their careers at these hotels.

Break a leg, a wish of good luck, is generally said to an actor or a performer, but never, of course, to a dancer. The superstition dates from classical Greek theater, when it was believed that the gods, who were fickle and sometimes perverse, would send the opposite of something wished for; so a wish for a mishap was used to try to trick the gods into bringing good luck. A similar expression to wish good luck, though heard less frequently in show business, is *in boca luca*, in the wolf's mouth.

To *corpse* is to frighten another performer on-stage, usually to provoke laughter, as in a prank in which a corpse is replaced with a live actor or actress. It also means to lose concentration, as a result of a blunder or prank.

Lay an egg, to fail, probably also comes from the British, in which a zero is called a "duck's egg" because of its shape. In American slang, a zero is called a *goose egg*.

Has any of this so far produced a smile, laugh, or best of all, a *yak*? *Variety* usually calls a laugh a *laff*, as well as a "yak."

This brings us to a common term in television, *laugh track*, the audio component of a comedic or other program in which audience laughter is inserted. If laughter does not occur when desired (the place is usually noted in a script by a *laugh line*, for a pause in anticipation of audience laughter), the tape can always be *sweetened* using a "Laff Box," or laugh machine.

About fifty years ago, Charles Roland Douglass (1910–2003) invented the *Laff Box* to produce a variety of laughter sounds like giggles, chuckles, guffaws, roars, and the other funny noises people make when tickled various shades of pink. The device enhanced or "sweetened" the sound track of programs that had live (but not lively enough) audiences, as well as those tracks without an audience. Douglass's invention is still used today, though sound engineers now rely on various computerized systems to mimic laughter.

There isn't a machine yet to make a *knee slapper*, a joke that generates a physical reaction, such as slapping one's knees—in the audience, not onstage! But maybe some day this too will be automated. A *belly laugh* is loud and so strong it shakes the stomach area.

A *sendup* is a parody or satirical takeoff. A *spoof* is a similar humorous imitation, but it also means a trick played on someone as a joke. The word was coined by Arthur Roberts (1852–1933), an English comedian.

A *sketch*, or *skit*, is a short piece of humorous or satirical writing, a comic play, or a funny scene, as on *Saturday Night Live*, a TV program that is primarily *sketch comedy*.

Likeajoke is a slang word used by writers of TV programs, particularly sitcoms, to describe a sequence that has the rhythm and form of a joke (with a *setup* and a *punch line*) but still isn't funny. Thus, it means, "Keep trying!"

Slapstick, or crude, physical comedy, has a literal origin in a wooden implement of the same name, used by a clown or vaudevillian to whack the buttocks of another performer for comic effect.

Masters of slapstick include Stan Laurel (1890–1965) and Oliver Hardy (1892–1957); Michael Richards (b. 1949), who plays the character Kramer in *Seinfeld*; and The Three Stooges. To jump to the answer of a favorite trivia question, The Three Stooges, whose reruns still get big yuks today, were actually played by six characters who teamed up three-at-a-time as the three classic buffoons.

The names of the three most enduring ones—Larry, Moe, and Curly—have become synonymous collectively with goofball behavior, including among upper management or politicians of every stripe. The stage names and life spans of these slapstick immortals were: Larry Fine (1902–75), Moe Howard (1897–1975), Curly Howard (1903–52), Shemp Howard (1895–1955), Joe Besser (1907–88), and Curly Joe DeRita (1909–93).

My mother had her own name for such antics, *slapstuff*, which indeed was appropriate; and her favorite practitioner was, not surprisingly, Lucille Ball (1911–89), the brilliant, screwball comedienne of stage, TV, and film.

Bob Hope (1903–2003), in contrast, was the master of *one-liners* or brief jokes, which he delivered with suave aplomb. The Marx Brothers were adept at almost all types of zany comedy. Here are their stage and real first names (and life spans): Groucho (Julius Henry, 1890–1977), Chico (Leonard, 1887–1977), Harpo (Adolph Arthur, 1888–1964), and Zeppo (Herbert, 1900–79).

In a common slapstick technique, called the *pratfall*, the performer would fall on his buttocks (*prat* is slang for the posterior part of the body), such as by slipping on a banana peel.

When you catch my comedy act, I may not use a slapstick, but I probably will have a few *rim shots*, which are rapid rolls of a drum followed by a cymbal clash, to call attention to *punch lines*. Actually, a drummer does a rim shot by using one stick to simultaneously hit the head and rim of a snare drum.

One of my favorite terms, *JTC*, means *joke to come*—a notation in TV scripts in optimistic anticipation that a writer will develop a joke or funny bit: So watch this space for my next performance, that is, edition, of this book!

CUTS: THE KINDEST, AND UNKINDEST ONES, TOO

ONE word can have several different meanings, which lexicographers call "senses."

The common word *cut* is a good example of a word with many senses. As a noun, "cut" can mean an opening, a decrease, the omission of a part of something, or the part omitted. As a verb, to "cut" means to reduce, omit, or eliminate. The etymology is simple—more than 500 years ago from the Middle English *cutten*, in turn derived from the Icelandic *juta*, to cut with a knife.

You can "cut" across, back, down, in, off, out, through, and up, and almost everyone should know what you're doing. Well, maybe not always. In music, a *cut off* is the point at which a conductor ends (cuts off) the playing with a gesture, such as a wave of the hand. In other media, the word "cut" has many specialized meanings, especially in film, printing, and television, and many of these technical terms appear in popular media.

For example, in the era of the letterpress, when lead-metal type was used, printers literally cut into a metal plate to produce a drawing, design, or other artwork. A *cut* thus was a block or plate engraved for printing, or the impression made from it. You've seen *die cuts*, which are slits or holes cut into a page, to insert a calling card or other item, or to reveal the artwork on the next sheet. The cutting press uses an engraved metal ("die") to shape or punch the openings. The word *cut* still is used, generally as a synonym for a drawn illustration (derived from "woodcut"), a photograph, or other artwork used in printing. That's why the text ("caption") that describes the photo also is called a *cutline*.

"Cut" takes on a completely different meaning in the

film business. Film producers, editors, and other movie people commonly refer to a "cut" as a total film, generally in an interim state, that is, in the process of being cut or edited further. A *rough cut* is an early stage of editing, in which the shots are assembled in proper sequence.

A *fine cut* is a finished work or print, ready for final approval, prior to reproduction. An *answer print,* or *first proof print*, is between these two stages.

A *director's cut*, or *director's fine cut*, is the last edited version of a film, as approved by the director. A *director's cut clause* in the director's contract guarantees the right of this approval. DVDs and videotapes now usually include the director's cut version, which contains scenes previously excised to shorten the theatrical version or to conform to certain standards, as a film rating.

Cuts are ubiquitous in films themselves. For example, a "cut" could be a transition (or *transition point*) from one scene to another (a *visual cut*) or one soundtrack to another (a *sound cut*). A *late cut* is made (generally unintentionally) slightly after the indicated moment, whereas a *delayed cut* is intentionally withheld to create suspense or other effects. A *straight cut* is a transition from one scene to the next without optical effects. A *cut-only editor* is a specialist in making transitions.

As a cinematic verb, "cut" is an instruction to end a scene or to shift from one scene to another. The symbol for this command is an index finger drawn across the throat. *Cut and hold* is a director's instruction to stop filming, but for the performers to remain in position.

In film and television, a *cutaway* is a reaction shot or a shot of an action, object, or person not part of the principal scene. It's also an insert, such as between two scenes of an interview subject, usually a brief sequence that shows the interviewer.

Back to other media cuts. *Cutback* is a return to a principal or earlier scene following a reaction shot or other cutaway. It's also called a *cutback shot*.

A *cutter* is a film editor who sometimes works in a *cutting room*. Though editing is now done digitally, "cut" terms still are used. The deleted scenes are called *outtakes*. "Left on the cutting room floor" is now a general expression for anything that is deleted or left out, or that doesn't make the grade.

Cutting negative is the process of cutting a negative to match the final "work print" (a positive), producing a *cut negative*. In film and television, "cutting" means the ending or stopping of a scene. *Cutting the action* is a technique in which the camera switches, or cuts, from one event or scene to another. *Cutting on the reaction* is an orderly sequence in which an event or scene is followed by its results, impact, or reaction. A *jump cut* is a transition in which an object has moved (jumped) from one place to another.

Cutting continuity is a list detailing the final cut, or finished print, containing information about camera setups, dialogue, and other aspects of each shot. A *cutting outline* is a guide sometimes used by a film editor, as in preparing a documentary or other compilation of cuts from existing films.

On stage, however, a *cutter* is a long, narrow flag (also called a "finger") that cuts off light, generally placed on a stand in front of a light.

"Cutting" also refers to a technique used by disc jockeys, particularly in nightclubs and associated with hip-hop, of playing identical records on two turntables and manually manipulating one of the records so that the music has a stammer.

Though records have been replaced by tapes and CDs, the term "cut" is still used by consumers, broadcasters, and recording engineers to describe a single section (a "band"), such as one song containing several different selections. A *cutting session* (or "cutting contest") is a gathering (session) at which jazz musicians attempt to surpass (cut) each other.

In the theater, "cut" has many specialized uses. For example, a *stage cut* is a narrow section of the floor into which a curtain can be rolled (a *curtain cut*) or through which scenery, props, or performers can pass.

A *cutout* is a piece of scenery cut out of a board to represent the silhouette of a building or other object. A *cutout drop* is a cloth, or drop, suspended from above the stage, with an opening so that scenery behind it is partially revealed. It's also called a *cut drop,* or in the United Kingdom, *cut cloth*. If there's more than one, the cloth that is in front (downstage) is numbered first, as in "cut drop one."

Cut-down scenery, sometimes called a *cut-down set* or vignette, is a small unit usually set in front of black drapes. A *cut scene* is a piece of scenery with an opening through which objects can be seen.

Scenographers (scenery designers), stagehands, and performers know all about these cuts. Much of the terminology is from the British theatre (as the English spell it). For example, a *cut in* is a performer who incorrectly interrupts another performer's speech. This faux pas is sometimes called "cut the cue," "bite a cut," or "cut bite."

In a newspaper or magazine, a *cut-in* is the insertion of a headline (a "cut-in head"), blurb, or other material (such as a quotation or excerpt) within the text of an article. A *cut-in note* is set in a margin adjacent to the main text, as in a textbook. In radio and television, a *cut-in* is the insertion of a local commercial or announcement in a program.

"Cutouts" are also ubiquitous. In outdoor advertising, a *cutout* is a visual device affixed to the molding or surface of a billboard. It either is three-dimensional or provides a three-dimensional effect, which explains why it's also called an "embellishment."

In publishing, a *cutout* is what every author abhors— it's a title deleted from a catalog, which then becomes a *remainder*, inventory sold at or below cost to clear it out.

"Cutout" also describes a title dropped from a record company's catalog.

Cut flush is the trimming of a book (such as paperbacks) with the cover and pages the same size, distinguished from a book trimmed with a cover larger than the pages. It's also called *trimmed flush*.

Cut list is a term at *The Wall Street Journal* and elsewhere that describes paragraphs and sentences that may be omitted to suit editing and space requirements.

A *cut sheet* is a numbered list of tapes ("sound bites"), with their exact times in seconds, that are available for use during a long program, such as a call-in radio show.

First cut refers to an early version of a work in process. To *make the cut* is to be retained after others have been eliminated.

To a printer, *cut off* refers to the maximum dimensions of paper, as limited by the size of a printing press, and also printed matter completely or partly missing from a printed sheet.

In broadcasting, *cut-offs* are specific times (usually for late-night broadcasts) after which a commercial cannot be aired. To a consumer, a *cut-off* can be an interrupted telephone call.

Though most writers now edit via computer, the term *cut-and-paste* still describes rearranging and editing text. Originally, it involved the actual cutting of previously printed or existing work and pasting it in a different order. The phrase sometimes is used pejoratively to describe a job hastily assembled from pre-existing material, and hence is unoriginal.

Have we missed any cuts, or did we manage to "cut the mustard" (do something with verve)?

But it's probably time to "cut out" now. And this, as Shakespeare's Julius Caesar said, "Was the most unkindest cut of all."

DOUBLES: NOT MORE OF THE SAME

DOUBLE means two. You know that. Major dictionaries list specialized meanings of "double": in baseball, card games, music, and other fields, plus dozens of "double" terms, ranging from "double agent" (an espionage mole) to "double-barreled" (having a dual purpose).

"Double" terms also are common in publishing and other media fields. For example, a *double dagger*, or *double obelisk*, is a reference mark used in footnotes. Traditionally, a first reference calls for an *asterisk* (*), a second a *dagger* (†), and a third a double dagger (‡). A *double letter*, also called a "ligature" or "tied letter," involves two letters joined together, such as œ, common in Latin and Old English. Reference books and professional journals still use *ff*, which refers to the following lines or pages. Printers use "double" to describe many paper sizes, such as *double demy,* derived from "demi-," or half.

A book with a *double title page* has two title pages facing each other, such as in two different languages. This differs from a *double-spread title page*, which contains a single title (and other information) spread across two facing pages. A *double truck* runs over adjacent or facing pages in a publication, such as a single two-page advertisement or editorial layout. This is also called a *double spread* or *double-page spread*, particularly in magazines. Just don't call it a "doublewide," which is a mobile home.

Assuming that you have not doubled over (in pain or laughter), let's take a broader view. A *broadsheet* is a full-size or standard newspaper, longer and wider than a tabloid. The actual size varies, as many dailies have decreased the number or width of their columns. A *broadfold* is a sheet folded to make its pages of greater width than depth, which is less commonly used.

A broadsheet sometimes is mistakenly called a *broadside*. A "broadside," indeed, is a large sheet of paper, but it's generally printed on one side and folded to a smaller size, often for use in direct mail or for door-to-door distribution. A broadside usually is greater in width than height. In fact, a *broadside page* is a page in a publication designed to read sideways, usually to accommodate wide tables or illustrations. (This horizontal orientation in books and word processing is also called *landscape*. The corresponding vertical orientation is called *portrait*.)

Let's move for a moment to film, theater, and other media fields more glamorous than printing. A *double* is a performer's understudy, or sometimes, a performer who plays two roles. To *double cast* is to assign two performers to the same role so that they alternate, or one is an understudy. A *photo double* is someone who is a look-alike who closely resembles a performer; a *stunt double* may not have as close a resemblance, but one close enough to take the falls and bruises on-screen for a performer.

A *double bill* theater program (a "bill") has two plays or other works. The film equivalent, the "double feature" with two movies on the same program, is no longer common. A *double broad* is a box-shaped light commonly used in film production. If you need enlightenment (a "double entendre"), a *broad* is a large floodlight and a "double broad" links two lamps, each 1,000 or 2,000 watts.

Broadside ballads, or "broadsides," were poems or essays printed on one side of a large sheet of paper and distributed or posted in England from the sixteenth to the nineteenth century. A *broadside* is also a large floodlight, a lighting unit used to illuminate a large area. "Gaffers" (the lighting people in film, television, and theater) call them "broads." If you work with photographers, you know that *broadlighting* is full illumination, such as a broad expanse of highlight directed onto the subject. Its opposite is *short lighting*.

Editors sometimes instruct writers to avoid a *broad-*

brush view (too wide or general); and *broad-brush criticism* (too wide or indiscriminate). *Broad-based* is an adjective (as a "broad-based" PR program) that means having a foundation or basis that is wide in range. If an editor calls your article "broad-based," accept it as a compliment, unless it's "too broad-based."

In business news reporting, *broad tape* refers to financial news services, particularly Dow Jones. The origin is from the precomputer days when these services transmitted stock prices to tickers (electronic devices) using wide sheets of paper, as compared to the price-transmission wires of the New York Stock Exchange and other markets that used narrow ticker tape. In recent years, computers replaced the tickers and their paper rolls, so that the financial news now flickers on computer screens, though broadcasters and others still use the term "tape" for stock quotes.

Broadband has become a popular word as a synonym for high-speed transmission. It describes facilities capable of transmitting data at faster speeds and in greater quantity and frequency ranges than the standard facilities for the voice or narrow-band channels used for slow (under 200 bits per second) transmission of data. A broadband network can transmit voice data and video signals simultaneously at speeds in excess of 2 million bits per second (bps).

Let's double back to other double terms in the media. In computers, to *double click* is to press a mouse button twice in quick succession to select a file or other function. In journalism, a *double column* article measures twice the width of a single column. A *double deck*, or "double-decker," headline has two units, a "main deck" and a "secondary deck," and each can run over several lines. A *double*, or *doublet*, is text inadvertently printed twice in the same publication. It's often seen, for example, in two sections of the same edition of a newspaper.

In a *double exposure* photograph, two images, the same or different, are made on the same negative, to intentionally produce a composite image or unintentionally a blurred or "ghost image." *Double weight* is a photograph printed on heavy paper.

Double-coated stock is paper coated twice on the same side. *Double-deckle* stock is paper with parallel irregular (deckle) edges. A *double-duty envelope* is a self-addressed return envelope with a sales message or other text that can be torn off. These envelopes are commonly used by credit card companies to promote special offers.

A *double postcard* is two attached postcards, usually folded and perforated, one addressed to the recipient (customer) and the other arranged to be removed and mailed to the sender (seller).

In publishing, *double numeration* involves numbered references combining the chapter number (of books) or volume number (of periodicals, particularly journals), with the page number. In textbooks, illustrations or tables often are similarly identified by the chapter number followed by the number of the illustration within the chapter, such as Figure 5.3 for the third illustration in chapter five.

In direct marketing, *doubling day* is the point at which half of the expected returns or results of a mailing are received, generally around thirty days after the mailing.

Printers, editors, and writers know that a *double loop* is a proofreader's mark, indicating words to be transposed. *Double-space* is typing with a full space between the lines of text (not two full spaces).

A *double take* is a delayed reaction to a remark or situation, such as startled surprise, often used as a comic device. *Double-talk* is ambiguous and deceptive talk, usually deliberately confusing. A synonym is *doublespeak*, obscure or ambiguous language that usually is meant to be deceptive; coined in 1949 by George Orwell (1903–50), British author, in his novel *Nineteen Eighty-Four*.

A German word that critics and columnists like is *dopplegänger*, a ghostly double of a living person. Think about that while chewing your DoubleMint gum.

FILM: HATS OFF TO THE BEST BOYS AND FOLEY EDITORS

IN the course of a lifetime, the average person watches several thousand movies. Most of them are from "Hollywood," a term that has come to mean film-making in America. Hollywood is actually a section of Los Angeles, founded in 1912. *Hollywoodization* is slang for the influence of the American film industry or the overdramatization of a process or event.

Slang names for Hollywood include "La-la Land" (a playful pun on L.A., the initials of Los Angeles), "Lotusland" (from the lotus plant in Greek mythology, which induced dreamy languor), and "Tinseltown" (*tinsel* means showy or gaudy, made from strips of cloth or metal that glitter). *Bollywood* refers to the prolific Hindi-language film industry based in Mumbai (formerly, Bombay), India, though many Indian cineasts find the moniker condescending.

The film industry also is called *screenland*, a reference to the "silver screen," the surface covered with silver-colored metallic paint on which films are projected. In recent years, "screen" refers to a single theater with one screen. Almost all theaters now are *multiplex* (also called *cineplex*), containing several screens, many with twelve or more.

At the end of a film (people in the business prefer this word to *movie*) a list of credits streams by, often for several minutes, particularly in films containing animation and special effects. Similarly, some of the credits appear in advertisements, particularly of the featured performers, the director, and other major participants.

Few people stay in their seats when the final credits roll by, but they reveal the roles of all the people who work behind the scenes of every production. Let's therefore take a closer look at this identification, called the "billing,"—and other film lingo—to gain a deeper insight into the movie-making business and how it functions.

Hollywood labor union regulations or special contracts often determine the type of placement of the credit listing on a printed program, marquee, sign, advertisement, television program, or film. The jockeying for the relative size, position, order of names, and other considerations can be extremely sensitive. For example, the Directors Guild of America decrees that the film director appear last in the opening or *head credits*, but first in the closing or *tail credits*.

The negotiations among the managers, lawyers, agents, publicists, and advertising people can be highly emotional, as they attempt to satisfy the various producers, directors, performers, and others involved in making a particular film.

The portion of an advertisement, poster, or other promotion of a film, or other work, in which the names (credits) are listed, is called the *billing block*. The "billing block title" follows the "artwork title" (the main title and the largest in size) and precedes the credits. Types of billing-block credits include *first billing* or "first position," which is 100 percent of the title (same size) or a portion of the title. Variations include *likeness billing* (same-size photo as that of another performer), *top billing*, *solitary billing*, and *staggered billing* (one name on the left, which is preferred, with the other on the right but slightly higher in an attempt to equalize their importance).

Readers are sometimes confused and amused when an ad has photos of three actors but their names appear in a different order. The person whose name is at the top, before the title, has "top billing." *Equal billing* means that names appear on the same line and height, though the importance can be considered as diminishing from left to right. In cases of extreme competitiveness among actors, the sequence of credits may be juggled from one advertisement or poster to another, in an effort to please everyone.

The "presentation" credit precedes the title and may be in the form of a "possessory" credit ("Steven Spielberg's") or a "special" credit ("Steven Spielberg Presents"). Different contractual rules apply to the precredits sequence that appears before the start of a film or TV program.

The numerous credits for producers of plays and films can be lengthy and of little interest to the audience, but all of those involved clamor for their proper billing. The crediting of performers sometimes is solved by listing them in order of appearance, alphabetical order, or in a special section at the end, starting with "Also Featured" or simply "And." You've sometimes seen this in the opening credits in the "crawl space" at the bottom of the screen of TV shows.

A *title designer* creates the opening and closing credits, which often are quite creative, involving animation or live action and including "title music" and sometimes a "title song," all generally produced by a "title company." Credits may be in the main titles at or near the start or in the end titles. Major credits that precede the artwork title are called "above the title," as compared to those that follow "below the title."

Now, let's turn to the roles involved in the actual making of a film.

Actors often begin their careers on the *casting couch*, a term so well-known that it's defined in dictionaries as a couch or similar piece of furniture in the office of an agent, producer, or other person (usually a man) who is in a position to boost the career of a performer.

In the era of the big studios in Hollywood, during the twenties through the mid-fifties, aspiring stars who granted horizontal favors on such couches were sometimes cast in parts that launched their careers vertically. Today, the *casting director* (the person who selects the performers in a film, television, or other production) is a prestigious position. The Casting Society of America is a New York-based organization of casting agents. The designation *C.S.A.* after a name sometimes appears in film and other credits, indicating membership.

The *casting file* is a record of performers, generally cross-indexed by talent, characteristics, and experience. The term "central casting" has become so well known that people refer to someone who looks like a definite character type or role (such as a cowboy) as "straight out of central casting."

The Central Casting Corporation, set up in 1926, still exists as a source of extras and bit players. It's located in Burbank, California, also the location of the studios of NBC Universal and Warner Bros. Nearby are Encino, Sherman Oaks, and other Los Angeles suburbs in the San Fernando Valley, popularly known as the "Valley." Of course, you've probably heard the, like, rhythmic speech of the "valley girls."

The *producer*—the individual or company in charge of financial, personnel, promotional, and other nonartistic aspects of the production—usually selects the casting director and the director and is influential in negotiating with the performers and their agents. The title of "producer" can include "executive producer," "co-producer," "associate producer," and other classifications.

The *associate producer*, who acts as deputy to the producer, ranks higher than an "assistant producer," just as an associate professor outranks an assistant professor. The associate producer, usually in charge of financial matters, has an important position, though director Billy Wilder (1906–2002) defined it as "the only guy who will associate with a producer."

The *director* takes charge of the performers, technicians, and others involved in the creative and technical aspects of the production. In most films, the director has the single most important position. Sitting in a special chair, usually adjacent to the camera crew, the director uses an eyepiece called a "director's finder" to frame, or view, a scene from different angles and sizes. You've seen this eyepiece hanging on a cord or chain around the director's neck. Quite popular, a director's chair can be bought in many stores; it's a lightweight, folding armchair with crossed legs and usually a canvas seat and back piece. Other key people sit in similar chairs.

The Directors Guild of America (no apostrophe) is an independent union of film and TV directors, and its initials, DGA, appear in film and TV credits.

The major filming, or "production," is preceded by *preproduction*, or planning, and followed by *post production* (usually two words in film credits, but one word, "postproduction," in dictionaries and general media).

The *assistant director* (AD) is responsible for considerable preproduction work. It's the AD who calls for "quiet on the set" and gives the order for the cameras to roll, followed by the call from the director for "action" to begin.

The *unit director* assists the director by directing the crew on locations outside of the studio or the main location.

The *director of photography*, or *cinematographer*, extremely important in the creative aspects of the production, supervises the lighting and camera crews, and others involved in the photography, and often works closely with the director in composing shots. The cinematographer also uses an eyepiece to evaluate lighting contrast and tone values; he or she rarely operates the camera. The American Society of Cinematographers, in Hollywood, uses the initials ASC, or A.S.C., found after the names of its members in film credits.

The *cameraman* or *camerawoman* actually operates the camera, assisted by a "first assistant camera" or "first camera assistant" (the focus puller) and a "second assistant camera" or "second camera assistant" (the clapper/loader). The camera operator sometimes is numbered and informally called *camera*, such as "first camera."

Cameramen and camerawomen produce *takes,* which are scenes, shots, or other uninterrupted components. Each time a scene is repeated, it is another take, indicated by a number, as "Take 2." *Rushes*, or *dailies,* are rough, unedited prints of a film, made the preceding day. An *outtake* is a portion of a film or tape that is not used (taken out) in the final version. Outtakes sometimes are shown at the end of the film or TV program, or in a documentary or other special program, particularly if they involve amusing flubs.

The *screenwriter* writes the screenplay for a motion picture. In anticipation of numerous revisions, the finished screenplay is called the "first draft," "final draft," or "temporary screenplay." Subsequent revisions by the same or other writers lead to a "second temporary screenplay," "third temporary screenplay," etc., and at last to the "final screenplay," which even may be further revised (resulting in the "first revised final screenplay," "second revised final screenplay," etc.), ending with the "revised final." In Hollywood slang, to *screenplay* means to move forward with a project. The credit, "screenplay by" or "screenplay author," indicates that the writer wrote the film script but not necessarily the original story.

A key job, often unappreciated by audiences, is the *editor* (formerly called "cutter"), who meticulously selects and arranges shots (scenes) during and after production, usually working closely with the director. The film editor edits the *workprint* (the first positive print made from the master negative) and dialogue "tracks" (a band on the film that is synchronized with the picture), but generally does not edit the tracks for music and effects, which are edited by the "sound editor." American Cinema Editors membership is indicated by the initials A.C.E. in film credits.

ADR, or "automatic dialogue replacement," is a film technique supervised by an *ADR editor*, for recording a track to replace one already recorded by a performer.

A common job with an intriguing name is *best boy*. As noted in the chapter on lighting, he or she (yes, the term applies to both) is an assistant or apprentice, usually to the "gaffer" (electrician) or the "grip." The origin probably is from the days when young laborers assembled for work in theaters and the gaffer called, "Give me your best boy!"

A *grip* is a handyman, stagehand, or general assistant. Originally, the person had to have a firm grip to carry or push equipment. Types of grips include "dolly grip," "key grip" (the chief grip), and "lighting grip."

If I had to choose my favorite arcane job, it's probably that of the people who create the *Foley*, which are replacement sound effects. The job is performed by a "Foley artist" or "Foley editor" (a sound-effects specialist), who uses a "Foley mixer" to add to the action sounds like footsteps or collisions, recorded separately on "Foley tracks." Foley work is done on a "Foley stage," where a "Foley walker," for example, follows a performer and adds appropriate sound effects. "Foley" also is used as a verb to indicate the addition of sound to film, as in "Foleying in." The credits for the Foley crew often appear at the end of movies, particularly in those films with extensive sound effects. Many viewers familiar with various photography and other credits are still not familiar with the Foley credit. The inventor was Jack Foley (1891–1967) of Universal Studios.

Another underrated job is that of the *art director*, or *production designer*, who is involved with all aspects of the ambience, including costumes, décor, and sets. "Sets," the interior or exterior locations of a film, or the scenes of a theatrical production, are discussed in more detail in the chapter, "Theater." A *set decorator* or *set designer* creates the décor. A *set dresser* constructs and decorates the set with set dressing, including props, furnishings, and related items.

Properties include anything except costumes and scenery, handled by property personnel. A "property" is also a script or a performer under contract, preferably a "hot property." The "property department" obtains and maintains the props, under the supervision of a "property master." The "property handler" places the props in accordance with a "property sheet" and a "property plot" or "property plan" (a layout of the location of the props). A "properties truck" is a portable cabinet for storage of hand, or personal, *props*, the small objects worn or used by a performer.

A *costume* is the clothing and accessories worn by a performer, generally designed or selected by a *costume designer*. A "costume maker" constructs the costumes, generally in a "costume shop" that is part of a film studio or an outside company (a "costume company"). The sewing is done by seamsters (men) or seamstresses (women). The costume designer can also select from collected items in a "wardrobe department" and supervises the *wardrobe supervisor*.

A *makeup artist* applies cosmetics and other materials for performers, on the face and other parts of the body. "Straight makeup" enhances an actor's features; "corrective makeup" is more extensive and changes features; while "character makeup" emphasizes specific traits, such as anger. "Special makeup," using latex masks, hairpieces, and other transformational materials (for instance, as used by a young performer to play the role of an elderly person), is applied by a "prosthetic makeup artist." The command, "Makeup!" on a set is a request to apply cosmetics, generally a touchup of powder by the "makeup department" (headed by the makeup artist). The "makeup call" is the time a performer must report to be made up. The union designation for the person who applies makeup below the neck is "body makeup artist."

To "film on location" involves shooting in an actual setting outside a studio. The "location manager" finds sites, with the assistance of location scouts. In "daily location work," a performer is not paid for overnight costs, as different from "overnight location work."

Special effects (FX, F/X, and SFX are the main abbreviations) involve visual effects produced optically, electronically, or by other artificial means, rather than direct recording of live action. They can include sound effects but generally refer to visual illusions. Manipulative camera or laboratory tricks include such standard opticals as "dissolves" (progressive blending of the end of one shot into the beginning of the next), "fades" (gradual change in intensity), "freeze-frames," "inserts," "split screens," "superimpositions," and "wipes" (one scene gradually replacing another as if it were wiping it off the screen), as well as a slew of digitally produced graphics and actions.

Special effects also include a "special-effects generator" (SEG), a device that creates special effects. The special-effects crew, managed by a "special-effects coordinator" or "visual-effects supervisor," works in a special-effects department or company.

Animation, the process of creating static figures that appear to move and come alive, originally was produced by painting on *cels* (transparent sheets of celluloid). Now it's done with computers. *Anime* is a style of animation, originating in Japan, using colorful graphics and often violent or fantastic themes.

A *focus puller* adjusts the focus of the camera during filming. It's primarily a British term, so when you see it in the credits you can assume that the production is British. The American term usually is "first assistant camera," abbreviated as 1AC. Similarly, "draughtsman" is the British spelling of *draftsman*, an artist who renders drawings, as in animation.

The person in charge of carpets, draperies, and other coverings is called a *drape*.

You've seen a *clapboard*, a slate board on which is written information about a scene to be filmed, such as the name of the director, the title of the film, the date, and the number of the take (shot); it is also called a "clapper," "clapper board," "slateboard," or "take board." The clapboard is photographed at the beginning of each take. An automatic clapper or automatic slate automatically aligns the picture (with a flashing light) and sound (with a beep). The "clapper boy" operates the clapboard.

The *clapstick*, used at the start of a shot, synchronizes the audio to the picture by means of a clapping sound. It is composed of two boards hinged together at one end and connected to the top or bottom of the clapboard. The "clapper" or "loader" operates the clapstick and loads the film. This position also goes by a number of names, including "second assistant camera," "second camera assistant," "clapper and loader," "clapper/loader," or "slateman."

An *extra* is a nonspeaking actor (male or female), as in a crowd scene, usually hired by the "extra casting director." Extras sometimes rapidly repeat the word "walla-walla" to create a background murmuring sound (called "walla-walla"). Try it. If it doesn't work, try the word "rhubarb" or simply mumble.

A *wrangler* is in charge of animals and sometimes also special equipment.

Hundreds of other jobs include caterers, composers, drivers, music creators, stagehands (who work on the construction of rigs, or scaffolding, lighting, and other equipment), and stunt performers. The *crew* is a general term for all of the workers except the performers. A "crew call" is a posted notice ("call sheet") for production personnel, such as the camera crew, indicating the time and place of the upcoming shooting.

[DOLLY]

Almost everyone has seen a dolly, *a mobile platform commonly used in factories and warehouses to carry all types of cartons and equipment. In the media, dollies come in all sizes and with a variety of attachments to carry a microphone, camera, or other items.*

As for the etymology, the probable origin of the mechanical dolly is not a child's word for a small doll, but rather *doily*, a small mat put under a dish or other item, like a platform. "Doily" is from a seventeenth-century *draper* (a maker of cloth) named Doyley (or maybe Doiley).

The child's toy—*doll* and *dolly*—started as nicknames for the woman's name Dorothy in the late sixteenth and early seventeenth centuries, then took on the meaning of an attractive woman, a sweetheart, and then a polite way of referring to a mistress. William Shakespeare (1564–1616) and Ben Johnson (1572–1637) used *doll* in this last context. Today, some Brits call an attractive young woman a *dollybird*.

In film production, dollies have many forms and functions. A *dolly shot* shifts the viewpoint of the camera, often carried out by a crew member called a "dolly operator," "dolly pusher," or "dolly grip," who sets the dolly in motion. The process is called *dollying*, *tracking*, or *trucking*.

To *dolly-in*, or "dolly up" or "camera up," is to move the camera platform closer to the subject. To *dolly-out*, also called "camera back," "dolly-back," "truck back," or "pull back," is to move the camera platform away from the subject.

In a camera on three wheels, the most common type used in TV, the *dolly mode* is a movement in which two wheels are fixed and one is used for steering.

The movement and appearance of certain dollies is the basis for their animal names. A *crab dolly* has four wheels and can move like a crab in any direction and into very small areas. A *cricket dolly* has a telescoping central column that can rise about 4 feet, whereas a *spyder dolly* has a hydraulic column. A *doorway dolly* is a narrow dolly that can move through a doorway. *Dolly tracks* or *camera tracks* are rails or boards on which a dolly moves. A *western dolly* has heavy wheels and can move over rough terrain, as in a Western movie. A *fearless dolly* is a small dolly, with a hook that can be maneuvered easily.

Many of these dollies were used in the making of the 1969 film, *Hello Dolly!*, but most of us remember only one, Dolly Levi, played by Barbra Streisand (b. 1942). However, before we dolly-out, let's not forget Carol Channing (b. 1923), the inimitable star of the stage play, whose signature song is "Hello Dolly!"

If you've worked on a film, you want it to have legs. *Legs* is the ability of a film or other work to attract sizable audiences on a continuing basis. A film that opens to a strong box office, but fizzles a few weeks later, has "wobbly legs," whereas a film that continues to be profitable week after week has "strong legs." Incidentally, a book with "legs" is so successful that it "walks out of the store." To "open wide," a film is shown initially in many theaters. To "go wide," a film moves from a few to many theaters. A *big picture* is a major production. Outside the movie business, "big picture" means the overall view or perspective of an event or situation.

The original expression uttered at the end of each day's filming was, "Wrap it up." Now, "wrap" means to finish, and "That's a wrap" marks the completion of a scene (take) or the entire production. A "wrap party" celebrates the end of the film's production. To "wrap on schedule three weeks later" is bad news for the producer.

One of my favorite terms is a *MacGuffin* (or "McGuffin"), a plot device or inanimate object in a film on which considerable action revolves, often in a suspenseful manner; but though it appears to be important, really isn't. The term was popularized by director Alfred Hitchcock (1899–1980). The origin is an old Scottish joke told by Angus MacPhail (1903–62), an English writer who worked with Hitchcock. In one version, two men meet on a train and the first man asks, "What's that package you are carrying?" (In another version, the package has been placed in the baggage rack.) The other passenger answers, "Oh, that's a MacGuffin." When the first man inquires what that is, he receives the reply, "A MacGuffin's an apparatus for trapping lions in the Scottish Highlands." To which the first man retorts, "But there are no lions in the Scottish Highlands."

And finally, comes the reply, "Well then, that's no MacGuffin!"

In Hitchcock's *The Lady Vanishes* (1938), the MacGuffin is a coded message in a piece of music. In *Notorious* (1946), it's the uranium ore hidden in vintage wine bottles. MacGuffins also appear in non-Hitchcock films, such as the statuette in *The Maltese Falcon* (1941), directed by John Huston (1906–87).

Movies were called *flicks*, or "flickers," because of the flickering light from the projector. A *popcorn flick* has mass appeal, particularly for viewers who like to eat popcorn during the film. A *chick flick* appeals to women.

Cinema is a movie theater or the movie industry, in general. It comes from the French, *cinéma* (and sometimes spelled similarly in English, with the accent mark), which in turn is from the Greek, *kinema*, or motion. "Cinema vérité" is a form of documentary film that stresses realism. It's from the French *vérité*, or truth. Here now are other basic cinematic terms.

A *soundstage* is a large soundproof studio, usually with interior stages, used in film production. At a major film company, the many soundstages resemble warehouse buildings and are numbered. (Some numbers, such as seven and thirteen, are omitted for superstitious reasons.)

A *spaghetti Western* was a movie set in the American West but filmed in Italy with a mostly Italian cast, with English dubbed in. Common in the sixties, these low-budget films sometimes featured American performers, notably Clint Eastwood (b. 1930), and were sometimes made in Yugoslavia or Spain. A *runaway production* is a film produced by an American company primarily outside of the United States, such as Vancouver or elsewhere in Canada, generally to save money.

A *horse opera*, or "oater," is a Western movie. A *biopic* is a filmed biography, a blend of *bio*graphy and *pic*ture. It's pronounced BI-oh-pic.

"Take five" or "take ten" are common instructions for a coffee or rest break. If a set is being prepared or if the director is not certain about the length of the break, the command may be, "Possible twenty," indicating that the respite may stretch to twenty minutes. "Take a forty-two" is an announcement of a meal break, as specified in union contracts.

MOS is a direction that no sound is to be recorded during the filming of a scene, or an indication that the film is silent. It's loosely derived from the German *mit-aus sprache*, without sound. The opposite, which is more common, is *SOF*, "sound-on-film."

Silent films were shown in a *nickelodeon*, a theater to which admission cost a nickel. (Now you know the origin of the Nickelodeon cable network.) The first nickel shows were shown in Pittsburgh in 1904. The next time that you go to a multiplex, I hope that you will watch the credits with a greater degree of appreciation and understanding. Of course, it will also cost you a lot more than a nickel.

In the first few decades of sound pictures, films were shown at major theaters in the downtown area of cities ("first-run theaters"), often with a stage show, and then moved to neighborhood theaters ("second-run theaters").

Radio City Music Hall opened in New York in 1932. With close to 6,000 seats, it was the world's largest movie theater. It was located on Sixth Avenue (now called Avenue of the Americas) and 51st Street, adjacent to Rockefeller Center. One of the first tenants at Rockefeller Center was the Radio Corporation of America, and "music hall" is a common term for a theater in the United Kingdom—thus the origin of the name Radio City Music Hall.

The *Rockettes*, the famous synchronized chorus line, debuted at Radio City Music Hall on opening night, December 27, 1932. Actually, they started in 1925 as the Missouri Rockets and were brought to New York by S. L. George (Roxy) Rothafel (1882–1936), who called them the Roxyettes, when they performed at his Roxy theater. The name was changed to the Rockettes when they moved to Radio City. In these early days of movie-going, it was common to show two feature films (an A-picture and a B-picture), plus one or more of the following: cartoon, newsreel, short subject or "short" (a travelogue or other subject), and "trailers" (previews of coming attractions). Oh, there also often was a serial, particularly on weekends, an adventure film that had weekly installments, called "chapters." All for a dollar or less!

A film *rating* is a classification to guide viewers, especially parents, with regard to matters of "taste"—sex, violence, and other sensitive content—designated by a standards organization. In the United States, the rating system before 1968, called the Production Code, was administered by the Code Administration of the Motion Picture Producers and Distributors of America. The system has since then been administered by the Motion Picture Association of America, using these five ratings: G (general audience); PG (parental guidance); PG-13 (parental guidance for children under 13); R (restricted, children under 17 not admitted, without an accompanying adult); and NC-17 (under 17 not admitted; prior to 1990, called X). Sometimes a preview (a trailer) has a G-rating even though the film itself may have a different rating. Film ratings are so commonly understood that they are used in everyday language about other media and subjects, such as a "G-rated party." *X-rated* is still used generically to indicate a film or work considered offensive, pornographic, or obscene.

A *studio* is a room with facilities for an artist, photographer, or other specialists, such as a recording studio, radio- or TV-station studio, or movie studio. A group of artists or photographers, or film stages, also may be called collectively a "studio," as well as the company itself (a "movie studio"). A "studio exterior" refers to an outdoor set constructed and often photographed indoors in a studio. A "studio manager," like a plant manager, oversees operations but not of specific filming, which is the responsibility of the film's director. A "studio picture" is a film made primarily in a studio and not on location. Incidentally, in the music business, a "studio album" is produced in a recording studio and not at an actual concert.

In the golden era of the American film industry in the first half of the twentieth century, the major film companies popularized the studio system of performers and others who were on staff or under studio contract, which is different from the methods of today's film packagers and independents (*indies*).

The *studio zone* is the area near a film studio. A shooting area outside the studio zone is called a "distant location" that normally requires lodging and travel reimbursement. In Los Angeles, the studio zone is located within a 30-mile radius from the former offices of the Alliance of Motion Picture and Television Producers, at the corner of La Cienega and Fairfax.

The world's first movie theater was opened in the Grand Café in Paris in 1895 by brothers Auguste Lumière (1862–1954) and Louis Lumière (1864–1948), who invented the Cinématographe, a combination camera-projector. Louis Lumière is considered to be the "father" of the cinema. *Lumière* is the French word for light. Was their name a coincidence or fate?

There now are about thirty-seven thousand screens in about six thousand theaters in the United States, including about six hundred drive-in screens in about four hundred drive-in theaters. (There are an estimated 328,000 screens in the world.)

In the film business, a theater, or chain of theaters, that shows films is called an *exhibitor* (abbreviated by *Variety* as *exhib*). Exhibitors rent films from the distribution units of the studios or other producers. During the first week, and sometimes the second, the exhibitor keeps 30 percent of ticket sales, and the percentage increases in succeeding weeks, up to about 65 or 70 percent. Plus the exhibitor keeps the income from the refreshments concession. You can imagine how much profit there is in popcorn and soft drinks!

If you want more information about the film business, "Let's do lunch," as they say in Hollywood. Contact me c/o Random House.

GEOGRAPHY: MADISON AVENUE AND OTHER MEDIA METONYMS

WHAT do Wall Street, Madison Avenue, Fleet Street, and Pennsylvania Avenue have in common? This is not a trick question, though I'm sure you can come up with a clever answer.

In the context of media lingo, the answer is that each is a *metonym*, a word or phrase substituted for another that it suggests or with which it is closely associated. (Lexicographers and linguists have several such words to describe common figures of speech.) Examples of metonyms include the "White House" for the president; "crown" for a monarch or royal power; the "boards" for a theatrical stage; the "stage" for the theatrical field in general; and the "bench" for the judiciary.

To linguistic purists, a metonym is not a "synonym," a word with the same or similar meaning as another, such as *president* and *leader*. However, a synonym can also be a figurative or a symbolic substitute, so the distinction can become blurred. For example, a thesaurus lists synonym-like substitutions for the same word, such as "Broadway" for theater, "off-Broadway" for experimental or low-budget plays, and "Tin Pan Alley" for popular music.

The New York Stock Exchange is located at 11 Wall Street in lower Manhattan, and "Wall Street" is a metonym known around the world, symbolizing American financiers and their economic and political clout.

Elsewhere in New York City, several ad agencies were located on Madison Avenue, and the name "Madison Avenue" loosely refers to the advertising agency business. Today, Madison Avenue, known for its posh stores and art galleries, remains the home of a few agencies and the Advertising Council, an organization that helps to conduct public service advertising campaigns.

"Fleet Street," an old street in London, once was the location of several newspaper and press offices and remains the general name for the British press.

Central London includes the neighbourhood (British spelling) of Soho, familiar to tourists and film audiences for its fashionable shops and colorful nightlife. The name comes from an old hunting cry. So it was logical that an area in lower Manhattan south of Houston Street was dubbed "SoHo" (note the inner capital letter). Filled with pricey boutiques and art galleries, SoHo has evolved into a downtown hip version of Madison Avenue.

Millions of tourists also visit "SoBe," the South Beach area of Miami Beach. Major media often refer to Miami Beach as Miami. Not true. The two cities are distinct and separated by Biscayne Bay.

"Pennsylvania Avenue" has become a metonym for the White House, whose exact address is 1600 Pennsylvania Avenue NW, Washington, D.C. The "Beltway" refers to the highways that surround the city, thus, "inside the Beltway" a metonym for Washington, D.C., or, more specifically, the political establishment, consisting of government officials, lobbyists, the media, and others associated with the federal government. The "Hill" is slang for the U.S. Congress, which meets in the U.S. Capitol building located on Capitol Hill in Washington, D.C. A common journalistic expression is "heard on the Hill."

People in the radio industry are familiar with an online newsletter, *The M Street Journal*, which covers radio industry news, including actions of the Federal Communications Commission (FCC). The name comes from the former address of the FCC, located for many years on M Street in Washington, but today on 12th Street SW.

Nashville, the capital of Tennessee, is also the country music capital. It's sometimes called "Music City" or "Music Town," which brings to mind Detroit, the home of automobile companies, known as "Motown" (motor town). "Motown" refers to a style of rhythm and blues music that originated in the sixties primarily in Detroit. Motown Records is now part of Universal Music Group.

Let's move on now to Peoria, a small city in Illinois. PR and advertising people want to know, "Will it play in Peoria?" when assessing whether a campaign or other project will be understood and appreciated in a typical small U.S. city. The term originated with touring theatrical troupes whose producers assumed that, if a show went over well in Peoria, it could succeed anywhere.

A common journalistic practice, particularly of headline writers, is to use the capital of a state or country to refer to the entire entity, such as "Washington" for the United States and "London" for the United Kingdom.

One of the best-known metonyms is "Hollywood." It's not a separate city—as is Beverly Hills, a metonym for wealth—but a section of Los Angeles. Many film studios were once located in or near Hollywood; the name now connotes the West Coast movie industry or the U.S. film industry in general. "Hollywoodization" is slang for the influence of the U.S. film industry or for the overdramatization of a process or event.

The editors of *Variety* and other entertainment trade publications delight in the use of slang and coined words (neologisms). "Tinseltown" was slang for Hollywood in the larger-than-life, glittering era of the thirties. "Tinsel" means showy or gaudy, from glittering strips of cloth or metal in fabrics or decorations. Hollywood historians credit Mrs. Deida (or Daida) Wilcox (1861–1914) of Kansas City for the creation of their city section's name. Wilcox retired with her husband in 1886 to a ranch in Los Angeles they named after the holly trees on the site.

One of Hollywood's attractions is a movie theater that was opened in 1927 by Sidney Patrick Grauman (1879–1960). The theater became famous for its courtyard; movie stars embedded their handprints and footprints in its cement walkway and the theater was renamed Grauman's Chinese Theater. In 1973, it was purchased by Ted Mann (1917–2001) and renamed Mann's Chinese Theatre. Now it's back to being called Grauman's Chinese Theater, and in the movie trade, simply the Chinese Theater.

The "Loop" is the downtown commercial district of Chicago, so called because the elevated railroad tracks circle (loop) around part of it. However, to be "in the loop" means to be part of an insider group that is privy to information. The opposite is "out of the loop."

Every state and major city has one or more nicknames. Sometimes it's an official name or slogan and appears on license plates, such as the "Sunshine State" (Florida). Sometimes, the name also refers to the people in the state, such as "Hoosiers" (Indianians), "Buckeyes" (Ohioans), "Hawkeyes" (Iowans), and "Badgers" (Wisconsinites). A complete list is found in *The World Almanac*.

Nicknames of cities often appear in newspaper columns and other media without further identification. I mentioned Motown and others earlier. Here are more:

"Beantown" (Boston), "Big Apple" (New York City), "Big-D" (Dallas), "City by the Bay" (or "Bay City") (San Francisco), "City of Angels" (Los Angeles), "City of Brotherly Love" (Philadelphia), "Gotham" (New York City again), "Second City" (Chicago; no longer apt, but still used), and "Windy City" (Chicago).

You know that the "Twin Cities" refers to Minneapolis and St. Paul. You're excused if you don't know the "Quad Cities": Davenport, Iowa, and three nearby cities across the Mississippi River in Illinois—East Moline, Moline, and Rock Island.

TV viewers know the locale of their favorite programs, such as Evergreen Terrace in *The Simpsons* and Wisteria Lane in *Desperate Housewives*. Wisteria, a woody vine, is named after Casper Wister (1761–1818), an American physician who first described the shrub with flowers that are bluish, lilac, or other colors. Botanists sometimes spell it "wistaria" because his name probably was Wistar.

GEOMETRY: THE SHAPE OF MEDIA THINGS

ONE of the most common styles of journalistic writing involves the *inverted pyramid*, in which the most important news elements (such as the five Ws—who, what, where, when, and why) are presented first, in the "lead," with increments of detail added in successive paragraphs. The structural image of a pyramid resting on its point seems misleading, as the beginning, or top, of a news story should be sharp and pointed. But the image is apt, in that an editor can chop off less important material, starting at the bottom, without adversely affecting the core story.

The pyramid is our lead-in to this essay about geometric shapes found in the media. Next, let's consider the "circle," which has numerous uses in the media. In a theater, for example, a *circle* refers to a tier of seats, such as the *dress circle* that encircles the main floor (the orchestra), so named because patrons of this section used to dress formally. A circle also can refer to a group of people with common interests, such as a *family circle*. (Now you know the reason for the title of that similarly named magazine.)

In photography and film, circled numbers on a "contact sheet" or a "camera report" (a list of shots or takes) indicate those images that are to be printed. These are called *circled takes* or *OK takes*. In contrast, in broadcasting, circles are placed around portions of a script that should not be read, such as cues and times.

A *circle of illumination* is the area of an image that is seen through a camera lens. Within this circle, the area that is the clearest is called the *circle of best definition*.

In film and television, in an optical effect called *circle wipe*, an image first appears as a dot in the center and then grows to full size while covering (wiping out) the preceding scene.

In broadcasting, a director may signal a performer to speed up by quickly moving the index finger in a circular motion. If you're in the midst of giving a speech and someone gives you this signal, it can be unnerving.

A *circular* is a letter, booklet, or other item, usually an advertisement, that is distributed (circulated) by hand or mail. It's sometimes called a *flier*, *flyer*, or *leaflet*.

A *circular file* is a euphemism for a wastebasket. An instruction to send a news release or other item to the "circular file" means to throw it away.

Arc (a curved shape) is also a media term. In film and theater, an "arc" is a high-intensity light (described in "Lights Up!"). *Arc out* is an instruction to move a dolly (mobile platform) on a graceful curve away from the action. It is also an instruction to a performer to move on a curved path in front of the camera, as it is less bold.

As noted in "Broadcasting," an *arc* is a series of programs. In a script, article, or other work, an "arc" is the line of progression of the story.

Arc of fashion is the general pattern of acceptance of a fashion or other item among different types of customers. Market researchers refer to "early accepters" or "early adopters," then "early followers," "general accepters," and "laggards."

A *cone* (a geometric shape with a circular base and curved sides that taper to an apex) is the name of a common type of floodlight (high-intensity light) in various sizes, such as "senior cone," "junior cone," and "baby cone."

In precomputer days, artists used a metal or plastic *triangle* to draw straight lines and right angles. A *triangle* also refers to a musical instrument consisting of a steel rod bent into a triangular shape. A common plot device is a *love triangle*, a romantic entanglement involving three people.

It used to be that an old-fashioned or boringly conventional person was called a "square." The term "square" is common in printing, typography, and publishing. *Square capitals* are simple, straight-line, all-capital (uppercase) letters, as in early Latin manuscripts. They still are used on tombstones, monuments, and for some company or product names.

Square serif is a group of typefaces with uniform strokes and vertical or horizontal, rather than curved, serifs. It's also called *block letter* or *slab serif.*

A *serif* is a short, thin line that projects above or below the main strokes of letters, such as a, l, and v, so that the letters do not have uniform thickness. Studies indicate that serif letters are easier to read in printed matter (and more graceful) than *sans serif* (typeface without serifs), which is why such excellent publications as *The New York Times* use serif typefaces. In 2003, *The New York Times* changed its headlines in the news and other sections to a new family of typefaces based on **Cheltenham.** The body text still is **Imperial,** a serif typeface created in 1957. It is not the commonly used **Times Roman,** which is named after the English newspaper *The Times* of London.

A *square book* is just that. Technically, its width can be three-fourths of, up to or equal to, its height. The format is common among art books or other large-size books, sometimes called *coffee-table books. Squares* also are the edges of a book cover that project beyond and protect the pages of the book.

At TV stations, *squares* are spaces on a grid filled in with the names of television programs on a proposed or actual schedule for each day. In transit advertising, a *square end* is a large area near the doors of a train or bus that is square or almost square, in contrast to the rectangular units in the middle of the vehicle.

A *sphere* is a round solid figure, such as a ball or globe. A *sphere of influence* (or *interest*) is an area in which an individual or organization has power to affect events and developments.

An *ellipse* is an oval shape. "Ellipsis," though not a geometric shape, is a media term from the Greek *elleipein*, to leave out. An *ellipsis* is the omission of a few letters, a word, phrase, sentence, or more that is considered to be superfluous or understood. It also may indicate a pause or passage of time, and sometimes is called *suspension points*. The omission or pause is indicated by a mark or series of marks, such as three dots . . . or asterisks***.

Here's a rule about "ellipsis points": three dots (. . .) refer to an omission within a sentence; but if the omission occurs at the end of the sentence, four dots are used (the fourth dot is the period closing the sentence). . . . To *ellipt* is the verb, though rare. Ellipsis (plural, "ellipses") sometimes is used by columnists to separate brief items. The best-known frequent user of ellipses was Walter Winchell (1897–1972), in his newspaper gossip column.

A trend is sometimes called a "curve." A curved line on a graph often is used to indicate trends. It's better to stay "ahead of the curve" than to fall "behind the curve."

Hyperbola is a geometric shape that can be generated from a cone intersected by a plane. The origin is from the Greek *hyperbole*, meaning to excuse. This brings us to *hyperbole* (pronounced hi-PUR-buh-lee), a figure of speech in which emphasis is achieved by exaggeration, usually designed for effect and not meant to be taken literally. Speakers and writers generally should avoid being "hyperbolic." On that note, we conclude our brief geometry media lesson. You're on your own with trigonometry, algebra, and calculus.

JOURNALISM: STOP THE PRESSES!

WE live in a world saturated with news, round the clock, 24/7. A major news event can clog the airwaves and fill print media for days. The credit and blame for this wall-to-wall coverage of breaking events goes to *journalism*, the profession of gathering, writing, editing, and publishing the news—for newspaper, magazine, other print, broadcast, and digital media. A *journalist* writes for these media. The origin of *journalism* is the Latin *diurnalis*, or daily. *Journalese* refers to the jargon of journalism and also to a writing style, characteristic of mass media, that emphasizes brevity and popular appeal. Sometimes the writing style can look deceptively simple, but can require great skill with words.

Press refers to print journalists or print media, and can now loosely refer to all news media and news writing. This chapter is primarily about newspapers—their basic terms plus a few of my favorites with colorful origins. Magazines and broadcast media are discussed in other chapters under those headings.

News is new or fresh information. The word comes from Middle English (about the twelfth to sixteenth centuries), when *newes* meant novelties, from the Old French *noveles*, in turn from the Latin *novus*, or new. (A popular, but erroneous, etymology says *news* stands for *n*orth, *e*ast, *w*est, and *s*outh.)

Hard news is the reporting of current events, whereas *soft news* is less current or urgent reporting, such as human interest and other features. The news department at a newspaper usually is located in a large open area called the *newsroom*. These days, reporters usually are seated in cubicles, each with a telephone and a computer, instead of a typewriter, as in not-too-distant years ago. *Spot news* is late-breaking news ("on-the-spot reporting"). *Enterprise journalism* involves investigative or other reporting initiated by an enterprising reporter or editor.

"Press" appears in the name of many newspapers, such as *Detroit Free Press*. Names of newspapers, however, more commonly include "News" (most frequent), "Times," "Journal," "Herald," "Tribune," or sometimes a combination of these, such as *International Herald Tribune*.

A *daily* newspaper is published five, six, or seven days a week. There are about fifteen hundred dailies in the United States, mostly published in the morning ("a.m. newspapers"). Newspapers published two or three times a week usually are grouped with once-a-week newspapers and are called *weeklies*, or *community newspapers*. There are about ten thousand weeklies in the United States. Incidentally, mass appeal popular newspapers, primarily in the nineteenth century, were sold for a penny and were called *penny papers*.

A newspaper is commonly called a "paper" or "papers" for short, as in "I read it in the papers." A *rag* is slang for a newspaper, particularly one that is sleazy or of poor quality.

A *newspaper chain* comprises a group of newspapers under common ownership. The largest is Gannett (described later in this essay). A *newspaper supplement* appears as a separate section prepared by the newspaper or an outside source. The largest supplements are *Parade* and *USA Weekend* (owned by Gannett), with millions of copies published each week.

A *free-standing insert*, or *fsi*, is a printed section or supplement, generally with advertising, inserted or stuffed into a newspaper or other publication. Sunday newspapers are loaded with them.

A *press association* is a news agency, or "wire service," such as The Associated Press and Reuters, that provides news and other material to newspapers and other subscribers. Initially, "newswires" were transmitted via telegraph wires, hence the continued use of the term "wire service." The material originally was received by wire machines (called "tickers") and printed on rolls of paper, in wire rooms, monitored by a wire editor. Now the services operate via computer.

The magnitude of AP alone is almost beyond belief: It transmits daily about twenty million words and one thousand images (photos). "Ripped from the headlines" is an expression used in radio, television, and other media, harking back to the days when wire copy was ripped off rolls of ticker paper.

To *go to press* (or *go to bed*) is to start printing a publication. *Presstime* is the length of time that a newspaper or other item is on press, the length of time the printing presses are running, or the time of day the presses start rolling. A *press run*, or "run," is the total number of copies of an edition or issue of a newspaper, magazine, book, or other publication.

A *press card*, or "press badge," is an identification carried or worn by an accredited media person. It is not the same as a *press pass*, a ticket that entitles a media person to free admission to an event.

An *edition* refers to the copies of a publication printed from a single typesetting, such as all the copies of a single press run of a newspaper. However, during the printing of an edition, the presses may be stopped for revisions and late news. ("Stop the presses!" is the electrifying command.) A "new edition" starts when the type is changed in a major way. A daily newspaper may issue a "city edition," "state edition," "national edition," "late city edition," or "final edition." A newspaper reporter or other person working within a short time from the printing of a specific edition is working *on edition*. The last edition printed is considered the "edition of record," which is the one filed online or in the archives and also sold by the back-issue department.

"Edition" also describes revised versions of books, so that a first edition could be rare and valuable to collectors. In broadcasting, "edition" can be a specific version of a program, such as a "sports edition."

Bulldog is the earliest edition of a morning newspaper, published the preceding night. A *bullpup* is the first edition of a Sunday newspaper, generally published at an earlier hour than the weekday papers, and sometimes printed in full or in part before Sunday. (For example, subscribers to *The New York Times* in the New York City area receive a large "bullpup" of the Sunday paper a day early, on Saturday, including the book review, magazine, arts, and real estate sections.) These canine words probably originated in the 1890s, when the *New York World* and other morning newspapers published early editions in time to catch the mail trains, with the newspapers fighting like bulldogs to make their deadlines and to outscoop each other. Another alleged origin holds that in 1905 William Randolph Hearst (1863–1951) urged the editors of his *New York American* to write strong headlines that would bite the public like a bulldog.

Cheesecake in newspaper and magazine jargon means a photograph or work of art with sex appeal, originally of a woman showing her legs above the knee. The originator probably was a *New York Journal* photographer, James Kane, who in 1912 photographed an actress on the rail of an incoming steamship and compared her to that favorite New York dessert, the cheesecake. "Cheesecake" was formerly a staple in the portfolios of press agents, particularly in Miami Beach, Las Vegas, and Hollywood. "Cheesecake calendars" adorned with reproductions of sensuous drawings were popular long before the advent of the *Playboy* centerfold (the middle pages) or the *Sports Illustrated* swimsuit issue. The masculine equivalent of cheesecake showing muscular men has been playfully dubbed *beefcake*.

An amusing term from the days when several daily newspapers competed in every major city, *lobster trick* refers to the early-morning working hours or dawn shift at a newspaper. Also called "lobster shift" or "lobster watch," it is again attributed to the publisher William Randolph Hearst, who frequently visited the presses during the early shift at the *New York American* and observed that the printers' noses were lobster-red, probably from visits to neighborhood bars. (One wag recently coined the phrase *bagel shift* for the same wee-hour work shift.)

An *extra* is a special edition put together to cover late-breaking or very important news. U.S. newspapers first published extras in the mid-nineteenth century, with newsboys running through the streets yelling "Extra! Extra! Read all about it!" The word EXTRA was emblazoned across the top of page one. Extras are rare in the television and Internet era.

Editorial is a general term for the news, features, and other nonadvertising material in a newspaper or other periodical. It also means an opinion piece, written by the editorial page editor or a member of the editorial board. *Editorial hall* is British for the newsroom. *Editorial well*, the part of a publication devoted to news and other nonadvertising material, sometimes refers only to the main section, or to the section that contains longer articles, such as the central section of a magazine, which does not include departments in the front or back. The total amount of space or time (usually expressed in column inches or seconds) allocated to nonadvertising material is called a *budget*, such as a "news budget," or a "budget" for a specific article or report.

The *editor* is responsible for the editorial or nonadvertising control of a publishing operation, such as the head of a department of a newspaper or of the entire editorial staff (sometimes called "editor-in-chief" or "editor in chief"). At a newspaper, the *executive editor* (ex. ed.) often combines business and editorial responsibilities, whereas the *managing editor* (m.e. or mng. ed.) supervises editorial departments, such as those headed by the "assignment editor," "foreign editor," "metropolitan editor" or "city editor" (c.e.), "national editor," "news editor," "picture editor," "state editor," "suburban editor," and editors of specific "beats" or sections.

A few newspapers, such as the *Chicago Tribune, The New York Times,* and *The Washington Post*, have an ombudsman, called a "public editor," "reader advocate," or "reader representative," whose responsibility is to independently review the newspaper's coverage of news for fairness and accuracy, and to explore any reader's complaints to the contrary.

A *beat* denotes a geographical area or subject category assigned to one or more reporters, such as the "City Hall beat." It's sometimes called a *run*, referring to the route. A "beat" can also mean an exclusive story that beats, or "scoops," the competition (to "get a beat"). In a "phone beat," or "beat check," the research is covered by telephone. "Scoop" is a common noun and verb in journalism and elsewhere. The word is from the German *schöpe* and *schöpfen*, and is discussed later in this chapter.

The *publisher* is the chief executive, often the owner or representative of the owner. At some periodicals, the publisher runs the advertising and other business areas, with both the editor and publisher reporting to the owner, who may have the title of president or chairman.

A *desk*, a department such as the "national desk," is headed by a "desk chief" and staffed by a "desk editor" and "deskmen" and "deskwomen." In the local news department, formerly called the "city desk" but now generally called the *metropolitan desk*, the "metropolitan editor" supervises the reporters covering the area in and near where the publication is headquartered. Many newspapers publish a separate metro section devoted to local news, or have regional editions, with separate staffs, for distribution in nearby counties or states.

Copy refers to the text of an article or other written work. The "copy desk," supervised by the *copy editor* with a staff of *copyreaders*, is the section responsible for editing the material turned in by reporters and other writers. "Copyediting" is the boot camp of journalism and many editors and reporters started as "copyeditors" or as "copy boys" (or "girls"), carrying copy and running errands. In this computer era, copy no longer is typed on sheets and carried, but the term still is used for digital texts. Arthur Gelb (b. 1924) and Joseph Lelyveld (b. 1937) both started as copy boys at *The New York Times* and went on to become acclaimed editors.

More extensive writing is handled by the *rewrite desk*, staffed by writers (formerly called "rewrite men") who receive copy from reporters, often by telephone, and write the actual stories. In *The Front Page, Lou Grant*, and other fiction about journalism, reporters call in from telephones at a news site and snarl, "Get me rewrite!" The rewrite personnel generally wear headphones and are fast typists. They do not receive bylines or other recognition, though their writing (not just typing) skills make them indispensable to news reporting.

A *byline* identifies the writer, in a line generally below the headline, starting with "By." A "byline box" sometimes appears at the end of the first column or the end of an article, containing a longer identification of two or more reporters (often in different locations), usually set in italic type or separated by a ruled line.

The editorial authority of a publication or broadcast medium results from its integrity, objectivity, and accuracy. An advertisement is biased on behalf of the advertiser and rarely is viewed with the same attention or respect as editorial matter. Although an advertisement may be set in all text to convey an "editorial look," it is customarily identified at the top as an "Advertisement."

Editorializing is the insertion of an opinion. When editorializing occurs in a news article that is supposed to be unbiased, readers may be skeptical of the publication's objectivity. However, the practice has become common.

Such articles may be labeled "Opinion" or "Analysis." A *think piece* is an analytical article (piece) or thoughtful commentary.

The *op-ed* page sits adjacent to (opposite) the editorial page and is set aside for columns by staff and syndicated columnists and articles by outsiders. In some cases, bylined op-ed articles and letters-to-the-editor appear on the editorial page itself rather than opposite or next to it. Some newspapers now have two pages of columns and articles, usually called "Opinion," following the editorial page.

The *masthead* area in a publication indicates its name and other information, such as year founded, personnel, motto, and statement of policy. Contrary to popular usage, the "masthead" is not merely the publication's name (called the *title* or *flag*, appearing on page one). This was mentioned in the essay "Body Parts," but bears repeating. The "masthead" generally appears on the editorial page of newspapers and on the contents page of magazines. The word comes from the top part of a ship's mast, which displays the flag of the country of origin. A *masthead editor* is a managing editor or other editor whose name appears on the masthead. A *masthead meeting* is a conference, usually convened every weekday morning, that brings together these top editors.

As also noted in the chapter "Body Parts," the *ear* is a box in the upper left and right corners of page one of a publication, generally a newspaper, flanking the "title" (also called the "nameplate" or "logo"). "Ears" contain weather reports (the "weather ear") or other messages, occasionally including advertising, particularly in newspapers outside of the United States.

Nonstaff writers include *freelancers* and *stringers*. In the Middle Ages, a "free lance" was a mercenary or an independent soldier, with a lance or spear, who sold his services. Carrying out this tradition, today's freelancers sometimes combat with editors, particularly about payment.

Because freelancers once were paid by the line, a

writer was called a *penny-a-liner*, though not necessarily paid a penny, but certainly a low rate. Now freelancers are paid a flat fee or are paid by the word, such as fifty cents (at trade magazines and newsletters) or a dollar or more (at major newspapers and magazines) per word.

A *stringer* is a correspondent, generally part-time, for a newspaper or other publication, who is not on staff. The origin is from "on the string," being paid a variable amount depending on the quantity of writing accepted by the editor. Some editors paid a part-time reporter by keeping the reporter's clippings tied together on a string and literally paying the reporter by the number of clippings or the number of column inches published, also perhaps measured with a string. Another possible origin comes from the era of hot metal, when type was assembled in a "galley tray." Each writer's lines of type were tied together with a string.

A *morgue* is a library, reference department, or collection, particularly at a newspaper or magazine. The word originates from the file of biographies prepared in advance of the death of prominent individuals. *The New York Times* excels in writing these obituaries-in-advance, often long pieces that, in the event of a death, can be used quickly, by adding an introductory paragraph about the circumstances of the death. The morgue sometimes is called a "clip file," as it is filled with *clippings* (articles that are clipped, or cut out), many of which predate the online editions of the publication.

Incidentally, an excellent source of articles previously published in newspapers, magazines, and other media, is Nexis, started in 1979. The name is a variation of the word *nexus*, a link between individuals in a group. A companion service, the Lexis system, is used for legal and accounting research. Today, the company and its brands, all called LexisNexis, are owned by media giant Reed Elsevier.

Obituaries brings us to the word "ghost," or *ghostwriter*, an anonymous person who writes speeches, articles, and sometimes, entire books, for attribution to others. In contrast, a *ghost word* is a spurious word, usually resulting from a typographical or other error and then repeated. The term was originated by William Skeat (1835–1925), an English lexicographer. A renowned example of a ghost word is the "Emmy" award, created by a typographical error of its original name, "Immy."

A *headline* ("head" or "hed") is a summary at the top (head) of an article. "Head to come" (abbreviated *HTK*) is a notation put on copy that the heading will be written and set later. Major newspapers sometimes have the embarrassment of accidentally printing this notation instead of a headline, particularly in the first edition. An *overline* is a caption set above a picture or art, or a line above a headline, usually flush left (at the left margin, without indentation). Some newspapers have a *summary blurb*, with more details, below the headline.

A *slug* consists of one or two words that identify an article or column. It may be taken from the headline or the name of the reporter or writer, and it's used for reference only during production, not intended for printing. It's also called a "catchline," "guide," "guideline," or "slugline." In the days of metal type, a metal line was inserted at the bottom of a column (called a "foot slug") or between a headline and the text (a "head slug"). Wire services still use the term "slug" to identify an article, and, as with HTK, the slugline occasionally accidentally appears in print. In computerese, a "tag" is a word or words that an individual attaches to online text or photos to identify the file. (More on tags at the end of this chapter.) The process is called "tagging."

Flush right, or "right justified," is the alignment of all lines at the right margin. It often requires "justification," the adding of spaces between words (or sometimes between characters) to fill out the line. Books, such as this, are automatically justified on the left and right margins. *Ragged right*, in which the type does not extend to the right margin, minimizes hyphenations and has a looser appearance—sometimes used adjacent to artwork. Some of the short articles in the *National Geographic* and other media are set "ragged right." (The term does not connote political bias!)

A *split head* is a headline of more than one line with a bad break between lines, such as a line ending in a preposition or a line with only part of a compound verb. Words are never hyphenated in headlines. The present tense often is used in newspaper headlines, even when referring to events that have already occurred, to enhance the sense of immediacy and because present tense verbs generally are shorter than past tense ones. A *blind headline* is a headline with no obvious meaning, such as a teaser headline on a magazine cover or in a tabloid newspaper. Even full-size newspapers use one-word teaser headlines, such as "Blast-off!" or "Guilty!" on the assumption that readers already know something about the event from the previous evening's broadcasts.

Writing that is *headlinese* has some of the telegram-like characteristics of a newspaper headline, but in an exaggerated way. It may be writing too staccato or overly compressed, have too many nouns (including the use of nouns as adjectives), or include ambiguous words or clichés.

A *broadsheet* means a full-size newspaper; while a tabloid, a smaller one. *Above-the-fold* is the top half of the page of a broadsheet and has more important articles than *below-the-fold*. A photo of a fire, given prominent attention in the top half of the page, usually page one, is called *flames above the fold*. In broadcasting, "Fire at 11" is a bulletin indicating that a fire will be reported on the 11 p.m. news. In the United Kingdom, a few broadsheets have converted to tabloids (the Brits call them "compacts"), and some conversions are likely in the United States.

[TABLOIDS: WOOD THIS!]

If you write for a tabloid or are an avid reader of one, be not ashamed. Tabloid simply means a newspaper of less than standard size. Originally published for mass appeal, tabloids featured large sensational headlines on the front page, and over time developed a disreputable reputation.

Tabloid journalism today generally connotes exaggerated, exploitative, and sensational articles with short sentences and lots of photos. "Tabloidization" means a change in emphasis from the factual to the sensational. However, both the *Christian Science Monitor* and Long Island's *Newsday* are highly respected tabloids, as are many other daily and weekly tabloid newspapers, as well as hundreds of trade and business tabloids, such as *Advertising Age*, *Computerworld*, *Crain's New York Business*, and *PRWeek*.

Preprinted advertising supplements inserted in *broadsheets* (full-size newspapers) usually are tabloids, as are *Parade*, *USA Weekend*, and other newspaper supplements.

The word "tabloid" means tablet-like (a flat, thin piece of stone or other material, commonly carrying an inscription). A British pharmacist, Henry Wellcome (1853–1936), developed a compressed medicinal tablet and, in 1884, trademarked it as a "Tabloid." (Yes, he's the one who partnered with American Silas Burroughs [1846–95] to form Burroughs-Wellcome, now GlaxoSmithKline.) Because the compact tabloid pill was easy to swallow, the word "tabloid" soon became the designation of smaller-sized accessible newspapers, featuring shorter articles and more illustrative material.

Publishers often shorten "tabloid" to *tab*, particularly in describing a Sunday or other supplement (called *supps*); for example, a "theme supplement," such as a "car tab" (covering an automobile show), "fashion tab," and "school tab" (back-to-school).

Large-size headlines, common in tabloids, have a colorful terminology. *Wood* is slang for a super-size headline, so large that it was set by hand, using old-fashioned wood type. Many editors use the verb, to "wood," to indicate large-size type, and the word sometimes is heard in films or TV shows about newspapers.

Another directive to print a large, bold headline is, "make the eagle scream," a reference to the drawing of an eagle flanking the title of some newspapers. Other slang for large-size headlines includes "banner," "ribbon," "screamer," "streamer," and "studhorse." A brief overline above a headline, photograph, or art is called an "eyebrow," "highline," "teaser," or "kicker." "Kicker" has other meanings in media, such as an attractive item, article (a *brite*), or photo used to brighten a page, sometimes in the left column to kick off, or start, the page.

A *reverse kicker* is a word or phrase set above a headline in larger type than the headline. It's also called a "barker," "hammer," or "hammerhead" and sometimes is underlined and followed by an exclamation point. It's often short and set flush left (no indentation) so that it somewhat resembles the head of a hammer.

At the supermarket checkout counters, the headlines of the tabloids are powerful factors in impulse sales. The editors who are responsible for these headlines are deft in combining hard news with puns, bold language, and other creative writing. In New York City, two of America's biggest circulation newspapers are tabloids—the *Daily News* and *New York Post*—which often front-page the same news with totally different headlines. And, sometimes almost all of page one is a headline.

A *minidaily* is a controlled circulation (free) tabloid containing short articles and "briefs" (usually one paragraph) distributed at the entrances to subway stations and other high-traffic locations, including coffee shops and retail stores. Designed to appeal to young adults, these advertiser-supported newspapers (some with as many as sixty-four pages) are different from *shoppers*, or community newspapers, which generally are weekly or semiweekly.

Metro, which is based in Luxembourg, now publishes many minidailies in Europe and the United States, including *Metro Boston*, *Metro New York*, and *Metro Philadelphia*. Philip Anschultz (b. 1939), of Denver, publishes the *San Francisco Examiner* and other free tabloids with the Examiner name in many cities, including the *Examiner Washington*.

Ironically, several major daily newspapers recently have launched minidailies, with quick-read formats produced by separate staffs who excel in edgy writing. In 2002, the *Chicago Sun-Times* launched the *Red Streak*, and the *Chicago Tribune* followed with the *RedEye*. The *Dallas Morning News* has *Quick*, and *The Washington Post* publishes the *Express*, both started in 2003. *Newsday* publishes *amNew York*. The Tribune-Review Publishing Co., which owns five small-circulation dailies in Pennsylvania, publishes the Pittsburgh *TRIBp.m.* If you don't have a minidaily in your city, you probably will see a Metro, Examiner, or similar tabloid soon.

Circulation is the number of copies sold by all the editions of a newspaper on one day. Many writers equate it with "readership," which is inaccurate since on average more than one person reads each copy of a newspaper, particularly on Sundays.

Verified statements of circulations of daily and weekly newspapers, magazines, and other media are provided by the Audit Bureau of Circulations (note the plural). You've seen the ABC logo on the publisher's page or elsewhere. A similar organization, BPA International (formerly Business Publications Audit of Circulation), audits and certifies business and other publications.

A *reporter* performs the basic job in journalism, gathering news and writing or broadcasting it. (A recent colloquial term coined for a reporter is *newsie*—not to be confused with "newsy," filled with news.) A "cub reporter" is a novice; while a "veteran reporter," very experienced. Reporters are categorized by the types of material on which they report, as indicated by their "beats," or areas to which they are assigned—such as "financial reporter," "general assignment reporter," "police reporter," or "sports reporter." A *legman*, or "legger," gathers news (runs "on the street" or elsewhere) and reports it to the writing and editing staff who put together the news story.

A *columnist* writes a regular feature or other article with a byline that expresses his or her own opinions. Sometimes called a "pundit" (expert) or "Brahmin" (culturally superior), a columnist may appear locally (in one newspaper) or syndicated to many subscribing newspapers. The most widely distributed column is the advice column *Dear Abby*, described toward the end of this chapter. (Don't confuse this with an *agony column*, a series of classified advertisements announcing missing individuals, pets, or other personal losses and problems.)

A "column" also means the standard vertical unit of space in a newspaper or other periodical. Editors describe the space available for news as "open columns." Advertisers use *agate lines* instead of inches to measure column depth; there are fourteen agate lines to a column inch.

The width of a column is generally measured in *picas*, expressed in *points*. One pica is twelve points, or 0.167 inch; six picas, or seventy-two points, equals one inch. The word "pica" (pronounced PIE-kuh) originates from the medieval Latin for "a table of rules used to select the correct church service." The origin, in turn, may be that the size and blackness of pica type on a white sheet can resemble a magpie, which in Latin was called a *pica* or *pie*. (*Piebald* means covered with spots, particularly black and white, as a "piebald horse.") Picas and points also are the units of measurement for the width and depth of characters and spacing between printed lines. This typeface is 9 points high and is set on a 13-point line; the measurement is expressed as 9/13 or 9 on 13.

A *web* is a large, continuous roll of paper, such as *newsprint* (paper lighter in weight and less white than the paper generally used in magazines and books) that can be fed into a rotary printing press (a "web press"). The web press prints continuously and at a high speed.

In case you've had enough technical terms, here are a few of my favorite lighter journalese expressions.

A *puff piece* is an article that extravagantly praises its subject. Publishers sometimes call a laudatory comment about the author or book, used on the book cover or elsewhere, a "puff," or more commonly, a "blurb" (discussed in the "Magazines" chapter). The origin of "puff" may be Mr. Puff, a character in *The Critic*, a 1779 book by Richard B. Sheridan (1751–1816), an Irish playwright best known for *The School for Scandals* (1777).

A *scoop* refers to an exclusive report in a newspaper or other medium. To "scoop," or "get a beat," is to top, beat, or outmaneuver a competitor by acquiring and publishing (or broadcasting) a major exclusive story. The origin is the Dutch *schoppe*, a bailing vessel or shovel, and the German *schöpfen*, to dip out or to create.

A *hack* is a writer who produces boring work. "Hack writer" is thus redundant as a term for a literary drudge. "Hack journalism" is uninspired (hence "hackneyed"), mediocre work. The etymology derives from London in the twelfth to fifteenth centuries, where an ordinary horse was used to pull a "hackney," or carriage. Hackney itself was a borough in East London. Today, taxicabs sometimes are still called "hacks."

"Hack" as a noun (meaning a rough cut) or a verb (to cut) has a different origin: from the German, *hacken*. A "computer hack" or "hacker" gains unauthorized access to (cuts into) data in a computer. The term has become so common that it sometimes can be a compliment, such as a "Google hack," a person who creatively and extensively conducts searches on Google.com.

New journalism is a form of writing with personal involvement and subjective interpretation, as contrasted with the objectivity of traditional journalism. It sometimes includes a composite character, invented quotations, and other techniques from fiction. The term was used in the sixties and seventies to describe the works of Hunter S. Thompson (1939–2005), Tom Wolfe (b. 1931), Truman Capote (1924–84), and others.

Gonzo journalism is a type of new journalism with reporting filled with bizarre or extremely subjective ideas or commentary, usually reflecting the alternative lifestyle of the writer. When Hunter S. Thompson first used the term, he said that "gonzo" was a Portuguese word that meant weird. Actually, the etymology is probably the Spanish *ganso*, a goose or fool; or Italian, *gonzo*, the shortened form of *borgonzone*, or foolish person.

Yellow journalism is exaggerated, exploitative articles designed to attract a mass audience. The origin was the use of yellow ink to print *The Yellow Kid*, about a troublemaker (the first successful comic strip character), created in 1895 by Richard Outcault (1863–1928) in the *New York World*, a sensationalist newspaper.

Back to serious journalism. *Libel* is defamation—a false, malicious statement, picture, or other material damaging to a person's reputation. "Libel" formerly referred to print media, but now includes all media. In fact, the Latin *libellus* is from *liber*, a book. *Slander* means oral defamation, as in a speech, rather than in print.

If it's old, been "killed" (thrown out or cancelled), or used—news is dead. *Deadline* is the latest date that something must be done or completed. Ironically, it originally meant a line around a prison area that prisoners were forbidden to cross lest they be shot. The first prison so equipped was in Andersonville, Georgia, for captured Northern soldiers during the Civil War.

The *daybook* is a list of news events, usually for that day or the following day, issued by the wire services in major cities.

The *dateline* at the beginning of an article indicates the city from which the news emanates and the date it was written, generally the day before publication, followed by a dash (—). Many newspapers omit the date. If the article was written in the same city as the headquarters of the newspaper, the entire dateline is omitted. The city usually is set in all caps (capital letters) and the state or country is omitted if it's well known. The *page dateline* is the complete date appearing at the top of a page of a daily newspaper, or the publication date at the top or bottom of each page or alternating pages of other periodicals.

Through a *pool*, a limited number of reporters, photographers, and broadcast crews (usually one of each) pool their resources to represent all those assigned to an event, resulting in *pool coverage*. You sometimes see the term *Pool photo* below a photo in a newspaper.

A *refer* (journalists pronounce it REEF-er), or *reefer*, is a notation within an article that refers the reader to a related article. A *pull quote* (or "pullquote") is a quotation that is taken, or pulled, from the text and set off or displayed as a "blurb" (excerpt), perhaps surrounded by ruled lines (a "pull quote box"). *More-on* is a brief item on page one that refers to an article inside. A *floater* is a photo and caption that appears on page one and is related to an article inside.

A *sidebar* is a news item, feature, or graphics with incidental information (sidelights) inserted within, adjacent to, or following, a related article. It is also sometimes surrounded by ruled lines.

To *jump* is to continue an article from one page to another. A "jump line," set in parentheses, boldface, or italics, appears at the end of the first portion of the "jump story," indicating where the article continues (called the "jump," "jump page," "breakover," or "carryover"). A "jump head" identifies the beginning of the continued portion. The *Los Angeles Times* has many long articles, each with several jumps. In contrast, *USA Today*, renowned for its sparsity of jump stories, usually jumps only the lead article (*cover story*) in each section.

The *jump line* in most newspapers is brief, such as "Continued on Page C4." *The Wall Street Journal* is more polite and helpful, with, for example, "Please Turn to Page C4, Column 1." Newspaper sections—such as the "Main Section" (major news), "Metro" (local news), "Sports," or "Business" sections—are identified by letters: "Page A1" is the first page of the first section.

Canning a story means writing an article about a forthcoming event in the past tense as though it already had happened. The story is then "put in the can," to be published just after the event—a dangerous practice, unless the "canned material" is checked and updated.

"Piece" is a multimedia word. Print and broadcast journalists commonly refer to an article, report, or broadcast segment as a *piece*. It's also a musical composition.

Journalists and government officials often refer to *The New York Times* as the "newspaper of record," an indication of its importance. Incidentally, when listing a group of newspapers, *The New York Times* uses a style in which "The" is part of the name (with a few exceptions, such as *USA Today*), in order to provide all of the names in a uniform manner. *The New Yorker* does the opposite (in spite of its name) and italicizes only part of the name, such as the Washington *Post* and the *Wall Street Journal*. In some cities, local readers have a nickname for their paper—such as the "Trib" (for the *Chicago Tribune*), the "PD" (*The Plain Dealer* of Cleveland), and the "Inky" (*The Philadelphia Inquirer*).

Following is information about a few major companies in the journalism field that are relevant to media lingo.

Advance Publications, headquartered in New York, owns newspapers, magazines (Condé Nast and Fairchild publications), and *Parade*, and operates a news service. It is headed by S. I. Newhouse, Jr. (b. 1928), the son of Samuel Irving (S. I.) Newhouse (1895–1979), who was nicknamed "Sie." The first Newhouse newspaper, acquired in 1922, was the *Staten Island Advance*, which started in 1896 as the *Richmond County Advance* and then became the *Staten Island Advance*. So that explains the name, Advance Publications.

Dow Jones & Company, headquartered in New York, was started in a basement at 11 Wall Street in lower Manhattan by Charles Henry Dow (1851–1902), Edward David Jones (1856–1920), and Charles Milford Bergstresser (1859–1923). The three men produced for distribution to subscribers in the area daily handwritten news bulletins, called *flimsies*. (In the era of typewriters, a duplicate copy of an article, usually made on yellow copy paper, was called a "flimsy.") These bulletins grew into *The Wall Street Journal*, started in 1889 as a four-page newspaper sold for two cents. Today, the *Journal* (as it's generally called) has a circulation of more than two million, with editions in the United States, Europe, and Asia. And the newsstand price now is one dollar.

The Dow Jones Newswires were started in 1882. The "Dow Jones Industrial Average" (DJIA) was launched in 1896, as an index of stock prices based on changes in a group of representative major stocks. (Note that "Dow Jones" is not hyphenated.) The DJIA is a barometer of the stock market and is quoted throughout the day on radio and TV, as well as in newspapers and other media, and generally is referred to as the "Dow," as in "The Dow hit a new high today."

Gannett Co., Inc., headquartered in McLean, Virginia, is America's largest newspaper group, with about one hundred dailies, with a total circulation of more than twenty-two million copies. The company was started by Frank E. Gannett (1876–1957) in 1906. Gannett's largest newspaper, *USA Today*, started in 1982 as a new type of newspaper. It became known for its short articles and colorful graphics, and has been the country's largest circulation newspaper (with more than 2 million copies) for many years.

Knight Ridder, based in San Jose, California, is America's second largest publisher of daily newspapers. The first Knight newspaper, *The Miami Herald*, was started in 1893 by the two brothers, John S. Knight (1894–1981) and James L. Knight (1909–91). Ridder was started by three of the five sons of Herman Ridder (1851–1915): Bernard H. Ridder (1883–1975), and twins Victor F. (1886–1963) and Joseph E. (1886–1966) Ridder. In 1926, the Ridders acquired the *Journal of Commerce*, first started in 1827.

The New-York Daily Times, started in 1851 by Henry Jarvis Raymond (1820–69) and George Jones (1811–91), became *The New York Times* in 1896.

In 1905, the *Times* moved to a building, called "Times Tower," on West 42nd Street, and the name of the nearby area (the intersection of Broadway and Seventh Avenue) was changed from Long Acre Square to "Times Square." The *Zipper*, started in 1928, flashes news headlines that move around the building, produced by an intricate system of thousands of flashing light bulbs. The same type of electronic billboard now is found on other buildings (including the News America headquarters, which includes the *New York Post*, near Rockefeller Center in Manhattan) and is used for advertising, as at airport terminals.

The New York Times News Service provides bylined columns and other material from *The New York Times* and other sources to about 650 subscribers. One indication of the importance of *The New York Times* is that New York Times News Service subscribers receive advisories in the late afternoon, with brief descriptions (called *frontings*) of the front-page stories the *Times* plans to use the following morning. (Actually, the *Times* starts printing its first local edition and its national edition the previous night, with the local edition available on newsstands before midnight.) The New York Times News Syndicate transmits columns and other material from many sources to more than two thousand clients around the world. *The New York Times* once was nicknamed the "Gray Lady," in reference to its conservative appearance, but that name no longer is used because, in recent years, the *Times* has excelled in color, graphics, and creative layouts.

Incidentally, America's national newspapers—*USA Today, The Wall Street Journal, The New York Times,* and *The Christian Science Monitor*—all have at least one commonality: They do *not* carry comic strips (but do print some political cartoons). Newspaper comic sections sometimes are called "funny papers" or the "funnies."

The Tribune Company, based in Chicago, is the nation's third largest publisher of newspapers. In ancient Rome, a "tribune" literally was an official who represented the commoners, and figuratively was a champion of the people. The *Chicago Tribune* was started in 1847; Joseph Medill (1823–99) was its editor and part-owner. The Medill School of Journalism at Northwestern University in Evanston, Illinois, is named after him. His two grandsons,

Robert Rutherford McCormick (1880–1955) and Joseph Medill Patterson (1879–1955), took over management of the *Tribune* in 1912.

Robert McCormick was a colonel in the U.S. Army in the First World War and was dubbed "The Colonel" by the Trib's staff. His grandfather, Cyrus Hall McCormick (1809–84), in 1831 developed a mechanical harvester that generated the family fortune. McCormick Place in Chicago, one of the world's largest convention centers, is named after Colonel Robert McCormick.

In 1921, the Tribune Company started WGN, a 50,000-watt clear channel radio station, taking its call letters from the *Tribune*'s slogan, "World's Greatest Newspaper." In 1925, the company moved to Tribune Tower, a neo-Gothic skyscraper on North Michigan Avenue, which has become a landmark. In 1981, the company acquired, from the Wrigley family, the Chicago Cubs baseball team, which plays in Wrigley Field. McCormick and Wrigley—two Chicago dynasties. Chew on that for a while.

Colonel Robert McCormick's cousin, Joseph Medill Patterson (1879–1946), moved to New York in 1919, and the Tribune Company acquired the *Illustrated Daily News*, a tabloid started in 1910. Two years later, Patterson changed the name to the *Daily News*, with the slogan, "New York's Picture Newspaper." The *Daily News* (that's its exact name, not "The New York Daily News," as it's often called in major media) became America's top circulation newspaper. For many years in the mid-twentieth century, its daily circulation was more than two million copies; and its Sunday edition, more than three million.

The *Daily News* was located in a building at 220 East 42nd Street. Even if you've never been there, you've seen its lobby with its huge, revolving globe, as it was the locale of the *Daily Planet* in the Superman films (the first in 1978). The Tribune Company sold the *Daily News* in 1991, and in 1993 it was acquired by a company owned by Mortimer B. Zuckerman (b. 1937), who also owns *U.S. News and World Report*. The *Daily News* now is located at 450 West 33rd Street, but you still can see its famous lobby at 220 East 42nd Street.

The Washington Post Company was started in 1877 by Stilson Hutchins (1838–1912) and was bought in 1933 by Eugene Meyer (1875–1959). He was succeeded by his son-in-law, Philip L. Graham (1915–63), and then by his daughter, Katherine Meyer Graham (1917–2001), who became one of America's best-known publishers.

America's largest news service is The Associated Press (note that "The" is capitalized), formed in 1848 and headquartered in Rockefeller Center in New York. The initials AP appear every day in parentheses in the datelines of thousands of articles.

Reuters Group plc, a publicly traded company headquartered in London, provides financial data to thousands of subscribers, as well as news, photos, and other material to print and broadcast media. Reuters claims to be the world's largest international multimedia news agency. Reuters America, Inc., is headquartered in Times Square in New York. Reuters was founded in 1849 by Baron Paul Julius von Reuter (1816–99), who was born in Germany. Note that his name did not end with an *s*, nor is there now an apostrophe in the name of the company. The newswire originally was called Reuters News Agency.

Bloomberg LP was started in New York in 1981 by Michael R. Bloomberg (b. 1942), who became mayor of New York City in 2002. The original business was to provide financial information to subscribers who leased Bloomberg computer terminals, informally called "The Bloomberg." Now, Bloomberg is a major international company providing business news to newspapers, radio and TV stations, and also owns a business magazine, TV channel, and radio station.

UPI, United Press International, is a news service formed by the merger of United Press and International

News Service. It once was a major wire service and its alumni (called Unipressers) include Walter Cronkite (b. 1916), Howard K. Smith (1914–2002), and Eric Severeid (1912–92).

Now, a brief section about *syndicates*, companies that provide articles, columns, comics, editorial cartoons, and other material to newspapers and other subscribers.

King Features Syndicate, Inc., New York, is the largest "syndicator" of columns and comics. It was formed in 1915 and named by its first president, Moses Koenigsberg (1878–1945). (*Koenig* is German for king.)

Universal Press Syndicate, Kansas City, Missouri, distributes *Dear Abby*, the most widely syndicated column in the world. Jeanne Phillips (b. 1942) writes *Dear Abby*, the advice column started by her mother Pauline Esther Phillips (b. 1918 as Pauline Esther Friedman). *Refrigerator journalism* is the taping of favorite clippings on refrigerator doors. As far as I know, there is no rating for this category, but I am confident that *Dear Abby* ranks number one. For many years, Pauline Esther Phillips shared syndicate leadership with Ann Landers, who was her twin sister, Esther ("Eppie") Pauline Lederer (1918–2002).

As a side note, we've been discussing the lingo of the "fourth estate," which is the press. You know, of course, that the first three estates are the clergy, the nobility, and the common people.

Newspaper writers used to signify the end of a dispatch with the number thirty, written as -30-. The origin may be the Roman numerals for thirty, XXX, which were used by telegraphers as a sign-off. Another theory is that the first telegraphed message to a press association during the Civil War ended with the number thirty, when it was common practice for telegraphers to end a message by indicating the number of words it contained, which then became the standard sign-off. The 30-symbol, called a "tag," has been replaced by many writers with -END- or a series of double daggers, generally ###.

LEADS: BUT, WAIT FOR THE KICKER

A *leader* is a person who guides, directs, or is in charge, such as an orchestra leader. The word has specialized meanings in journalism, music, printing, and other media.

In music, a "leader" is a conductor and also the principal performer in an orchestral section, chorus, or other group. A principal performer in a play or other production, such as a *leading man* or *leading lady*, has a "leading role" (the *lead*). The terms "leading man" or "leading lady" are seldom used in the United States these days, and "lead" is preferred. The *leading candidate* in politics is the one ahead of the other candidates in the polls.

Lead (pronounced LEED) is one of the most important aspects of journalism. Newspaper editors often use phonetic spellings, such as *graf* for graph or paragraph, and *lede* for lead. In journalism, a *leader* or *lead article* is a major article that "leads" a page or section of a publication. The word originated at *The Wall Street Journal* to designate a major article, generally involving investigative reporting or extensive analysis, that appeared in the far left, or far right, column of page one. The *Journal* calls it a *leder* (pronounced LEED-er). In England, the principal editorial is called the *leading article*.

Today's redesigned *Journal* has expanded its headlines, which now stretch over two or three columns. The term *leader* also is used at other publications. Leaders usually appear in the A-section (the first or main news section) of a newspaper. *A1* is the designation of a *page 1* article in the first section. (Editors use numerals for page numbers, instead of spelling them out.)

The *lead sentence* is the first sentence of a news release or article, just as a lead article begins a section or page. The most common type of "lead sentence" is the *di-*

rect lead, the workhorse of journalism, which may be a traditional, factual exposition (a *summary lead*), an anecdote, a quotation, question, or perhaps a clause, phrase, or single word. The other basic type is the *delayed lead*, a more leisurely approach often used for soft news and features, or by the newsweekly magazines, to set the scene or establish a mood. A *grabber* is humorous, startling, provocative, or human-interest material, often used in a lead sentence or paragraph to grab the reader's attention.

In film, a "leader" is a length of film joined to the beginning of a reel for threading through the camera or projector or any blank framed film used to link other film. A *black leader* or *opaque leader* is black film, without images, used in film and tape editing. A *tail leader* is one tacked on at the end of a film.

In printing, a "leader" is a series of dots, dashes, or other characters that lead horizontally across a page or column, from one item of text to another. Leaders are sometimes used in lists or in tables of contents, where a series of dots links chapter titles and page numbers. A *universal leader* is a series of dots; a *hyphen leader* is a series of dashes.

Other "leading terms" in the media include *leading light*, an important and influential member of a group; and *leading question*, contrived to elicit or suggest a specific answer during an interview. A newscast "leads" with the most important item. In marketing, a *loss leader* is an item offered at cost, or even below cost, to attract customers. There's also *leading edge*, the foremost position, originally a nautical term for the edge of a sail facing the wind. (And, by extension, "bleeding edge" connotes the painful tribulations of a pioneer in any field).

A *new lead* (also called *new top,* and sometimes written by editors as *nulead* or simply NL), is an update or fresh beginning. A *lead-all* is an article that covers various elements of a news event, accompanied by related articles on the same page or elsewhere.

In broadcasting, a story may begin with a *perspective lead* (one that relates the report to previous events), a *quote lead* (a quotation), a *new story lead* (when an event is reported for the first time), a *folo lead* (a follow-up to an earlier story), or a *segue lead* (a transition, generally to a related story). Local TV news often is akin to tabloid journalism, with the motto, "If it bleeds, it leads."

In a *broadsheet* (a full-size newspaper), the *lead story* usually appears on the upper (above-the-fold) right side of page one; with the *off-lead*, the second most important story, usually on the upper left side.

A *soft lead* is the style of the features that increasingly appear in major newspapers, particularly for feel-good and service articles, and usually revolves around human interest stories. A "soft lead" does not start with the traditional five Ws (who, what, where, when, and why) of hard news.

A *feel-good article*, which may be a first-person report, is the opposite of a *feel-bad article* about a death or other tragedy. Both of these sagas are often about celebrities and are promoted on *feel-good* or *feel-bad covers*, respectively.

A *service article* includes information that is useful or of service to the reader. These articles appear everywhere, particularly in the food, home, hobby, and other publications still called *service magazines*.

Let's move on to the other *lead* (pronounced LED), which refers to the heavy metal called "lead." In the days of metal type, a thin strip of metal called *leading* was used to insert space between lines of metal type. The term is still used in the nonmetallic digital era for the space inserted between lines.

Double leading means twice as much space between lines as usual, as on page one and the editorial page of newspapers. *Leading out* is the insertion of extra spacing between lines. *Extra leading* is an instruction to add white space, such as between two blocks of type or at certain locations throughout a manuscript. *Primary leading* is the line spacing used in the general body of a text, whereas *secondary leading* entails a different amount of spacing, for instance, between paragraphs or in a specific section of the work. *Negative leading* is the cramming of type into a line space that is smaller than the type, such as 12/10 (12-point type on 10-point leading), which will result in overlapping of lines.

Millions of "lead pencils" are still used, though the name is a misnomer since they have a core of graphite (a form of carbon), not lead. The origin of the word is that graphite was once called "black lead." Writing pencils are graded by degree of hardness: 1 (softest), 2 (most common), 3, and 4 (hardest).

Television viewers of celebrity trials and countless other programs are familiar with "sidebars," conversations between lawyers or prosecutors and a judge at the side of the bar, or railing, in a courtroom. But another definition prevails with writers.

A *sidebar* is a news item or feature inserted within, adjacent to, or following a related article. It's sometimes called a *side story* or *with story*. When it appears after the main story, it's called a *follow*, a common term at news services and newspapers.

Sorry! I nearly got sidelined into a sidebar. Let's return to leads (LEEDS). *Lead time* means preparatory period. In journalism, it's the period of production: the time between the completion of a manuscript and its publication, or the interval between the medium's deadline for receipt of advertising or editorial material and the time of its appearance in the publication. Monthly magazines usually require several weeks or months of "lead time" for receipt of proposed editorial material prior to publication.

Lead to come (usually abbreviated LTC) is a notation on copy, often made on a developing story sent to an editor or printer, to indicate that the beginning section of the article will follow. "Lead" also means a tip about a possible news story or idea.

Let's move on to other media that also use leads. In film, *lead* is a space left in front of a moving subject. In thrill scenes, the *lead space* is reduced or omitted to heighten the tension.

The *lead sheet* is a musical accompaniment score for use by the conductor, and includes the music and lyrics and the names of the composer, lyricist, publisher, and copyright date.

Had enough leads? If not, let me lead you to *lead line* (also called *leader line*), which is a line that leads to and points out an item, as in a diagram. It may end in an arrowhead. In theater, a *lead-through* is a rehearsal.

In marketing, a "lead" is a tip or information about a prospective customer. *Leadflow* is the volume of such leads over a given period of time. *Lead generation* is the stimulation of marketing "leads," as through advertising and public relations. *Lead shortfall* is an insufficient number of leads, generally in comparison to a predetermined goal.

With all this attention to leads, let's not ignore the importance of a great ending in all media. On a TV or radio broadcast, an inconsequential, humorous, or even zany final item is called a *kicker* or *zipper*; in print media, a *hooker*.

And, here's my hooker: One of my favorite words, *weenie*, is slang for a gimmick or trick device dangled in front of the viewer or reader to tantalize him or her, like a frankfurter or wiener (pronounced WEEN-er). I pronounce my last name, Weiner, as WINE-er, though some with the same name prefer WEEN-er.

LIGHTS UP!: FROM PEEWEES TO BRUTES

LIGHTING is a key component of film, television, theater, and other performing arts, and lighting lingo often appears in articles about these media terms.

Gaffers use hundreds of technical and slang terms to describe lighting equipment. Some are so common—such as "footlights," "highlight," "limelight," and "spotlight"—that they also occur in everyday language.

A *gaffer* is the foreman of a stage crew. In film and television, the "gaffer" is the head electrician in charge of the other *juicers* ("juice" is slang for electricity). The term originated in England in the sixteenth century when the word *gaffer* was an altered form of *godfather* or *grandfather*. In the nineteenth century, a foreman or overseer was called a "gaffer," particularly in the United Kingdom, and the word also meant a master glassblower.

As noted in the "Film" chapter, the *best boy* is the principal or first assistant to the gaffer, and sometimes is called "best boy electric." The term may have originated in the days when young laborers assembled for possible work in theaters and the gaffer shouted, "Give me your best boy!" These days, women have these jobs too, but they are still called "best boys."

Lighting engineers, who are in charge of the gaffers and lighting crew, distinguish between a *lamp* or *luminant* (the bulb or tube) and a *luminaire*, the fixture that includes the lamp, reflector, support, housing, and cable. To *lamp down* is to replace a lamp with one of lower wattage. A "lighting technician" is called an "electric," a "lampy," "lights," "sparks," or "sparky."

So as not to get too technical, let's use "lights" as the

general term. Lights used in film and other media include the *key light*, or "principal light," which tends to produce strong contrasts (*hard light*), and *fill light* for less contrast (*soft light*). Lighting that is dimly lit and has strong contrast is called *low-key lighting*; while *high-key lighting* has lower contrast. *Flat lighting* produces a minimum of shadows and very little contrast. Supplementary lights include a *back light* (to illuminate the subject from behind), *accent light*, and *effects lights* (for specific areas of the subject), *base light* (diffuse or soft illumination of a larger area), and many sizes of lighting instruments, ranging from small bulbs to "arc lights," "floodlights," and "spotlights."

An *arc light* is a high-intensity light, generally with a carbon filament. The arc- or arch-shaped flame between two adjacent electrodes is the lighting agency. An *arc follow spot* focuses on or follows a performer.

A *floodlight*, or *flood*, is a high-intensity light, generally with a reflector, that fills (floods) the area.

Footlights, or *foots*, are a row of lights along the front of a stage. They are so common that the word often refers to the theatrical field in general. *Footlighters* are performers.

A *spotlight*, or *spot*, is a light with a directed beam. In general, to "spotlight" is to focus, draw attention, or give favored treatment. To *steal the spotlight* is to change the focus of attention, as from one person to another. A *torm spotlight*, which is mounted on the side of a stage, is named from *tormentor*, a curtain or piece of scenery on the side.

To be *in the limelight* is to be the focus of attention. The origin is the stage light in which lime (calcium oxide) was heated to incandescence. Similarly, to *highlight* is to emphasize. To have one's name *up in lights*, as on a Broadway theater marquee, is to receive an electrifying acknowledgment of success.

Here's a lightning-fast look at light terms:

A *light bridge* is a narrow platform above the front area of a stage, on which are mounted lights and other equipment. A *light curtain* is a bank of lights, on or in front of a stage, directed toward the audience or that are high-intensity so that they serve as a curtain or wall. A *light leak* is unintentional light seen through a crack in the scenery or another opening. A *light meter*, or *exposure meter*, measures the amount of illumination on a subject, used to determine the settings on a camera. A *light rehearsal* is a rehearsal of lighting changes and cues, not a superficial, or light, run-through. A *light stand*, or *pipe stand*, is a support for lights. If it has one or more horizontal arms, it's called a *light tree*. A *light tower* is a vertical pipe or structure to which spotlights or other lighting fixtures are attached. It can also refer to a "light stand" or "light tree."

A *bar* is a horizontal metal tube from which lighting equipment or scenery is suspended. It's also called a "barrel," "batten," or "pipe." A *batten* is a narrow strip of wood or metal that fastens or makes secure the lighting or scenery, as in "batten down the hatches" (compartments) of a ship.

Several lighting terms have personal derivations. An *emily*, for example, is slang for a *broad*, or floodlight. It has one lamp so it's also called a *single broad*. The term probably was first used by a gaffer who had a friend named Emily.

Many luminaires are named after people or companies. The commonly used reflected light devices called *fresnels* are named after Augustin Jean Fresnel (1788–1827), a French physicist. He pronounced his name fray-NELL, though Americans say fruh-NELL.

Century lights are commonly used spotlights but their origin may stump novices. It's not because they've been used for a century: The name refers to the original company, the Century Lighting Company, which no longer exists, taken over by Strand Lighting.

Klieg lights are powerful, wide-angle carbon arc lamps used at so many premieres and other events that their name is generally known. Most people correctly pronounce them KLEEG, but often use the misspelling of "Kl*ei*g." The lamp was invented by the German American brothers John Kliegl (1869–1959) and Anton Kliegl (1872–1927).

Barn doors are hinged flaps or blinders on the front of a spotlight to control the beam of light. They're also called *flippers* or *shutters* and are akin to the doors on a farm building. To *barn door* is to adjust the flaps. Incidentally, *barney*, the sound-deadening housing around a camera, probably has a similar agricultural origin. A more colorful derivation is an old comic strip, *Barney Google*, in which a racehorse named Sparkplug wore a tattered blanket. Another possibility is that the two humps on the camera magazine resembled Barney Google's eyes.

A *PAR light* is a spotlight with a *p*arabolic (curved) *a*luminized *r*eflector. PAR is an acronym for these words or short for "parabolic." The inventor was Clarence Birdseye (1886–1956), better known for developing methods for quick-freezing foods; and the light sometimes is called a *birdseye*.

A *bazooka* is a device on a catwalk that supports lighting units. Second World War veterans know that bazookas launched armor-piercing rockets, and were named after a funny-sounding horn popularized by comedian Bob Burns (1896–1956), who in turn named it after the slang word *bazoo* (meaning mouth or nose), probably from *bazuin*, the Dutch word for trumpet.

One of my favorite lights is called an *inky dink*, or *dinky inky*, or simply *inky* or *dinky*. It's a small incandescent ("inky") lamp. *Dinky,* which means small, comes from Scottish.

Here are a few other delightful lighting terms. A *cookie* (also called "cuke," "kookie," or "template") is short for *cukaloris*, a piece of netting or cardboard with shapes cut out to cast patterns of light on stage scenery (*Kukaloris* was used in ancient Greek theater). A *nookie,* or *nook light*, is a small light. A "nook," you know, is a corner or small area (and "nookie" or "nooky" can have a sexual connotation). A *strobe*, or *strobe light*, produces high-intensity, short-duration light pulses. The Greek *strobes* means "twisting around" and "stroboscopic" lights create the illusion of movement (*strobing* or *strobe effect*), popular in discos and at rock music concerts.

Lighting slang often refers to the size or intensity, such as "peewee," "tweenie," "ace," "baby," "junior," "senior," and "brute." A *peewee* is really small, perhaps with a 50-watt bulb. A *tweenie* is between 500 and 1,000 watts. An *ace* spotlight has a 1,000-watt bulb, while a *baby* can be anything smaller. To "kill the baby" means to turn off the light. A *junior* generally is 1,000 to 2,000 watts. A *senior*, common in films, generally has a 5,000-watt lamp. And, a *brute* is bigger than a senior, with a high-intensity arc spotlight; for example, a *maxibrute* is really big, usually with nine 1,000-watt lights. (A *minibrute* is smaller.)

All of this glowing jargon should be illuminating. Here are a few others: *basher* (or *handbasher*, a small portable lamp with a scoop-shaped reflector); *deuce* (a 2,000-watt lamp, also called a "junior"); *midget* (a small lamp, usually 200 watts, also called a "mini"); *pup* (a small lamp, usually 500 watts); and *tenner* (a 10,000-watt spotlight). If you already knew these terms, your name should go *up in lights*. So, let's *hit the lights*—turn 'em on, turn 'em up—and here's hoping that you rate a maxibrute.

MAGAZINES: FROM THE MIGHTY
AARP TO THE TARGETED *ZYMURGY*

ALMOST everyone reads one or more of the more than 13,000 consumer, business, professional, and trade magazines published in the United States and Canada. The etymology of *magazine* is the French word *magasin,* derived from the Italian, *magazzino.* The original meaning was storehouse, and indeed, a magazine is a storehouse of information.

A *magazine* (or, to be slangy, a *mag*) is usually printed on glossy or shiny (coated) paper, which reproduces color photographs and art much better than the uncoated paper used by newspapers and most unillustrated books. Types include "newsmagazines" (one word), "business magazines," "special-interest magazines" (such as those covering sports), "shelter magazines" (homes), "men's, women's, adult" (*Playboy*, and others with big circulations, especially in barber shops and beauty salons), and mags that are sold or distributed by controlled circulation, such as "inflight" (no longer hyphenated) and membership publications. A few Sunday newspapers include magazines; the largest in circulation is *The New York Times Magazine*.

A magazine sometimes is referred to by its publisher as a *title*. America's top circulation publication remains *AARP—The Magazine* (formerly called *Modern Maturity*), a bimonthly with a circulation of about twenty-three million; followed by the *Reader's Digest* (U.S. circulation about ten million; insiders call it *The Digest*).

The major women's *service magazines* (containing recipes and other services)—formerly called the "Seven Sisters"—are, in approximate order of circulation, *Better*

Homes & Gardens, Good Housekeeping, Family Circle, Ladies' Home Journal, Woman's Day, and *Redbook*. The seventh, *Rosie* (formerly *McCall's*) no longer is published. The group should be renamed the Eight Sisters (even if it's not alliterative) to acknowledge *O, The Oprah Magazine* and *Martha Stewart Living*. Two common misspellings involve the names of *Ladies' Home Journal* (plural, apostrophe after the *s*) and *Woman's Day* (singular, apostrophe before the *s*).

Trade magazines (also called "trade journals," "trade publications," "trade books," or simply the "trades") are business publications that cover a specific industry, such as *Advertising Age* and *Adweek* in the advertising field. (In book publishing it's the opposite. As noted in the "Books" chapter, trade books are distributed to the general public as distinguished from reference books, textbooks, and other more specialized books outside of the general market.)

A *zine*, short for *magazine*, is a publication devoted to a specific subject, usually without advertising and irregularly printed or posted on a Web site. A *fanzine* is a magazine, usually produced by an amateur devoted to a celebrity or special interest, such as science fiction.

Insiders often call a magazine a *book*, such as a "women's book," probably because publishing a topical magazine has a lot in common with book publishing. *Front of book* (sometimes hyphenated) means the first section, usually including the contents, a letter from the publisher or editor (an *ed let*), letters-to-the-editor, and other departments preceding the main section (called the "editorial well"). Advertisers consider "front-of-book ads" to be more desirable, as indicated by *Vogue, Vanity Fair*, and other successful, high-profile trendy mags.

Back-of-book (hyphenated) material comes at the end, sometimes including listings, classified ads, and an essay or department that regularly appears on the high-readership last page. This area or "backyard" also includes the continuations (called "jumps") of articles from the front or middle sections.

The *staff box*, or list of personnel, sometimes lists editorial people on one page and publishing and production people on another. The listing often includes contributing editors, usually freelancers not on staff.

The *contributor's page* has information about authors, photographers, artists, and nonstaff contributors to that issue. A brief identification about the author appears at the bottom of the first or last page of an article. Everyone has seen it but few know the exact name: it's called a *bionote* or "bio block."

An imaginative insider term is *violin piece*, meaning the lead story (first major article) that sets the tone for the magazine, particularly if it's a *theme issue* (devoted to a single subject).

Magazines are so common that their jargon has been picked up by other media people. For example, newspaper editors refer to a "magazine layout," which has large areas of white space, wide columns, and other elements akin to the arrangement of material in a magazine. Similarly, a "magazine-style program" on radio or TV, such as *All Things Considered* and *60 Minutes*, presents interviews and feature segments instead of just a succession of news reports.

Many magazine editors use lingo that is specific to their publications. In some cases, the jargon has been picked up by other magazines and newspapers, and even by freelancers and readers.

Time-ese is a style of writing used by *Time* featuring puns and other wordplays, verbs preceding their subjects, and other juxtapositions. The style is less common in the magazine now than before 1990. *Time* neologisms include cinemaddict and Technicolorization.

Wallenda is an in-house term at *Newsweek* for a senior editor or other "high-fliers." The Flying Wallendas were a renowned troupe of circus aerialists; the best known was Karl Wallenda (1905–78).

Editors at *Forbes* and other magazines refer to the theme or core of an article as the *nut* (or "nut graf" or "nut paragraph"). The term probably originated at *The Wall Street Journal*, where the third paragraph in a page-one feature generally has more of the facts or essential information—nut or kernel—than the first two paragraphs.

Several magazines have nicknames or abbreviations that are used by newspaper writers and others. Examples are "Cosmo" (*Cosmopolitan*), "Esky" (*Esquire*), SI (*Sports Illustrated*), and EW (*Entertainment Weekly*). "Cosmo" is so well-known that its spin-off magazine is *CosmoGIRL!*. The British call a magazine that appeals to young men a *lad mag*. A *skin mag* is a magazine that emphasizes nudity or seminudity. The film equivalent is a "skin flick."

One of the most unusual titles of a magazine probably is *Zymurgy*, published by the American Homebrewers Association. "Zymurgy" means the study or practice of fermentation, as in winemaking and brewing beer.

Variety, a weekly magazine that is "the bible" of the entertainment industry, probably has coined more words than any other publication (covered in the chapter, "Show Business").

Incidentally, a "vogue word" is not a neologism coined by *Vogue* magazine, but a word or phrase that is coined or emerges from obscurity and quickly becomes popular. Current examples include "faith-based," "flip-flopper," and "reality-based." The popularizer of "vogue-word," Henry Watson Fowler (1858–1933), was the English lexicographer who wrote *Modern English Usage*, once the most popular guide for writers.

Vogue, however, is responsible for *vogueing*, a styled version of modeling, as on fashion-show runways, based on poses from the magazine. The models are referred to as "voguers."

[NEW YORKER-ESE]

For many years, The New Yorker *was a closed society with jargon known only to its staffers. Here are several words that are now known by others, including one that has made its way into general dictionaries.*

Casuals at *The New Yorker* means informal fiction and nonfiction articles. Have you ever submitted a funny headline or other item to *The New Yorker*, hoping that it will be used as a "filler" at the end of an article? Fewer appear now than in previous years, but they still are avidly read; *The New Yorker* calls them *newsbreaks*. Hardly any outsider knows that term.

Profile at *The New Yorker* means an article about an individual. It often runs for many pages or is broken up into two or more issues. The word, popularized by *The New Yorker*, now is used by many editors and writers, though usually for a brief biography, and is in major dictionaries.

Here's one that I bet you did not know: Look at *The New Yorker* and you will see a stripe running along the inner (left) side of the front cover, called the *strap*. Typical of *The New Yorker's* meticulousness, the "strap" entails a novel technique to ensure that the entire front cover art is visible, regardless of the thickness of the spine (which can eat into some of the front cover). It was started by Rea (pronounced RAY) Irvin (1881–1972), the magazine's first art director, better known for his creation of Eustace Tilley, the distinguished-looking character who has become the mascot or symbol of *The New Yorker*. The drawing of Tilley appears atop the "Contents" page. It originated on the cover of the first issue (dated February 21, 1925) and has appeared in various poses on anniversary covers. (For two years, in the late nineties, there were no anniversary issues.)

The New Yorker is unique in many other ways. It modestly omits a staff box, though it has a page (or part of a page) with information about contributors. It also omitted "Contents" as a separate page until 1988. The magazine is meticulous in its fact-checking. Its typographical style is distinctive, particularly its use of diacritics and other accent marks. For example, it's the only mass-circulation publication that puts a diaeresis (identical to an umlaut) over the second vowel in words with the same vowel repeated consecutively, as in "reëlect" and "coördination"—and, of course, in words like "naïve" or "Brontë"—to indicate that a vowel is pronounced separately.

Let's move on to the terminology for the parts of a magazine (its anatomy). "Cover 1" is the outside front cover; "cover 2," the inside front cover; "cover 3," the inside back cover; and "cover 4," the outside back cover. (These terms are also used for paperback book covers.) They are also known respectively as "first cover," "second cover," and so on. Since mag covers 2, 3, and 4 usually contain advertisements (cover positions are charged at a premium rate), editors refer to "cover 1" as *the* cover.

A *gatefold* is a large sheet (usually wider than the other pages) that is folded over so that the resulting folded page is the same size as the other pages, while the extension can be opened or swung out like a gate. It makes for a spectacular pullout or cover (a "gatefold cover") and is often used by advertisers (for a "gatefold ad"). Gatefolds can be produced in various sizes, such as a "single gatefold" or "double gatefold."

The top of the cover usually features the publication's

name set in a distinctive manner, called its *logo* (shortening of "logotype"), *flag*, or *nameplate*. Nearby are the *cover price* (also called the "street price" or "newsstand price") and the *cover date*, not necessarily the date of publication, but instead a date in the week, month, or other period following the actual date of issue or circulation. Magazines sold on newsstands thus will not appear immediately outdated. Note the spelling of "newsstand"—one word with a double *s*." In the United Kingdom, they are called "news stalls"—two words.

Newsweek and other "newsweeklies," as well as weekly newspapers, use the term *date week* as a reference point, relative to the publication date, for dates in an article. For example, if the publication date falls on a Friday, as with many weekly newspapers, the "date week" comprises the seven days ending on that Friday. Thus, a news event that occurred during the preceding six days is referred to only by the weekday, such as a "fire on Wednesday," whereas an event occurring seven or more days before the publication date falls outside the "date week" and is referred to by its calendar date.

Covers are especially important for magazines sold on newsstands and at other retail outlets. The "cover stock" (glossy and heavier than the inside pages), "cover ink," "cover art," and "cover photo" (perhaps featuring a "cover model" or "cover girl") are factors that influence single-copy sales.

Major articles, particularly the *cover story*, are promoted on the cover with *coverlines*, akin to newspaper headlines, and usually a related photo. A "cover story" can also mean a false account intended to deceive, or "cover up." Incidentally, a few trade and professional magazines print advertising on the front cover. A notable example is *Publishers Weekly.*

To "go long" is an expression used by magazine editors to indicate an article that is longer than average; for example, twenty thousand words is generally considered long.

Most magazines are bound with wire staples. You can see the two or three staples in the middle of the center spread, where the two facing pages lie in the exact middle of the publication. Because these adjacent pages are printed on the same sheet, they sometimes have an advertisement, photo, or other graphic material suited to running across (bleed) the center space (gutter).

The two common types of stitching are *saddle* (or *saddle-wire*) *stitching* and *side* (or *side-wire*) *stitching*. In the former, a section (signature) is laid on the "saddle," or arched part, of the stitching machine ("stitcher"), which feeds a continuous roll of wire (instead of individual staples, as in your desktop stapler), fastening the pages through the middle fold of the sheets. In the latter, the stapling goes through the side near the spine and the pages cannot be opened completely flat.

Thick magazines and books usually use glue instead of stitches or staples, a process called *perfect binding*. These magazines also have a "spine" that connects the front and back covers and that carries the name and date of the publication on it.

The *center spread* (two facing pages in the exact middle of a magazine) may have an order card stapled in. Some consumer magazines also have several other cards that are inserted but not affixed, called *blow-in cards*, or *blow-ins*, because an air machine literally blows them in during binding. Perhaps they should be called "shake-outs" because that's what most of us do to them.

Many business, trade, service, and other magazines also have reader-response cards, dubbed *bingo cards*, usually a full page, bound-in, with perforations so that they can be torn out and returned in the mail. A typical card has many numbers on it (as in the game bingo), enabling readers to circle numbers to order products, brochures, or other materials from a number of advertisers or participants. A *tip-in*, or *bind-in*, card is bound into the publication, such as an advertisement printed on heavier stock than the rest of the magazine. The term also means a special illustration inserted separately and bound into a book.

The "front of book" of many magazines includes columns and departments. A *column* expresses the opinions of the writer, the columnist, who usually is one person who writes on a regular basis, such as in every issue of a magazine. A *department*, in contrast, is a section on a specific topic, which may not be written by the same person in each issue, and sometimes is not bylined. Magazine columnists often are not on staff, whereas almost all departments are staff-written.

Many magazines have a distinctive symbol or typographical ornament to mark the end of an article, appropriately called a *tailpiece* or "end mark." At *Forbes*, a boldface **F** is placed at the end of the last line (flush right); at *Fortune* an *F* in *reverse type* (printed white) in a black square immediately follows the end of an article.

The line between magazines and newspapers can sometimes get blurred. Magazines are usually different from newspapers in their appearance and tend to be smaller, published less frequently, and bound. A "magazine supplement" is a section of a newspaper in the format of a magazine or tabloid newspaper. *Parade*, distributed in more than three hundred newspapers, calls itself a "Sunday magazine."

About one thousand new magazines are started every year in the United States. Most of them fall by the wayside. The successful publications often are those targeted to niche markets, such as ones involving shopping, hobbies, or new industries. Magazine publishers pay for the *rack slots* (called "pockets") at the checkout counters and elsewhere in supermarkets and other stores.

The comics industry has its own lingo. A *comic book* is a magazine with a series of captioned drawings, often of an adventure story and not necessarily humorous. A *comic strip*, usually in a newspaper, is a series of drawings in a horizontal sequence of several panels, generally captioned with the conversation of the characters.

A *cartoon* is a humorous or satirical drawing, usually published alone, as on an editorial page (an "editorial cartoon") or elsewhere in a newspaper, such as in "comics sections," or in other publications. Cartoons generally fill one frame or panel, but can run for two or more panels. The word cartoon was derived from the Italian *cartone*, the heavy paper on which drawings were made in preparation for murals, tapestries, or other works of art.

A *balloon* is a circular, oblong, or other space indicated as emerging from the mouth of a speaker in cartoons or comics. A smooth-bordered balloon usually indicates speech, while a balloon drawn with a jagged or broken line (a "scalloped balloon") means thoughts. A line, called a *pointer*, generally runs from the character to the balloon. One of the first comic books to make extensive use of thought balloons was *The Amazing Spider-Man*, launched in March 1963. Incidentally, "balloon" also is a show-business verb for "forgetting lines" of dialogue.

Let's return to general magazine lingo. A common word is *volume*, which means a book or one of the books in a set, or, in magazines, newspapers, and other periodicals, a series of issues. All the issues of a periodical for a specific period, generally a year, are bound together in a volume designated by a number. Following are representative styles of indicating the volume number.

The New Yorker started its volume-number system on its first day of publication and changes it annually on its anniversary date. Their style, which is the most common, is to use Roman numerals for the volume number and Arabic numbers for the issue number with a comma between them. Other magazines use a colon, line, or simply a space to separate volume and issue numbers. The volume number usually appears on the contents page of a magazine, and atop page one (the page dateline) below the name of a newspaper.

While on the subject of volume numbering, take a look at *The New York Times*. Founded in 1851, *The New York Times* changes its volume number annually but uses consecutive numbering for its issues. Each time it stops its presses for an editorial change or change within an edition, a dot is removed. Thus, the first or earliest edition has four dots, while later editions have two, one, or no dots, after the volume number. If you subscribe to the national edition, as I do, it's printed early and usually is a "four-dotter." If you live in or near New York City, you can buy a four-dotter late the previous night or get a later edition the next morning. When the *Times* stops the presses to make a correction and update a page, it prints + at the top of the revised page. Sometimes you'll see ++. Now that you know about the dots and plus marks, test your knowledge the next time you are with *Times* buffs.

Returning to magazine lingo, a *running head* (copy editors abbreviate it as RH) is a headline or title repeated at the top of each page or on alternate pages of a publication. It's also called "running title." A *running foot* or *footline* is a title repeated at the bottom of each page or alternate pages. *Running text* or "straight matter" is continuous text in the body of an article, not the headlines, captions, or blurbs (also called "inserts").

Media jargon includes other running terms. Before I run, let's end with two terms that are used by many magazine editors. The first is *warm-and-wonder*, which appropriately means an upbeat feature. The second is *blurb*, a common word in several media. For example, it is a summary or excerpt of an article used before or within the article and also as promotional copy, such as on a book jacket or record cover. Journalists sometimes refer to inconsequential material, such as a promotional quotation, as a "blurb." The word was coined by American humorist Gelett Burgess (1866–1951) in his 1907 novel *Are You a Bromide?* in which a character was given the name Miss Belinda Blurb "to sound like a publisher."

MEDIA: MARSHALL McLUHAN WAS RIGHT

RADIO, television, the Internet, billboards, books, film and other media are communication vehicles that link producers and other sources with their audiences. Technically, *media* is the plural of *medium*, though *media* is so common that it is used as a collective noun, taking either a singular or a plural (my preference) verb. Canadian writer Marshall McLuhan (1911–80) was a pioneer in understanding how modern media convey ideas and emotions: "Hot media," such as print, transmit high-definition data with minimum involvement of the recipient; and "cool media," like television and the telephone, transmit low-definition data and require more of the recipient's participation. McLuhan's most famous quote is from his 1964 book, *Understanding Media*, in which the first chapter was titled, "The medium is the message."

The origin of *medium* is the Latin, *medius*, meaning middle, as in communications links. People "in the media," as well as advertisers, public relations consultants, and others who work with the media, use many terms that start with *media*. Here are a few.

Internal media are communication channels within a group, such as employee newsletters; while *external media* are the channels outside of a group, such as radio, television, newspapers, magazines, and other mass media that reach the masses. A *media buyer*, working in the media department of an advertiser, advertising agency, or media-buying service, purchases advertising space or time. It's not to be confused with a *media center*, a department or area, as in a school, with a variety of audiovisual equipment and services. The coordinator of such a department, a "media specialist," sometimes is called a "learning resources specialist" and is assisted by support personnel, including "media aides" or "media technicians." However, *media class* is not an educational term but refers to a category or type of medium, such as magazines or newspapers. A specific publication or entity within a class is called a *vehicle*.

In Canada and other countries outside of the United States, common terms include "media luncheon" (to wine and dine the press) and "media officer" (an executive or government official involved in press relations).

Media blitz, a buzzword among advertising and public relations people, involves the intensive scheduling of all types of advertising and publicity targeted to a particular market, demographic audience, or type of media. *Media coverage* means the percentage of the potential audience, the actual number of readers or viewers, or another measurement of the "reach," or effectiveness, of an advertising or public relations campaign. "Media coverage" can also mean a list of the publications and stations that print or broadcast publicity relevant to an external campaign.

A *media tour*, a common PR technique, covers an itinerary of cities or markets in which a spokesperson is sent, generally for a day or two. A *media escort* makes arrangements, provides transportation, and accompanies the interviewee.

Media training has become a big business—counseling, rehearsing, and preparing individuals for interviews on TV programs and other media. Provided by a media trainer, the sessions often take place in a TV studio to simulate an actual interview. A *mediagenic* person is attractive and appealing to TV viewers, newspaper readers, and other media audiences.

A *media event* is a newsworthy occasion conceived and set up by a public relations practitioner and designed to attract media attention. The term frequently applies to the photo opportunities ("photo ops") and other events at which public officials, including the president of the United States, are captured on camera in highly favorable (sometimes artfully staged) settings.

Media imperatives is a method of classifying audiences into categories in which one medium is imperative and commands greater attention than another medium. For example, in a newspaper-TV comparison study, a newspaper imperative indicates a high level of newspaper reading compared to a low level of TV viewing (the dream audience of newspaper publishers!).

Media mix is the combination of communication vehicles chosen to achieve the goal of an advertising or other campaign. A *media plan* contains the specifications of an advertising campaign, including reasons for their selection, media cost options, and media strategy. A "media planner" working in the media department of an advertiser or advertising agency selects the media appropriate to the plan and likely to reach the target audiences and achieve the objectives of the campaign. The plan often uses a *media model*, a mathematical formula to enable comparison of costs and benefits of different advertising schedules.

The material or form used by an artist, composer, or writer also is called a "medium." (The plural is *media*.) A "medium" also is a person who claims to be able to communicate with the dead. In this case, the plural is *mediums*. Finally, the most common meanings of "medium" are: something midway between extremes (I like my steak medium rare), an intervening substance through which something else is transmitted, and an agency by which something is accomplished or transmitted, such as a transportation medium, or, in our frame of reference, a communications medium, such as these very words on the printed page.

The world's largest media company is Time Warner, Inc., which includes many top circulation magazines, as well as film (Warner Bros.), Turner cable networks, WB Television Network, HBO, AOL, and other companies. Following is a brief summary of other major media companies:

Bertelsmann AG, one of the world's largest printers and publishers, including Gruner + Jahr (Europe's leading magazine publisher) and Random House (America's largest book publisher).

Walt Disney Company, owner of ABC, ESPN, and other radio and TV networks and stations, film companies, and, of course, theme parks. Walter ("Walt") Disney (1901–66) created Mickey Mouse in 1928.

General Electric Company, majority owner of NBC Universal, including Universal Pictures, TV stations, theme parks, and NBC, Telemunto, Bravo, CNBC, MSNBC, USA, and other networks.

News Corporation, owner of Twentieth Century Fox, Fox Broadcasting Company, the *New York Post,* and other newspaper and TV channels in Australia, Asia, and elsewhere.

Reed Elsevier Group, publisher of several thousand scientific journals and magazines, and owner of Lexis-Nexis.

Sony Corporation, owner of Sony Pictures, Metro-Goldwyn-Mayer (MGM), and co-owner (with Bertelsmann) of Sony BMG Music Entertainment.

Viacom, Inc., owner of Paramount Pictures, DreamWorks, MTV networks (with one hundred channels around the world), and Nickelodeon. In 2006, CBS Corporation became a separate company, including the CBS and UPN TV networks, radio and TV stations, Showtime, and other companies that formerly were part of Viacom.

These and other companies are included in "Broadcasting," "Journalism," and other chapters of this book. All of the companies, except Bertelsmann, are publicly owned, so for more information, get their annual reports and see their Web sites.

POTPOURRI: BALLYHOO AND OTHER MEDIA MISCELLANY

A "potpourri" is a mixture, and that's what this chapter is: a miscellaneous collection of media-related terms that somehow don't quite fit in any of the other essays. In the seventeenth century, the French word *potpourri* described a stew made of different kinds of meat, and literally meant rotten pot. But I hope that this media potpourri is more akin to the "potpourri" mixture of dried spices and petals used to perfume a closet or other area.

Going down the alphabet, let's begin with a few common words with colorful origins that start with B. *Barnstorm* means to travel about the country, particularly to small towns, to give political speeches, and for baseball exhibitions or other events. The word comes from the days when barns or barnlike buildings, called "barn theaters," were used for plays and speeches. Actors and politicians who made extravagant gestures were called "barnstormers."

A *barnburner* is an event, speech, or other item that is very exciting. In the 1840s, the antislavery wing of the New York State Democratic Party was accused of trying to "burn down the barn just to get rid of the rats."

Incidentally, *bandwagon* (the wagon that carries a band in a parade) connotes a particular activity that has suddenly become fashionable or popular. Supporters who "jump" or "climb on the bandwagon" of a politician or group can create the "bandwagon effect."

A term that has become common, though not found in most standard dictionaries, is *big-box store* (or *retailer*), a large-size store, often with over 100,000 square feet in space, that has a plain boxlike exterior. Originally, the term did not refer to the size of the cartons, but now the connotation to some is that of a warehouse that sells large-size containers of foods and other items.

To "think out of the box" is to be creative by going beyond the confines of whatever delineates a problem or idea.

The "Journalism" chapter discussed "beats" and "scoops." In general, *scoop* refers to the latest or inside information about something, as in "What's the scoop?" To "get a beat" is to beat a rival by obtaining an exclusive story (a "scoop") or by gaining another advantage. Other media uses of *beat* include music (a regular and rhythmical unit of time), theater (a brief pause, a count of one), and the principal theme of a story, such as its *heartbeat*. A *beat sheet* is a detailed scene-by-scene outline of a proposed film or summaries of programs in a TV series.

A *bellwether* is an indicator, predicator, or trendsetter. A *wether* is a castrated ram (a male sheep), with a bell tied around its neck to lead the flock.

A *billboard graf* is a paragraph in a newspaper or other work with the theme, an announcement, or the "reason why." It's sometimes called the *nut graf*.

A *blog*, which is a blending of We*b log*, is a Web site set up by an individual as a personal diary (a "log"). Blogs started only a few years ago, and it's estimated that there are now more than twenty million of them. Many blogs have links to other sites and a few are creative magazines or professional newsletters. Blogs constitute a major new medium, the ultimate in the democratic free press and instant communication of opinions.

"Bloggers," like e-mailers, have their own initialisms, such as *MSM*, or "mainstream media." In the "blogosphere," a *blog swarm* is a barrage of blogging on a specific issue, often to the point where it attracts the attention of the MSM.

"Boldface" is the title of a gossip column in *The New York Times* about celebrities. Their names appear in **boldface** type. The term, *boldface names*, now is used by laypeople to refer to VIPs. Boldface names often are involved in *pseudo-events*, contrived by public relations people, primarily to obtain publicity. The term *pseudo-events* was coined in 1961 by historian Daniel Boorstin (1914–2004).

Brainstorming sessions are common in advertising, public relations, and other fields. The origin of the term was discussed by Michael Quinion in the September 18, 2004, issue of his "World Wide Words" e-mail newsletter (*www.worldwidewords.org*). In the nineteenth century, *brainstorm* was a British medical term for a transient fit of insanity. About 1920, the term was used in the United States as a flash of mental activity leading to a bright idea. This evolved into "brainstorming" as a spontaneous group discussion to generate ideas to solve problems, create names and activities, and pursue other creative purposes.

A *bromide* is a platitude or trite statement, the origin of which is "potassium bromide," once commonly used as a sedative and headache remedy and still an ingredient in Bromo-Seltzer. "Bromides" (or "broms") are commonly used in photography, though less in the digital era. The term also refers to a photographic print that has been treated with silver and bromine.

Bulk circulation is distribution of multiple copies of a publication to one place, such as *USA Today* to hotels, for redistribution to individuals.

Media lingo has many other *b*-words, including *buzzwords* (technical terms that cause a buzz and have become popular), but it's time to say bye-bye to the *B*s. In radio, *bye-bye* is slang for a transition phrase used by a broadcaster to indicate a locale change, such as, "That's all from here in Baghdad, and now back to New York."

A *call-and-response routine* is something that you've seen and heard but you may not know the nomenclature: It is a dramatic technique of politicians, clerics, and labor leaders in which the speaker asks a series of questions and the audience answers them in unison.

Capes is short for "capabilities," a presentation of credentials by an advertising, public relations, or other firm to a prospective client.

A *cheat sheet*, or *crib sheet,* is a piece of paper with the answers to questions, lines of dialogue, or other information for surreptitious use by a speaker, performer, or person taking a test. The Germanic *krippe* referred to a woven or braided item, particularly a basket. Thieves used "basket" as in the slang expression, to "put in a basket," for petty theft. Incidentally, "crib-sheet" also is slang for a plagiarism.

A *cheesehead* is slang for a stupid person. Chicago sports fans originated the word by calling Wisconsinites "cheeseheads." Fans at Green Bay Packers football games retaliated by wearing Cheesehead hats.

I capitalized "Cheesehead" because it's the registered name of hats in the shape of cheese wedges and other products made by Foamation, Inc., of Milwaukee. Wisconsin is renowned for the making of cheese, but as someone who lived in Madison, Wisconsin, for many years, I strongly object to "cheeseheads" because *cheesy* is slang for something that is inferior or in poor taste. I can live with it, because one origin is from the Urdu (similar to Hindi), *chīz*, or thing, so that a "big cheese" is an important person. So, say "cheese," and I'll smile.

Two current slang terms are *props*, as in to "give props," and *crunk*. The first is from "proper respect." The second, an amalgam of c*r*azy and d*runk*, means energized, stirred up, or really wasted.

Chick lit is a book (literature) genre that primarily appeals to young women (chicks). The largest categories of buyers of fiction books are young women (particularly the zealous readers of Harlequin Books and other romance novels) as well as older women. (And by punning extension, *kiddie lit* refers to books that appeal to children.)

Claptrack is absurd, insincere, nonsensical, or pretentious language or ideas. I hope that this word does not apply to this book, though it has a fascinating origin. In the eighteenth century in England, playwrights used rants, rhymes, and other rhetorical devices, and actors enhanced them with flourishes as a trap to catch a "clap" (applause).

A *cliffhanger* is a tight contest or tense situation in which the outcome is uncertain until the end. The term originated in the era of movie serials in which each suspenseful episode or chapter ended with the hero or heroine dangling over a cliff or enmeshed in some other precarious situation.

To "connect the dots" is slang for "to follow a path," as of a series of events leading to a conclusion. The origin is from the rebus of dots that can be connected to produce a drawing.

Academics like the word *corpus* to refer to a collection of works, such as all of the publications of a specific author (dead or alive) or a body of work on a subject.

A *crossover* refers to a work in the style in which a singer or other creative person has not been associated, usually to appeal to a wider audience, such as from country to popular music. A "crossover hit" can be a recording or other work, such as a film that is successful with a Latino, black, or other major demographic niche.

A *dialer* is slang at *USA Today* for a quickly accessible and quotable expert.

Among the many meanings of *dish*, one that has become popular in recent years is "to gossip," from to "dish it out," meaning dispense something in an indiscriminate manner. It's also a noun, as in "What's the dish about ____?" *Page Six*, a page in the *New York Post* containing news and gossip about celebrities, is used generically to refer to newspaper columns, blogs, and other media devoted to gossip.

In the media, slang words that crop up constantly to describe a foolish or boring person include "doofus," "dorf," "dork," "flathead," "geek," "nebbish," "nerd," and "newt." There may be slight variations in the meanings of these words, but you'll have to ask a slang linguist (a slanglist?) to differentiate the fine points.

A *dweeb* is an earnest student, akin to a "nerd." A *goof*, or "goofball," blunders or wastes time ("goofs off"). A *yo-yo* vacillates, or goes up and down like a Yo-Yo toy. A *highbrow* is an intellectual or cultured person and a *lowbrow* is the opposite, though not necessarily a "dimwit" (stupid person). What's your favorite word for a bore? *Egghead* (an intellectual with a bald head shaped like an egg) and *jerk* are definitely passé. *Wonk* can be a compliment (a person who studies a subject thoroughly, as a "foreign policy wonk") or a criticism (a person who studies excessively, as a "grind"). We don't know the origin of "wonk," but I do know that *grind* is from Middle English (twelfth- to sixteenth-century) *grinden*, meaning to rub away or pulverize.

Though a *geek* may be a socially inept person, the word more commonly refers to a person with an intense or eccentric devotion to a subject, such as a "computer geek." In carnie (carnival) jargon, a "geek" is a performer who does wild or disgusting actions. The Dutch word *gek* meant mad or silly, so you may get "in Dutch" (disfavor) if you use the word "geek" indiscriminately.

Elevator music is innocuous, instrumental music: *Muzak* has almost become a generic name for this. The company was started by George Owen Squier (1865–1934) as Wired Radio, Inc., and now is Muzak, LLC, in Fort Mill, South Carolina. Muzak has "come out of the elevator" and changed considerably in recent years. It now provides what it calls "audio architecture"—a variety of music, voice, and sound for stores, restaurants, hotels, and other venues, where the type and tempo of the music varies, depending on the time of day and customer demographics.

An *elevator pitch* is a brief description of a company or product, so brief and well prepared that it can be given during the minute-or-less ride in an elevator with someone who might ask about your convention badge!

An *emoticon* is an *emot*ional *icon*, an expression of emotion or other colorful language, usually witty, originally typed with punctuation marks or other characters. The first, and best known, was the smiley :-), which, if viewed sideways, resembles a smiling face. Several hundred smiles, frowns, winks, and other emoticons are now commonly used in e-mail, as are acronyms, such as IMHO, "in my humble opinion."

Face the music is to accept the consequences of one's actions, even if unpleasant. The nineteenth-century origin may be from an inexperienced performer who had to courageously turn to the audience, thus facing the orchestra pit with its more seasoned, and critical, musicians.

In this computer era of instant messaging, *fax* (short for *facsimile*, or exact copy) is still widely used in homes and offices. Facsimile transmission over telephone lines became so common in the eighties that it is now used as a noun, a verb (to "fax" a document), and an adjective (a "fax number," the telephone number dedicated to a fax machine). The plural is *faxes*. A "fax attack" (or blitz) means a campaign in which many messages are sent, as to a governmental official. A "fax hacker" is a person who uses a fax machine to send unrequested messages. "Facsimiles" (exact copies of writings) were made as early as the sixteenth century. The word comes from the Latin, *fac*, from the verb *facere*, or make, and *simile*, a noun form of *similis*, or like. "Fax" also is slang for "facilities."

A *franchise* is authorization provided by a government agency (such as a cable system franchise) or licensed from a company (such as McDonald's) to a group or an individual to provide a specific service or product. The grantor is called the "franchisor," and the recipient, the "franchisee." In recent years, the word has acquired other definitions. In sports, a league grants a "franchise" to a group to operate a team. The team is called a "franchise" and a star on the team is a "franchise player." A company with an extremely dominant position in a category or area also is dubbed a "franchise." From this, in the media, a dominant series of programs or films may "have a franchise," such as *CSI* and *Law & Order* (crime franchises) and *The Simpsons* (animated sitcom franchise).

FTE, or "full-time equivalent," is a collection of freelancers and part-time employees that is equal to one full-time employee. It's a designation of the workforce at newspapers and in other industries.

GAT, or "good anytime," is a notation on a newspaper article indicating that it is timeless. It's also called an *evergreen*.

Get is a TV slang noun for a celebrity who is a hard-to-get potential interviewee. Of course, it's also a verb, as in "Get me the president!"

Grin and grip is a traditional photo of two people smiling and shaking hands on the occasion of receiving an award or at another newsworthy event.

A *gypsie run-through* is a special performance of a show to enable working dancers (called "gypsies") and other performers to see it, such as on a Monday night or other off-time.

Hometake is slang at *People* magazine for photography at the residence of a subject accompanied by a noncontroversial or "soft" interview.

Laydown is the distribution of a book to retailers. The "laydown date" is the day that a book actually goes on sale, which is often before the official "publication date" ("pub date" or "release" date).

Mise en scène is the staging or the overall composition or arrangement of a scene, including performers, scenery, and lighting. It's from the French *miser*, or "agreement," hence the process of combining the elements of a scene.

To *nail* is to fix, secure, or hit squarely. To "nail a story" is to validate all sources and complete all research prior to publication or broadcast.

You've seen *paparazzi*, the aggressive photographers, especially freelancers, who take candid photographs of celebrities, often to the distress of the subjects. The singular is *paparazzo*. Señor Paparazzo was a character in *La Dolce Vita*, a 1960 film directed by Federico Fellini (1920–94). The origin probably is from the French, *paperasse*, or waste paper (akin to trash).

A *peg-box* is a sentence that describes the gist of an article (its "peg" or "theme"), usually placed below the headline and identified with a bullet, ruled lines, or boldface type.

To *pipe* is to play, transmit sound, or distribute a signal, as in to "pipe in." In media lingo, to "pipe" means to fake, as with a journalist who "pipes a story" by making up characters or events.

In film, television, and theater, to *plant the flag* is to announce the opening day of a new film, TV series, play, or other work. Film producers jockey to establish an opening weekend (usually Friday), particularly during the summer, to open a major movie in the hope that producers of a similar type of film will open at a later date.

Potus, or POTUS, is an acronym originally used by the Secret Service and now by the media and others to mean the President of the United States. It was first used in the sixties during the Johnson Administration to identify the phone line in the president's office (the Oval Office) and other phone lines of the president's aides.

A *Rolodex* is an index-card unit with removable cards on a revolving spindle or in a tray, originally made by the Rolodex Corporation. Note that it's capitalized as a trademarked name. Lobbyists, press agents, event planners, fund-raisers, and others are credited in the media for their Rolodex collections of VIP names, addresses, and unlisted phone numbers, whether or not they use the actual Rolodex cards. The manufacturer is Sanford Corporation, Oak Brook, Illinois. There's also an electronic version, made by Franklin Electronics Publishers.

Salted peanuts, a slang expression at *Time* magazine, are brief, easy-to-read items.

"The Scottish play" is the name given *Macbeth*, the tragedy set in Scotland by William Shakespeare (1564–1616), by superstitious actors loath to say the play's name. Legend has it that the actor cast as Lady Macbeth in the first production (in 1606) died backstage, cursing the play. The hex has remained, abetted by many disasters associated with the play, so actors continue instead to refer euphemistically to this work of the bard.

Scuttlebutt is gossip or a rumor. The probable origin is from a "scuttle butt," a cask ("butt") with a square hole ("scuttle," probably from the French *escoutille*, a hatchway) cut into it. Before the twentieth century, sailors gathered around this drinking barrel to gossip. So the meaning of "scuttlebutt" is akin to today's *water-cooler gossip*, informal conversation among office workers gathered at a water dispenser or other communal area.

Sheetcake is a small, rectangular confection, flat like a sheet, used by newspaper editors and others for low-cost celebrations, such as circulation milestones.

To *shrink* is to reduce, but at *Cosmopolitan* magazine and other media, it means a quote; and, paradoxically, the process of adding quotes is called "shrinkage."

Signature has become ubiquitous as a reference to the name of a person or product and its identifying characteristics. Magazine articles and other media use "signature" as shorthand for an individual performer's way of walking, dancing, or talking; for his or her theme song; or for other audio and/or visual identification of a person or program. A television network refers to a *signature show*, meaning the program that is its most popular one and which reflects the network's special interest or primary demographics.

"Signature" terms are common in several media. As to the etymology, about 500 years ago *signature* was Latin for the signature of a sovereign on an official document. The original verb, *signare*, meant to sign or mark.

In advertising, the "signature" is the name of the advertiser, generally found at the bottom or end of an advertising message, sometimes accompanied by the advertiser's symbol or logo (logotype).

In music, the "signature" is a sign at the beginning of a staff (the five horizontal lines and four spaces between them, on and in which music is written) to show the "key" (called *key signature*), or time. The *time signature* establishes the meter or rhythm by indicating the number of beats in the measure or measures that follow.

In printing and publishing, a "signature" is a large sheet of paper that has been printed, folded, and trimmed. The section of a book or other publication obtained in this manner may consist of four, eight, twelve, sixteen, or more pages and is also called a *gathering* or *quire*. When printed signatures were folded by hand, the folders initialed their work; hence the word "signature." The first signature of a book is not lettered or numbered, as it would be on the title or first page, and is unnecessary; so that signatures usually start with B or 2.

The *signature title* is an abbreviated form of the author's name and/or title of a book, printed toward the inner margin of the first page of each signature. This identification generally is used only with lengthy books and appears on the same line as the *signature mark*, which is a dot, line, number, or other indication on the first page of a signature to indicate the sequence of gathering.

Television viewers are familiar with a *signature montage*, a series of brief scenes at the beginning of a TV news program, sitcom, dramatic series, or other TV show to introduce the program. Among the best-known "TV signatures" are the ticking clock that opens *60 Minutes* and Tony Soprano driving through the Lincoln Tunnel to New Jersey that opens *The Sopranos*.

A recent usage is the *signature block*, an attachment, usually at the end of e-mail and other messages, identifying the sender with a name, address, and sometimes other information. It's called a ".sig" (pronounced dot-SIG). Until 1991, reviews in *Variety* were not bylined and ended with a nickname, invented name, or simply the reviewer's last name, called a *sig*.

The first *signature fragrance*, Chanel No. 5, was introduced in 1921 by French couturier Gabrielle "Coco" Chanel (1883–1971).

John Hancock (1737–93) was the first signer, in 1776, of the Declaration of Independence and his name became a synonym for "signature," as in "put your John Hancock here." It's sometimes erroneously called a "John Henry," perhaps a reference to Patrick Henry (1736–99), best remembered for a speech that included, "Give me liberty, or give me death." Though a member of the Continental Congress, he was not one of the fifty-six signers of the Declaration of Independence.

And thus indeed, "signature" is a multimedia term. Let's move on to other media lingo.

Spam is that nearly ubiquitous unsolicited e-mail, usually advertisements, sent to many recipients, often in the millions, by "spammers" who "spam." The common use of the word probably is from its repetition on the British television comedy series, *Monty Python's Flying Circus*. Large quantities of SPAM, a canned seasoned meat product, were consumed by U.S. soldiers in England during the Second World War. It's still made by Hormel Foods Corporation, of Austin, Minnesota. The trademark is an acronym for *sp*iced *ham*.

Spinach demand is slang used by editors and others to indicate an article or other work that requires great concentration by the reader or viewer. The origin is from Popeye, the comic strip character who ate spinach to increase his strength. Elzie C. Segar (1894–1938) created the strip in 1929, and it is still distributed to newspapers by King

Features. Fleischer Studios, headed by Max Fleischer (1883–1972), produced about six hundred animated Popeye cartoons; some still are shown on The Cartoon Network.

A *squawk box* is a loudspeaker, part of a public address system that includes one or more microphones, used in offices, stores, and elsewhere for announcements.

A *stemwinder* is a long, boring speech. Before quartz, all wristwatches required winding at the stem and people at a long sermon or speech sometimes would ostentatiously wind their watches to indicate their impatience or boredom.

A *Telestrator* is an electronic device that enables a sports, weather, or other broadcaster to draw arrows and other lines and shapes on a freeze frame or other television image. Invented in 1981 by John Madden (b. 1936), a sports commentator and former NFL head coach, the original technique involved a pointer, but now the effect can be achieved by touching a screen with a finger. The device is made by several companies and the name also has become a verb, to "telestrate."

In a *tell-all book*, the author candidly describes, perhaps with the assistance of a journalist or ghostwriter, his or her experiences with a famous person or in a famous place; for example, to have worked in the White House in Washington or the Royal Palace in London. A more recent term is a *tell-some*, a memoir that partially reveals private or sensitive information.

A *thumbsucker* is jargon for a superficial or ponderous article resulting in reader discomfort, alleviated by thumbsucking. It also sometimes describes an article filled with speculation, as compared to a more factual report.

A *tick-tock* is a time line, or chronology of events. It has become a popular term with journalists and government press officers (particularly at the White House), as in "give the tick-tock."

Top is a word used in many popular media expressions. "Top-ten" lists of best-selling books, DVDs, and other items regularly appear in newspapers and magazines. "Top" can mean the beginning of a work, as in "top of the script" or "top of the story." The "top deck" is the main part of a headline. "Top" also can mean uppermost, as in "top billing" for a "top performer" placed at the "top" of an advertisement or program. For a performer, to "top a line" is to execute a line of dialogue at a greater intensity or with greater effect than the preceding line. To "top a laugh" is to outdo the preceding joke.

"Over the top," a term that is a common critical reference to theatrical and other performers, means to an excessive degree. The origin goes back to the First World War when an order to "go over the top" directed soldiers to climb out of their trenches. After the war, it connoted courage and then evolved to mean to go beyond reasonable limits.

"Trailers" are common in film, radio, and television as vehicles and other forms. In broadcasting, a *trailer* can be a short, blank strip at the end of a reel of tape, a promotional announcement at the end of a radio or TV program about a forthcoming program, or a commercial attached to the end of a program or another commercial.

Movie audiences are familiar with *trailers*, short films that promote a forthcoming motion picture. In recent years, trailers have become longer and more elaborately produced, so that viewers sometimes feel that it's not necessary to see the full movie. Another change is that the trailers now precede the movie, and there are more of them in theaters and also on videotapes and DVDs. The original "trailers" (in the twenties) were called *coming attractions*. They followed or trailed the feature movie, which is how they got their name. They also were shown between the movies of a double feature. Audiences call them "previews" or *prevues*, but the film industry still calls them "trailers" or "movie commercials."

In theater, a "trailer" is a single curtain that is drawn

across the stage. It's also called a *draw tab* or *French tab*. One etymology leads to another. In this case, "tab" is short for "tableau curtain," which when pulled, reveals a "tableau," a striking dramatic scene, generally involving a grouping of silent, posed performers.

A "trailer" also is a van or other vehicle on or near a film, TV, or other site, for use as a dressing room, control unit, or other purposes. A *production trailer* has facilities for the control of filming, taping, or broadcast. A *star trailer* is for one person and usually has a star on the door. A *double banger* accommodates two people. (Don't ask for the origin of that term!) A *honey wagon* usually is for more than two people and includes a toilet and dressing room. The origin is from *honey bucket*, a slang term for a bucket or container that was used when a toilet was not available.

And now, trailing clouds of media lingo, I leave the trail with the origin of "trailer." The verb "trail" is from the French *trailler*, from the Latin *trahere*, to draw or pull.

The *velvet rope* is a barrier at a disco or event to exclude people who are not members, are not on the guest list, or are otherwise undesirable. It may not be made of soft velvet and it does not provide soft treatment.

Woodshedding means practicing on a musical instrument. The origin is from the use of a woodshed as an isolated place in which to practice. The word sometimes is used by performers to indicate going off alone to practice music, dialogue, or other actions. In broadcasting, "woodshedding" is the marking of a script to indicate pauses and other inflections, as with a slash mark (/) for a pause, a double slash (//) for a long pause, an underline for emphasis, and double underline for heavier emphasis.

[INITIALISMS]

Here's a roundup of a handful of initialisms (abbreviations formed from the initial letters) that are common in the media.

AA means "author's alteration," a revision made by the author to typeset copy other than to fix a typographical error (called a *PE* or "printer's error").

APR, "annual percentage rate," are initials that appear in bank advertisements and are rarely spelled out, though many readers think that it refers to adjusted percentage (or principal) rate (or return). *APY* stands for "annual percentage yield." *APR* also means "accredited public relations," a title given to members of the Public Relations Society of America who pass an examination and meet other standards.

CC stands for *closed captioning*, a method of superimposing typed text, as of an audio track, over a television image, usually as a crawl across the bottom of the TV screen. It is invisible on ordinary TV sets and is made visible with a decoder that can be used by hearing-impaired viewers.

CPM, "cost per thousand," indicates the cost of advertising for each one thousand homes reached by radio or TV, for each one thousand copies circulated by a publication, or for each one thousand potential viewers of an outdoor or other advertisement.

DNA (desoxyribonucleic acid), the material in chromosomes that carries genetic information, has given rise to the current slang use for "DNA" to refer to the personality or character (the essential nature) of a person ("It's in his DNA") or the theme or orientation of a publication, business, or other entity.

P.i. stands for *per inquiry*, a common system in which an advertiser pays a TV station or other medium for an advertisement, based on the number of inquiries received from potential customers in response to an ad, not based on the normal time or space cost of the ad.

Q score is a term that appears in the media, particularly advertising and TV columns. It's a qualitative market research technique, developed by Marketing Evaluations, Inc., of Manhasset, New York, to determine the familiarity of TV programs, personalities, and products. TV newscasters, talk show hosts, and other broadcasters check their Q scores the way that producers check their Nielsen ratings. The Q stands for "quotient."

Everyone in marketing (particularly retailing) knows that an *SKU* (pronounced SKEW) refers to a "stock-keeping unit." Every color, size, and style of an item in a store has an "SKU number" that identifies it as a distinct product.

As I stated in the "Introduction," I have omitted computer jargon, as there are many books and Web sites covering the subject. However, here's some information that may explain the meaning surrounding some digital products and other technologies that have become immensely popular and also influence the media.

Google, Inc., in Mountain View, California, is the world's largest Internet search engine. Millions of people find out just about anything by going to *www.google.com* and doing a Google search. In just a few years, the word has become a verb, to "Google" and "Googling." The company, started in 1998 by Larry Page (b. 1971) and Sergey Brin (b. 1972), is based on the mathematical term, "googol," which is ten raised to the power of one hundred, or ten followed by one hundred zeros. The term was coined by Milton Sirotta (b. 1929), the nine-year-old nephew of U.S. mathematician Edward Kasner (1878–1953).

MP3 is a digital format for playing music and other audio that can be downloaded (transferred from a computer or other server to your own computer or other device). I'll bet that millions of users do not know that MP3 stands for the file extension "MPEG." The Motion Picture Expert Group (MPEG) is an industry group that has developed compression standards for moving images that can be downloaded on a computer. The "3" refers to "layer 3," which removes superfluous information. MP3 is a system that transfers audio files by compressing them into very small units and then storing them in portable players (an "MP3 player") and digital audio services.

In recent years, a controversy (involving lots of lawyers) developed about free downloading (ultimately deemed to be illegal) of MP3 files of copyrighted songs and music from Web sites, notably by Napster, Inc., in Santa Clara, California, an online music service named after the company's founder, Shawn Fanning (b. 1981). In high school, Fanning had nappy (frizzy) brown hair and was nicknamed "The Napster." He dropped out of Northeastern University, in Boston, after his first semester and created Napster in 1999, at the age of eighteen. Lingo introduced by Napster includes *song-swapping*, in which downloaded music is sent from one person to another. Fanning left Napster and the company was acquired in 2002 and relaunched in 2003, in Los Angeles, as a fee-based legal subscription service for online music. Now, Apple Computer's iTunes Music Store, the leading download service, sells music for the Apple *iPod*. The term *podcasting* means the transmission of music and other audio and video to online files that can be downloaded onto an iPod or other MP3 player.

Magazine and newspaper writers, and other media people, often use prefixes and suffixes to create new words. For example, *mega-* means very large, and *über-* comes from a German word that means super. A *megabyte* is a unit of information, about one million bytes.

A *megaflop* is a colossal failure, the opposite of a *megahit*. "Mega" sometimes is used as a word by itself, such as a *mega news story*. In the same vein, *meta-* means beyond or higher, as in a "metascandal," which is similar to a "superscandal."

Nano- means very small, from the Greek *nanos*, or dwarf. "Nanotechnology" deals with the very small (a "nanometer" is one-billionth of a meter), such as atoms and molecules. A recent term, *nanopublishing*, denotes a small, low-budget publishing operation, such as an on-line publisher or a blog.

As a prefix, *ana-* means up, back, again, or similar to. An "anachronism" is something that exists at other than its proper time, such as earlier or out of its proper order in history. An "analogy" is a similarity between things that are otherwise unlike. As a suffix, *-ana* indicates the sayings, writings, anecdotes, facts, or other material about a person or place, such as "Americana" or "Victoriana."

A word that has become a common media suffix is *-wise*, meaning in the manner of or in regard to. Media people love to add "-wise" to just about any noun to make it an adverb or adjective, such as "foodwise," "moneywise," and "saleswise." (Such constructions were once hyphenated, but now they usually are written as one word.) Lexicographers consider these wise-words inelegant or improper in style, but acknowledge that otherwise they are OK.

One of my favorite words is *wow,* a bon mot that is an exclamation of amazement, or as a verb means to impress or excite. It's a common word in the performing arts; to "wow" is to "be a great success," as in the "wow factor" or "wowing an audience." No, it's not an acronym, such as "way out of this world." The etymology probably is from an old English expression, "I vow."

A potpourri, a mixture, also connotes a literary or musical medley. I hope that you have enjoyed this medley and not found it a stemwinder or thumbsucker.

PUBLIC RELATIONS: A PR PRIMER

WHAT'S your reputation? Almost everyone wants to be highly regarded and have a good or positive *image*: the concept or character projected to others. Professional communicators often are retained to identify and improve the image of a person, such as a politician or other celebrity, as well as a company or other group. It's called "polishing an image," and these communicators work in the field of public relations. The media frequently use public relations jargon, sometimes pejoratively.

These days *PR* (also P.R. or p.r.) is the common abbreviation, used both as a noun and a verb. Journalists and even the general public say that a company should "PR something," which usually means to promote even without a strong rationale. As a longtime public relations professional, I cringe when I hear, "Don't PR me," though it's better than being told instead, "Don't give me any BS," or some other vulgarism.

Let's start this public relations primer with a few basic definitions. "PR people" (or PRP for short) still do *not* have a commonly accepted definition of public relations, believe it or not. So, here's mine: Public relations means "the activities and attitudes intended to analyze, adjust to, influence, or direct the opinions of people, in the interest of an individual, group, or other source."

If you read the definition slowly, it may seem less cumbersome or pretentious. Or, consider this simple example familiar to most of us: an organization with good public relations has a favorable image or reputation, perhaps as a result of the publicity, publications, speeches, events, and other PR activities it engages in.

In its broadest sense, public relations includes advertising and all forms of communication. In a narrower sense, however, the field generally excludes advertising except for institutional, or goodwill, advertising or other targeted advertising. The PR field is categorized by the specific groups (called "publics") to which it makes appeals to accept, support, or reject certain public policy decisions, political candidates, or products and services, so that PR may involve "community relations," "employee relations," "financial relations," "legislative relations," and "general-public relations."

A "public," as a smaller group within the general population, is linked by common interests, such as the "reading public" or the "voting public." A related word that has become popular is "stakeholder," a person with a particular interest or concern in something, ranging from an issue as general as "clean air" to something as specific as the stock of a particular company. "External publics" are those outside an organization—for instance, potential customers—whereas "internal publics" are members, employees, and others within an organization or group. The expression to "go public" is to make something known. Ideally and in its broadest sense, PR helps an organization and its publics to mutually adapt, and/or to achieve the cooperation of other groups of people.

Public affairs sometimes is used as a synonym for public relations, but more often the former term refers to activities that are considered to be in the public interest. In a corporation, a "public affairs officer" or "public affairs director" is involved with external publics, not with employees (part of "internal affairs") or shareholders.

In the military, a *public affairs officer*, or PAO (formerly called a "public information officer"), is in charge of communications with the media and other groups. The White House and other governmental entities still use the term *press secretary* for their on-staff PR official.

The area adjacent to the assembly hall of a legislature is called a "lobby," an area open to nonlegislators, including individuals who congregate there to meet and influence lawmakers. That's the etymology of *lobbyists*, the PRP who undertake to "lobby" on behalf of special-interest groups ("lobbies").

Financial relations people communicate on behalf of public companies to shareholders, government agencies, the media, and others. If you own stock in a public company, you receive annual reports and other information, and are familiar with such terms as *10-K*, which is an audited report of a company's financial results, filed annually with the Securities and Exchange Commission (SEC).

In recent years, business media often refer to Regulation FD and the Sarbanes-Oxley Act. Regulation FD ("Fair Disclosure") is an SEC regulation issued in 2000 prohibiting public companies from selectively disclosing information to security analysts, bankers, and others before it's disclosed to the general public. The Sarbanes-Oxley Act (SOX), which became a federal law in 2002, is named after Sen. Paul Sarbanes (b. 1977), a Democrat from Maryland, and Rep. Michael Oxley (b. 1944), a Republican from Ohio. A section of SOX requires public companies to report on the effectiveness of their internal controls on accounting accuracy and other key data, and also mandates taking action to correct weaknesses, fraud, or errors.

Marketing communications (*marcom*) is the use of special events, publicity, and other techniques to promote products and services. Many PRP, uncomfortable with the word *publicity*, prefer the term *media relations* for the relationship between an individual or group and the communication channels (media) they employ.

In return, the media sometimes refer to a PR person as a "publicist." *Publicity* is a technique in which information from an outside source—usually a PR practitioner—is used by the media. Publicity is not advertising, which is the purchase of time or space in the media. Publicity may be called "free advertising," which, of course, is somewhat of an exaggeration, since the client pays for the services and expenses of the publicist.

Flack is a demeaning synonym sometimes used by the media for "press agent" or "publicist." The word probably was used first by *Variety* as a term for "press agent," stemming from the Second World War term for antiaircraft, which in turn emanated from the German *Flak*, an abbreviation of *Fliegerabwehrkanone*, an antiaircraft cannon. Thus, a publicist is a "flak-catcher."

Four of the most common PR tools are called "news release," "news advisory," "press kit," and "video news release." A *news release* (formerly called a "press release") is an article sent as a suggestion to the media. It's informally called a "handout" since it originally was handed out or distributed (released) free.

A *news advisory* (or "press alert") is an announcement of a forthcoming event, such as one provided by a PR source to the media. It usually lists the five Ws (who, what, where, when, and why), particularly the "news peg," of a forthcoming event or announcement, as at a press conference. Broadcasters prefer "news conference" or "media conference," as "press" connotes the print media, but the terms "press conference," "press show," and "press table" remain ubiquitous.

A *press kit* is a collection of materials provided by an outside source—such as a PR practitioner—to the media (a "press list"). The releases and other materials usually are enclosed in a portfolio or press kit cover.

A *video news release* (VNR) is a news or feature recorded on videotape, sent by a public relations source to TV stations. The radio equivalent is an *audio news release*. In 2005, the media reported and editorialized extensively about VNRs that did not clearly identify their sources, particularly those coming from government agencies. In fact, VNRs have been widely used by PRP and broadcast on TV networks and stations for decades.

Another PR technique is the *satellite media tour* (SMT), in which several interviews, generally on TV but sometimes in other media, are conducted during a specific period, such as over one or more hours. The interviewee—author, actor, political candidate, or other person—sits in a studio and is interviewed via satellite by broadcasters and journalists who are located elsewhere.

A *public service announcement* (PSA) is broadcast free by radio and TV stations. The announcement usually is provided by government agencies or nonprofit organizations and considered to be in the public interest.

Public relations people (PRP) are ingenious in their efforts to obtain media attention. For example, news can be created by setting up a contest, exhibition, race, or other special event that credits or involves the sponsor.

On the problematic side, *crisis management* is a process used by public relations practitioners to communicate with the media and other publics about an oil spill, product recall, or other difficulty, usually in accordance with a "crisis management plan."

This brings us to a controversial word among PRP, *spin*, presenting information with a particular point of view. PRP strongly resent being called "spin doctors" probably more than "flacks." PRP may sometimes appear glib, but their PR work often is based on extensive research. For example, they frequently conduct a "communication audit"—a professional review and evaluation of the history, policies, practices, needs, problems, and other aspects of the behavior of an organization—before setting out to improve the credibility of their client. (A shortened form, *cred*, now appears in *The New York Times*, with no explanation.) PRP these days like to talk about CSR, "corporate social responsibility," as a "cred booster."

To *frame* is to form or articulate, as when PRP frame a story, theme, or campaign. The process is called "framing." The origin of *frame* is the Old English (before 1150), *framien*, to be useful.

[SPIN DOCTORS]

Baseball pitchers, tennis players, and other athletes all know that to put a twist, or spin, on a ball is a desirable skill. Off the sports page, spin *can be a new angle, fresh approach, or twist, as in to "put a spin" on a story or project. An older meaning is to draw out a lengthy story, or "spin a yarn," as on a spindle.*

In recent years, political commentators and journalists usually use "spin" pejoratively: To "put a spin" on a statement means to use language to twist or manipulate a position, concept, or event. The interpretation or modification (the "spin" itself) is designed to alter the public's perception—and sometimes to divert attention from the real issues.

Spinnish, a play on the word "Spanish," is a humorous name for the language of *spin control*, or the management of communication. A *spin doctor* is an expert at "spin control," primarily in politics. He or she might call a "spin moratorium," or truce, with the political opposition. The goal thereby is to project a "positive spin" instead of a "negative spin."

Many writers and public relations people have undergraduate and graduate degrees in journalism and mass communications. My brother-in-law, David Linton, has a Ph.D. in *media ecology*, the study of the relationship between communication channels and materials (the media), on the one hand, and our society and environment, on the other.

"Media ecologists" often criticize spin doctors and others for polluting our media environment. I hope that I merit a green rating, particularly if I end here with a prescient line by English poet Alfred Lord Tennyson (1809–92) from his 1842 poem *Ulysses*:

"Let the great world spin forever down the ringing grooves of change."

Let's press on with some PR-related press terms. A *press list* is a collection or series of print and other media, such as that compiled by a public relations practitioner prior to a news event. A *press aide* is an assistant to a government official or an executive who deals with the media. A *press gallery* is an area in a legislature or other building for observation by reporters and other members of the media.

Though some publicists refer to a collection of clippings as a *press book*, in the publishing business the term has a different meaning: a limited edition of a book, often signed by the author. "Press" has many meanings. For example, a book publisher, particularly at a university, often has "press" in its name, such as New York University Press.

PRP set up special events and other activities to create "buzz," or excitement, particularly by "word-of-mouth" (oral communication) or *viral marketing* (product promotion by customers and others that spreads rapidly like a virus, usually via e-mail and on the Web). A *plug* is a mention or showing of a product, book title, or other credit. The origin of "plug" as publicity is from newspaper editors' use of fillers or other text to fit into (plug) a hole, or open area on a page. A press agent today sometimes is called a "plugger."

Boilerplate, a block of copy that may be picked up and reused, such as a sentence or paragraph describing a company and its products, often is the standard last section of a news release. The term is also used for any type of clichéd material in journalism, public relations, and advertising, and especially by lawyers for standard or formulaic legal language. It is also called "fill" or abbreviated by journalists as *A.O.T.* (any old time).

Many newspaper syndicates started in Chicago, including the American Press Association, founded in 1882 in the same building as a sheet-iron factory. Chicago printers dubbed the noisy American Press offices a "boilerplate factory." The term *boilerplate* soon was used derogatorily for the mechanical stereotype plates generally provided as single columns by news syndicates. Editors were criticized for filling their papers with plate matter cut into fillers and shorts, often on the basis of space rather than content, a process known as "editing with a saw."

PR campaigns often are targeted to the *grassroots*, the most basic level of an activity or organization. As generally used, *grassroots* refers to the dispersed membership of an organization, or to the anonymous, scattered holders of opinions or attitudes. PR consultants sometimes refer to the leaders of grassroots groups as *grasstops*.

Lobbyists and PR professionals often conduct campaigns to influence *gatekeepers*, the opinion makers, media people, and others who control or influence the flow (they keep the gates) of information to the grassroots or other groups.

Communication through the grassroots often takes place via the *grapevine*, the circulation of rumors or unofficial information within a network of individuals, spread out and connected like grape-bearing vines. "Grapevine news" transmitted along the "grapevine telegraph" may be authentic information or unfounded gossip. In contrast, in journalism, "grapevine copy" is timeless and can be used any time.

On the other end of the authenticity spectrum, to *Astroturf* is to create a grassroots movement that does not really originate with the common people, but is artificial. Astroturf is the name of a synthetic grasslike carpet, developed in 1967 by Monsanto Industries and now made by AstroTurf Industries.

A *pressure group* is an organization of people that advocates a viewpoint and attempts to influence government officials, legislators, and others by means of lobbying, letter writing, publicity, and other techniques.

Propaganda is communications intended to influence public opinion, often with a nefarious connotation, particularly when the source is not disclosed. An Italian word, it's from the Latin *propagare*, to propagate or spread.

Before we close, here is some PRP jargon whose exact meaning often gets blurred.

Social reporting is the providing of information, as in annual reports to shareholders (a euphemism for "stockholders"), about the environmental, health, safety, and other nonfinancial activities of a company or other entity.

Convergence, an in-word a few years ago, is the occurrence of two or more things coming together, such as audio, video, and computer information.

Scalable, which is a jargon adjective among market and opinion researchers, refers to the capability of being measured (scaled), such as a program that can be increased in measurable increments.

Many advertising and public relations people blithely use -*metrics* as a suffix for the application of statistics or mathematical analysis to a specific field—for example, "customer satisfaction–metrics"—even when it might be difficult to meaningfully quantify such key elements. More generally, *metrics* means a standard of measurement of the attainment of specific objectives.

In the same vein, *benchmark* is a standard by which a product, process, or project can be compared or judged. A common term, for example, is the Federal Reserve's "benchmark interest rate."

PRP also use common words, such as "deliverable," "end-to-end," and "leverage," sometimes without hesitation about their aptness. *Deliverable*, for example, as an adjective means capable of being, or about to be, transported, distributed, or delivered. What is usually meant is

THE SKINNY ABOUT...MEDIA LINGO

an objective, measurable, and identifiable goal—or the ability to provide specific end results—for a client.

In public relations and related fields, *end-to-end* is akin to cradle-to-grave, goal-to-conclusion, or more generally the delivery of services that attain desired goals.

One of the dictionary definitions of *leverage* is the "power to influence a person or situation to achieve a particular outcome." As used by communicators, "leverage" refers to a positional advantage, such as social or political leverage.

Three other normally easy-to-understand words are so overused by public relations consultants that they have become hackneyed: "integrated," "multifaceted," and "turnkey." A typical PR cliché is an "integrated, leveraged program that is scalable," which means that all of the related components provide specific advantages and the results can be measured at fixed intervals. And, delving further into PR clichés, such a "convergent program is deliverable with benchmarks and end-to-end actions that are identified in metrics." Obviously, it also is "turnkey" (ready to start immediately). Incidentally, the earliest sense of turnkey was a jailer. Maybe users of these pretentious words should be jailed in a small metrics cell.

ROLL, RIGHTS, RELEASE:
THREE MEDIA Rs

"LET'S roll," the battle cry of hero Todd M. Beamer (1969–2001) on September 11, 2001, aboard hijacked United Flight 93, has become part of our nation's history.

The word *roll* is commonly used in everyday language and in the media. A *roll in the hay* (or *sack*) is a euphemism for intercourse. *Rolling in money* means to be very rich. *On a roll* is experiencing sustained success. *A roll* is a register of names, such as a "roll of honor." A *roll* is also a list of names of members, voters, or attendees; a cylindrical mass or shape; a rapid succession of sounds, as in a "drumroll," and a revolving tool used in bookbinding. Now on to media lingo.

In film, a *roll* is a reel or spool of tape or film. As a verb, to "roll" is to move, revolve, or play a film or tape. Early manuscripts, rolled on a rod, were called *rolls* or *scrolls*.

Let's roll on to specialized uses in the media. Perhaps the best known is *roll* (also *roll it* or *roll 'em*), a director's order to begin operating the movie camera. A few seconds later, when the camera reaches operating speed, or is "rolling," the command "Action!" is given to the performers. In live TV, the *roll cue* applies simultaneously to the camera operator and performers. *Roll focus* is a direction to begin or end a scene out of focus, simply by adjusting the lens while filming or taping.

In theater, to *roll them in the aisles* is to delight an audience. A *roll curtain* is rolled around a batten, or pipe. It's also called a "roll drop" or "roller drop."

In broadcasting, a *roll-in* is the insertion, or "cut-in," of a commercial into a program, sometimes for an extra *roll-in charge*.

A *rolloff* (also "roll off" or "roll-off") is a gradual loss of signal clarity of a radio or TV station at the edges of its transmission band—what you hear when the radio station is not exactly tuned in. Generally, a "rolloff" is a gradual weakening of sound. A "bass rolloff" is a gradual reduction in the low frequencies (bass); a "treble rolloff," the high frequencies (treble).

Quite different, a *rollover* is the vertical movement, or "flutter," of a film or TV picture due to improper vertical synchronization. It also means a repeat of a program immediately following the first broadcast, a type of scheduling common on cable channels.

In film and television, *rolling titles* are credits that roll up from the bottom of the screen; they also are called *crawl titles, creeping titles,* or *running titles.* Originally, *the roll-up titles,* or credits, were printed on a strip of background material and rolled on a revolving cylinder so that they appeared to crawl up the screen.

Rolling terms are common in other media. A *rolling billboard* is a panel truck or other vehicle that carries an electronic, painted, or printed display. The truck drives around or parks in specific locations, such as near a convention hall.

Rollers are common in printing, particularly the revolving cylinders, usually made of hard rubber, which spread the ink. The *cocking roller* is the guide roller that feeds the paper in a web-fed printing press. A *roll-up* is a check of the first impressions produced in a press run.

In marketing, a *rollout* is a movement of a product into new markets, such as a regional or national rollout following test marketing. It's also a mailing to a full list of names after a test mailing.

There's more, including *roll-film camera* (you know about that), *rolled edges* (of a book), and *roll-back mixing* (a technique of rerecording sound).

Before I roll away, permit me to squeeze in a homonym (a word pronounced the same way as another word, but with a different meaning and spelling): The word is *role*, a character or part in theater and other media. A *leading role* is a principal part. A *title role* is a character named or referred to in the title of the play or other work, usually the most important or one of the key roles. A performer *in role* has identified with the part in accent, gait, and other mannerisms.

Once the presses, cameras, or recording tapes roll, creative properties are being made, to which their owners claim rights.

Rights involve a legal claim or title, such as the authorization to use copyrighted material. Rights are a big part of the publishing, film, and music businesses, in which the copyright holder owns the material and the right to publish or reproduce it, so let's get to rights jargon right away, particularly in publishing.

All rights reserved is a printed notice that any publication or other use requires the consent of the copyright owner. The publisher generally controls the subsidiary rights, which can be more valuable than the original book itself, and can include sales to book clubs, serialization, syndication, excerpts in other media, broadcasts, motion pictures, records, foreign translation, adaptation, printing in other formats such as paperback, and even sales of components such as the title, character rights, or the general theme.

The jackpot for a book author can be the *dramatic rights* for dramatization as a play, film (*film rights*), or television show; *foreign rights,* and *syndication rights.* Right on!

The term *serial rights* often refers to sales to periodicals, which themselves are called serials. *Prepublication serial rights,* or *first serial rights,* pertain to the serialization of sections of a book prior to its publication; *postpublication serial rights,* or *second serial rights* (also called *reprint rights*), involve use, in another medium, of material from a book after its publication. *Simultaneous*

THE SKINNY ABOUT...MEDIA LINGO

rights are sold at the same time to two or more noncompeting media. *One-time rights* are for a specific use; the opposite of *all rights*, which means unlimited use.

Other rights include *U.S. serial rights*, *North American serial rights*, *foreign serial rights,* and rights for "condensation and abridgment," "translation," "merchandising," and other ingenious means of producing income for the author and his or her entourage of agents, lawyers, and rights specialists. One of these specialists deals with *rights clearance*, the process of finding the owner of the title, music, or other "intellectual property" and obtaining permission, free or for a fee, to reproduce all or part of the work.

A special type of rights is called *residuals*, royalties or payments to performers and others included in broadcast programs, commercials, plays, and other works for use beyond the original contract. A TV series that goes into reruns can produce big money over a period of many years. Ask Jerry Seinfeld (b. 1954). The payments are made according to formulas developed by the American Federation of Television and Radio Artists (AFTRA), Screen Actors Guild (SAG), and other unions.

In publishing, *residual rights* remain with or revert to the author or other copyright holders. Claims or obligations of "residual rights" are of vital importance to freelancers, particularly with regard to rights and royalties arising from the reproduction or reuse of material, after the original use, in other media, such as the Internet.

The word *right* has a fascinating origin. In Old English (about a thousand years ago), *riht* meant straight or direct, and hence, right (correct). The English derived the word from the German *recht*. Elsewhere in Europe and parts of Asia, *reg* meant straight or put in order, from the Latin *regere*, to rule.

Rights are not simple, as Thomas Jefferson (1743–1826) understood when he wrote in the Declaration of Independence "that all men are created equal; that they are endowed by their creator with certain unalienable rights, that among these are life, liberty, and the pursuit of happiness; that to secure these rights..." (If you are a careful reader, please note that this quotation is correct. Jefferson wrote *unalienable* though most of us say *inalienable*.)

Jefferson lived fifty years after the Declaration of Independence. Can you imagine what would have happened if he had retained the rights!

Release is a ubiquitous term among writers, particularly in the film, music, and public relations fields. Everyone knows its common meaning. To *release* is to set free or let go; and as a noun it means being set free or the art of letting loose. The origin is simple. The Middle English *relesen* came from the Old French *relaisser*, which evolved from the Latin *relaxares*, to loosen.

From its meaning as a deliverance or authoritative discharge, lawyers use "releases" as agreements, to give up or surrender a claim or a right. Many of us have signed releases (often without reading the "fine print") with publishers and others. Advertisers and public relations people use a *model release* for a professional model or other person to grant permission for the use of his or her name, likeness, or words.

A film, record, book, or other work also is called a "release." When it's just issued (released), it's a *new release*; when it's no longer available, it's *out of release*. A film, book, or other work that is extensively distributed is in a *wide release*.

The *release date* is the date or time at which an article or other item may be published, broadcast, or used. It appears atop or at the end of a news release, usually with the notation, "For Immediate Release" or "For Release."

In the movie business, a print of a film that has been screened and approved for showing is called a *release print*, which is made from a *release negative*.

Release camera informs the camera operator that the

shot has been completed. *Release crew* and *release studio* are commands to stop work or move on.

Context is everything. To a landlord or tenant, a *lease* is a contract and to *re-lease* is to renew the contract (the hyphen is used to distinguish it from *release*).

In music, a "release" is the act or method of ending a tone. Musicians sometimes call a contrasting or transitional section of a song a "release," though a more common word is *bridge*. If you're a singer or musician, you know that a "release" is the third group of eight measures that supplies a connection (bridge) between repetitions of the melody.

A current usage describes the issuance of computer software. The first version of a program is called *release 1.0* and subsequent revisions are numbered 1.1, 1.2, etc. A major revision is called 2.0 and then there are subsequent *release numbers*, 2.1, 2.2, etc.

In public relations, "release" refers to distribution. Thousands of *news releases* are distributed every day to the media. They have not been replaced, though the means of distribution now is via e-mail and fax, as well as postal mail.

There's more, such as "release buttons" on some telephones, to end a call, but I'll release you now, which, of course, is called *release* (or *released*) time.

SHOW BUSINESS:
A PRIMER FOR TYROS

SHOW business is a very broad term that refers to all of the performing arts, including broadcasting, film, and theater, as well as carnivals, circuses, concerts, fairs, nightclubs, and other live entertainment. This chapter features slang terms in *show biz*, including the colorful lexicon of *Variety*, the premier news magazine of TV, Hollywood, and Broadway.

Some of *Variety*'s neologisms (coined words) and abbreviations have become part of our everyday language, such as *B.O.* (box office) and *tunesmith* (a songwriter). Others are what linguists call a "nonce word," coined for a special occasion but generally used only once.

A "portmanteau word," or blend word, is created by fusing two other words, such as *sitcom* (from *sit*uation *com*edy). A "portmanteau" is a suitcase that opens into two compartments. Such linguistic creations are also called "centaur words," after the half-man, half-horse creature of Greek mythology. Now, let's get on with the show.

A *show* can be a play or other performance, as well as a radio or TV program. Performers are called "show folk" or "show people." A "showgirl" is an elaborately costumed woman in the chorus of a musical or variety show. A "showman" is a producer, ideally a possessor of a dramatic flair called "showmanship." A "showstopper" is a part of a scene that receives so much applause that it interrupts the show. A "show town" is a locality where productions are presented; a good show town has a generally favorable audience, a bad show town does not. A "show-wise audience" is sophisticated. To "put" or "get the show on the road" is to send a play or other work on tour or simply to start an activity.

In show business, bigger is often better. Circus shows take place under a *big top*, the main tent of a circus. *Big time* denotes a high level of success. The term originated in the days of vaudeville, when theaters with mass appeal that had three performances a day were called "small time," while elite theaters (like the Palace on Broadway) with only two daily performances were called "big time" and featured big-time performers.

The term *show business* covers a variety of shows. The American Guild of Variety Artists (AGVA) is an AFL-CIO union in New York of circus, nightclub, and other performers.

Vaudeville, or variety shows, was a type of entertainment, popular especially in the first half of the twentieth century and before, that consisted of singers, dancers, comedians, and other performers (*vaudevillians*). The most famous vaudeville producer, Florenz ("Flo") Ziegfeld (1869–1932), pronounced ZIG-feld or ZEEG-feld, produced elaborate musical reviews featuring the glamorous Ziegfeld Girls. The host of a variety show or other program, including the moderator of a seminar or other event, is called the *master of ceremonies*, "MC" or "emcee," for short.

A *cabaret* is a restaurant, café, or nightclub with entertainment, and also the entertainment itself. It's a French word, pronounced cab-uh-RAY (or CAB-uh-ray).

A *carnival* is an amusement show, usually with games and rides, that travels by truck around the country. "Carnie," "carney," and "carny" are slang for "carnival" and also carnival workers. A "carnival" also is a program of festivities, as a "winter sports carnival" and the revelry period before Lent.

Carnivals and circuses often include *sideshows*, which take place in auxiliary areas, sometimes requiring a separate admission charge. "Sideshows" were more common in the mid-nineteenth to early twentieth centuries, when they included dancers, magicians, sword-swallowers, weightlifters, and a variety of people who carnies called "freaks" or "geeks" (often billed as "wild men").

A *circus* is a traveling show with acrobats, clowns, and other performers, including circus elephants and other trained animals. In ancient Rome, a "circus" was an area, usually circular, in which horses and other animals performed. A "three-ring circus" is a big circus with simultaneous performances in each of the three rings (areas). A current use of "circus" is to refer to frenetic activity, such as a *media circus* with its extensive coverage of a person or event.

A *showboat* is a steamboat or other boat with a theater. In the nineteenth and early twentieth centuries, showboats carried troupes of performers up and down the Mississippi and other rivers. Paul Robeson (1898–1976) played Joe in the 1936 film, *Show Boat*.

Let's move from venues (places) to lingo. A *canary* is slang for an unidentified noise during a performance. A *Bronx cheer*, or "raspberry," is a sound of derision, made by expelling air forcefully between the lips. The term probably originated in the early twentieth century in a vaudeville theater in the Bronx, a borough of New York City, when a raucous audience booed an act with this sound.

To *cut the comedy* is to get serious. *Cut to the chase*—now a common expression that means speed it up, get to the point, or move to the action—is based on a film instruction to cut out slow passages and move directly to the chase scene. Let's do that by moving to several media terms that refer to the end, or death.

Death denotes a failure, as with a show that "dies" or is "death at the box office." To "die" is to do poorly, as with a show that dies on the road or a performer who dies standing up. Incidentally, *drop-dead date* is the last day that a writer or other creative person can deliver a manuscript or other material in time to be produced. If you don't deliver by then, "you're dead."

A "flop" is a failure; it's a variant of "flap," which was imitative of the sound of a movement. A "clinker" also is a failure, a mistake, or a sour note (to "hit a clinker"). The Middle English (twelfth- to sixteenth-century) *clinken* imitated the ringing sound when hitting glass or metal. The British sometimes call something admirable or superior a "clinker," probably from the clinking of glasses in a toast; so when a show is called a "clinker," the meaning depends on which side of the Atlantic Ocean ("the pond") you are.

More desirable is *boffo*, a box office hit, a *Variety* coinage that was mentioned in "Comic Relief." *Whammo*, an exclamation to express startling action, is slang for an even bigger hit show. A hit is sometimes called a *click* and, more often, a *socko*. A "sock line" is a punch line or climax of a joke or scene. To "sock it" is to emphasize, or punch up, a part of a script or other item.

Fan mail is such a common term that we sometimes forget its etymology. "Fan" is short for "fanatic," though its modern connotation has softened to mean an ardent devotee (pronounced deh-vo-TEE and spelled with two *e*'s, no accent mark). Most fan letters are requests for autographed pictures. An *autograph* is a person's own signature or handwriting, but many celebrities assign this chore to their assistants. "Autograph" is from the Latin *autographus*, meaning written with one's own hand.

Fanfare in television and theater indicates introductory music. The origin is from the French, *fanfarer*, to blow trumpets, and the current meaning is a loud flourish of trumpets. From this evolved the connotation of a noisy or showy display, like the ones frequently made by ardent and admiring fans.

A *gig* is a job or live performance, particularly by musicians. A *go-see* is an audition; the term is common among fashion models.

A *fake book* is a collection of music used by musicians, compiled illegally (no copyright fees paid) and generally inserted in a folder or binder.

Leerics are song lyrics that are sexually suggestive. It's from *leer*, a sly look. A *crooner* is a singer, usually a man, who softly sings (croons) sentimental songs. Though it may sound like a slang word, the origin goes back to before the sixteenth century, when the Dutch *krōnen* meant groan or lament. A *warbler* is a singer and a *chanteuse*, or "chantoosie," is a female singer, particularly in nightclubs. It's a French word, from *chanter*, to sing.

A *mash-up* (a *mash* is a mixture) is slang for a remix—a song or other music that is made by superimposing all or part of one or more songs or other music over an existing song or music. It's usually illegal and called a "bootleg." "White-label music" is a recording that is made anonymously (without a label or other identification), such as a bootleg recording made as a computer file.

From *mash-up* we go to *mosh pit*, the area in the front rows, particularly at a stadium. "Moshing" is a violent style of dancing ("slam dancing") in front of the stage at a rock music concert. The dancers are "moshers." The origin is *mash*, to crush.

Dancers have many nicknames, including *hoofer* and *terpe* (from Terpsichore, the Greek muse of dance). A *leg lady* is a chorus girl who appears in a "leg show." A *gypsy* is a dancer who is prepared to move quickly to a new show or city, like a Gypsy wanderer.

A performer who is functioning well or employed is "on," the opposite of "off." "On" also means through the use of, or through the medium of—as a performer who is "on stage," "on radio," "on television," but "in film," or a musician who is "on guitar" or another instrument.

A quick check is called an *o-o*, or "once over," as when a stage manager gives the "o-o" to the stage set.

"Over the top" is an exaggerated, unconvincing performance. A performer who overacts or exaggerates is a *ham*. The word may come from the inept actors who desired to play Hamlet, or it may come from the ham fat formerly used by actors to remove makeup.

Payola is money or favors given to disc jockeys and broadcast producers to promote a record or other item, an illegal, common practice especially in the mid-twentieth century. The term also is slang for bribes to legislators, judges, and others. From this evolved *plugola*, a bribe to a broadcaster or other media person to get a free mention (plug) of a movie, product, or other item.

A *roadie* is a person who travels with rock musicians when they are on the road, to handle equipment and run errands (usually paid more than a *gofer*, who does minor errands). A *groupie* is an enthusiastic fan, sometimes a person (usually a young woman) who follows rock music groups or other celebrities, often with the hope of having sexual relations.

A *roast* is a program, usually a dinner at which the guest of honor is the butt of jokes. The roasts at the Friars Club (no apostrophe), a theatrical club on East 55th Street in Manhattan, often are televised, with most of the expletives "blipped" (deleted).

To *scale the house* is to set admission prices for different sections of a theater or other venue. *Stuff* is theatrical slang for a dance number or other specialty. "Do your stuff" is an encouragement said to a performer of a specialty act, such as a juggler.

A *split week* is a week on the road in which a touring performer or group works in more than one place.

In the performing arts and all fields, a *star* is a prominent individual with popular appeal. "Star billing" involves large type ("star letters") used atop an advertisement or playbill. A "star entrance" is the first appearance of a leading performer in a production. A *superstar* is an extremely prominent person, perhaps characterized by a "star complex," an affectation of superiority. A "star maker" is a producer or other person who develops a star performer, for example, starting with a neophyte who has extraordinary charisma or potential, called "star quality." The "star system," as practiced by the film studios several decades ago, favored leading performers. A "star turn" is an act in a variety show performed by a top comedian or other popular performer.

The star symbol has been used for ratings for centuries. In school, a gold star was affixed to a paper to indicate a top grade. Movie reviewers rate films with stars or half-stars. A top rating gets four stars; close to it is three and a half stars. Restaurants are also rated with stars: Four stars denotes extraordinary. In the hotel field, five stars is tops.

A negative review of a book, film, TV program, play, or other work is called a *pan*. The origin probably is from being hit by a frying pan. It's also used as a verb, meaning to criticize severely, as to "pan a play." However, to "pan out" is to turn out well or be successful, probably from the pan used to wash dirt in searching for gold.

Take is the amount of money, the gross receipts, taken in at a sports or other event. It's also called the *gate*, from the gate at sports arenas. "Gate cut" is a percentage of the admission, or gate receipts. A "gate-crasher" is a person who gains admission to a party or other event without paying or being invited.

An *agent* performs services on behalf of clients. In show business, an "agency" arranges for placement in a film, TV program, or other work of an actor, director, or other client and negotiates payment, in return for a commission or other payment. A "literary agent" represents authors. *A&R* is the abbreviation, particularly at music recording companies, of "artists and repertoire," the designation of the person in charge of talent (artists) and the work they perform. Agents often arrange for their clients to go to a *tryout*, an audition. That term also applies to an experimental performance, perhaps in the hope of moving on to full production.

[TIN PAN ALLEY]

*To composers, songwriters (who are called "lyri-
cists"), and publishers,* Tin Pan Alley *is a synonym for the popular music industry and also
any area where music makers gather. It could
be Nashville, Hollywood, or, more likely, the
Times Square area of Manhattan.*

The origin of the phrase was the area below
Times Square where, in the twenties, many
music publishers were located, on 28th Street
between Fifth and Sixth avenues. Some of their
upright pianos had paper behind the steel
strings, resulting in a tinny sound akin to a tin
pan. Earlier in the twentieth century, many
sheet music publishers were located near Union
Square (14th to 17th streets), an area that
housed several vaudeville theaters; but "Tin Pan
Alley" was not used until they moved uptown to
28th Street.

In 1931, an eleven-story brick building was
built near Times Square on the west side of
Broadway near 49th Street. The address was
1619 Broadway and the Brill Building (as it became known, named after one of the eventual
owners, clothier Samuel Brill) was filled with
small offices, many of which were occupied by
music publishers and songwriters. Many song
pluggers (promoters), musicians, performers,
and others in the pop music business hung out
in the building, on the wide sidewalk in front,
and in nearby restaurants. For several decades,
the Brill Building and Tin Pan Alley were synonyms for the music business. A similar neighborhood in London is found on Denmark Street.

The Brill Building still exists, though it's
no longer a music Mecca. The West 49th Street

corner still is the home of Colony Records, a renowned store. Though Tin Pan Alley may never have been an actual alley, its memory lingers on, even for those with a tin ear.

The jargon of Tin Pan Alley is widely used in our general language. For example, a *riff* is a short passage or scene that often is repeated as variations on a theme, in a film, novel, or other work. In music, particularly jazz, a "riff" is a constantly repeated phrase.

The process is *riffing*, in which a musician "riffs" or plays a "riff." A new slang use of "riffing" means to jive, provoke, or pick up the energy level. It probably is an altered version of "refrain," though its origin may be "riffle," as in leafing through a book.

In music, a *bridge* is a connecting passage between two sections of a composition. I'll finish this sidebar appropriately with some bridging "song" expressions.

A *songfest* is an informal gathering of people for singing. A "song-and-dance man" is a leading male performer in a musical show, whereas a *songbird* is a woman singer. A "song and dance" is general slang for an evasive explanation. A cover is a singer who sings a version of a popular song of another singer.

To *work for a song* is to work on the cheap. To *break into song* is to start singing. A *songbook* is a publication with a collection of songs, usually words and music. It's also all the songs of a particular composer or period.

Variety, the show biz weekly, and *Daily Variety*, published in Los Angeles, delight in using abbreviations, shortened forms, colorful synonyms, and coined words, especially in their headlines. For example, *affil* for a network-affiliated station, *anni* for anniversary, *aud* for audience, *indie* for independent, *Chi* for Chicago, *Cincy* for Cincinnati, and *Gotham* for New York City.

Many *Variety* words end with *x*, such as *crix* (critics), *pix* (pictures or movies), and *tix* (tickets, also called "ducats"). One of *Variety*'s most quoted headlines reads, "Sticks Nix Hick Pix," meaning that rural audiences were not interested in films about rural life. The writer showed restraint, as it could have been "Stix Nix Hix Pix," and is often quoted that way.

A *web* is *Variety* lingo for a broadcast network, including the "Alphabetical web" (ABC), "Eye web" (CBS), and "Peacock net" (NBC).

Variety claims that it was first to use such now-common terms as "sex appeal," "deejay" (from *disc* and *jockey*), and "flack" (a publicist, also called a "praiser").

Starting in 1951, *Variety* used *blockbuster* to describe a film that has an enormous budget and/or is an enormous success. The term now is in general use to refer to something that is extraordinarily effective or notable. The origin is from the Second World War, when a "blockbuster" was a bomb capable of destroying a city block.

In the film business, the term *blockbuster* was used before 1948 to describe a film that was so attractive that it was booked individually into theaters and not as part of a block (group) of films. This illegal practice ended in 1948 when a court decision forced the separation of film production and exhibition by the same company.

[*VARIETY* LINGO SAMPLER]

- *ankle*: to leave or quit

- *cleffer*: a songwriter (from "clef," the symbol written at the beginning of sheet music to indicate the pitch or key)

- *glitterati*: celebrities in publishing and other literary fields

- *helmer*: a director (from "helmsman," one who steers a ship)

- *ink*: to sign a contract

- *keys*: slang for major, or key, cities

- *lenser*: a photographer or cinematographer

- *mitting*: applause; "heavy mitting" is strong applause. (A "mitt" is a glove and slang for a hand.)

- *nut*: the operating expenses of a theater or other company that are to be recovered

- *p.a.*: a personal appearance

- *pic*: a picture or movie

- *preem*: a premiere

- *shutter*: to close a show

- *sked*: a schedule

- *skein* (pronounced SKANE): a television program series (from a "skein" of yarn, a quantity wound around a coil)

- *solon*: an authority or pseudo-authority (from Solon, a Greek statesman and one of the framers of the democratic laws of Athens in the sixth century, B.C.E.)

- *tentpole*: a success

- *tyro*: a beginner; such as a "tyro scribe," a new writer (from the Latin word meaning recruit)

Variety avoids some words, such as *money,* which it prefers to call "coin," but has a variety of synonyms for a "week," or similar short periods of time, including "canto," "frame," "go-round," "inning," "lap," "romp," "round," "sesh," "sessions," "stanza," "stint," "turn," and "whirl." I guess *Variety* considers "week" a weak word!

One of the most common words in show business is *up*, used in many expressions to indicate greater intensity (as in "turn up the sound") or excitement (as a performer who is "up"). In contrast, a performer who falters or forgets lines is said to *be up* or *go up*. It's all in the context. To be "up for a part" is to be considered for a role. Common directives also are "bring up the lights" and "up the music."

"When the fat lady sings" means "the end," supposedly in answer to a child's question at an opera, "When will it be over?"

SPORTS: A MEDIA GRAND SLAM

SPORTSWRITERS (note: one word) and sports broadcasters (called *sportscasters*) are renowned for their extensive use of jargon, coined words, and colorful language, so much so that many have been dubbed "colorcasters" (borrowed from "colorcast," to broadcast in color).

Many sports terms have spilled over into our everyday language, and are used in speeches and news stories, particularly about elections and other contests. During major sports events, such as the Olympics, World Series, and Super Bowl, athletes and nonathletes, fans and nonfans alike, read and hear the slang of sports, essential today to understanding more than just athletic competitions.

Examples of widely used sports media slang include "grand slam," "hat trick," "Hail Mary," "slam dunk," and "sudden death." If you know their meaning and origins, you'll be prepared to follow more than just sports plays.

Let's start with one of the most commonly heard terms, *jock*. We have *computer jocks* and *science jocks*, who are enthusiasts in their respective areas. *Jock*, slang for a male athlete, is also often used pejoratively to connote a nonintellectual. The word has nothing to do with disc or horse jockeys. It's short for *jockstrap*, an elastic belt worn by men while engaging in athletics that has a pouch to support the genitals. It's also called an "athletic supporter." Oh, "jock" also is slang for penis.

The basketball version of success is a *slam dunk*, a shot in which the ball is pushed (dunked) through the basket, scoring a *field goal* for two points. Business people and others refer to "slam dunk" as a foregone conclusion or certainty, or to defeat or dismiss decisively.

Another synonym for success is *grand slam*. In baseball, a *home run* (a smash hit beyond the playing field usually into a spectator section) made when there are runners on all three bases results in the maximum score for a single play, or four *runs*, and is called a *grand slam*. The term "grand slam" is also used in bridge (the card game) and other sports. The four major professional tournaments in golf and tennis also are called the *Grand Slam*. A player who wins each one of the grand-slam events in succession achieves a "grand slam."

The football player who successfully completes a *Hail Mary* also is greeted with cheers. Usually made in desperation in the last seconds of a game, a Hail Mary is a long pass to potential receivers in the *end zone* (the rectangular area behind the goal line where touchdowns are scored). The chances of the ball being caught may be enhanced with prayer. The term comes from the first words of the "Ave Maria" (the Latin prayer to the Virgin Mary), which are "Hail, Mary." If the prayer is unsuccessful, and the Hail Mary falls to the ground, the game may end in a tie and then go into an additional period, called *sudden death*, because it ends the moment one team or participant scores. The term "sudden death" is also used in connection with elections and other nonsports contests.

During the 1991 Gulf War, a risky military offensive that involved a flanking (side) maneuver was called a "Hail Mary" by General H. Norman Schwartzkopf (b. 1934). In the military, to "flank" is to protect the side of a unit. In football, a "flanker" is an offensive player who runs from a position closer to the sideline than the rest of the team.

Go-to is used in football and other sports to indicate a player who is relied upon to make important plays. In general use, a "go-to guy" (or other person) is someone who can be relied upon to get the job done, particularly in a clutch, or critical situation, as one relies on a *clutch player* (a "clutch hitter," "clutch pitcher," or "clutch runner"). *Clutch*, meaning emergency, also is a common word outside of sports.

As our "national sport," baseball probably lends its jargon more than any other sport to commonly used non-sports contexts. "Pitch" and "catch" have many meanings among writers. Before I review them, may I note that to *get to first base* means "to accomplish the first step in an undertaking," and is often used to refer to how far the male gets in a romantic or sexual encounter. (You're on your own in getting to second or third base.) To *score* (or *hit*) *a home run* is to be successful or go all the way (sexually or otherwise).

Pitch is a common verb (to throw) and "pitcher" a common noun in several sports, particularly baseball. Among salespeople, writers, and publicists, a "pitch" means the process of suggesting or proposing an article, interview, or idea. To *make a pitch* is to present a proposal, especially in a pressured or fast-talking manner. To *make a pitch for* is to promote, usually by speaking in favor of a person or a project. A *pitchman* is a high-pressure salesperson or advertiser, particularly a person who sells novelties from a sidewalk stand or carnival booth.

Positive connotations include *in there pitching* (working hard and enthusiastically) and to *pitch in* (to set to work energetically). However, *pitch into* connotes to attack someone verbally or physically. A *pitched battle* is one closely fought with great intensity, where the line of combat is relatively fixed (settled) before the action.

In printing, "pitch" is the horizontal spacing of characters. "Fixed-pitch" is equal spacing between characters; "proportional-pitch" is varied spacing. *Pitch-black*, or "pitch-dark," is extremely dark, as in pitch or tar.

The etymology of "pitch," meaning a throw, is from the Middle English *picchen*, to pick; whereas the origin of "pitch," meaning the sticky substance, is from the Middle English *pich*, fat.

In music, "pitch" is an element of a tone or sound that is determined by the frequency of the sound waves. The greater the frequency, the higher the pitch. A "high-pitched" story or other work shows intense feeling that can be shrill (from music) or lofty (from sports). Or it could be a high-pitched (steep) slope or roof.

Here are a few catchy terms used in the media. Watch out for *catch*. It can mean attractive (a "catchy design") or easily remembered (a "catchy tune"), but also tricky or deceptive (a "catchy question"). A *catchword* is an often-repeated word. A *catchphrase* is a slogan, or other often-repeated phrase, used to catch or attract attention.

To an editor, a catchword is a *guide word* at the top of a page, column, or section that labels or indicates the subject. "Catchwords" were used for the first time in the fifteenth century in a book about ancient Rome, published in Venice, Italy; they were also called *custodes.*

When used as a guideline (also called a *slug* or *slugline*, from the days of lead type), the "catchword" or "catchline" (a mark, symbol, or other identifier) is used in proofing copy but not retained in the final printing.

Many years ago, mass-appeal newspapers sold for one cent a copy and were called *penny papers*. A *catchpenny article* had a headline or introduction designed to attract (catch) attention. (Incidentally, a *penny dreadful* was an inexpensive paperback novel, popular in England in the nineteenth century, usually featuring crime, adventure, or violence. The U.S. equivalent was a *dime novel*.)

Returning to catchwords, in the theater, the facial or body movement by a secondary performer to distract attention from the primary actor, as by pretending to catch a fly (the insect), is called *catchflies*. In photography, a lamp placed near the camera to produce a glint (reflect or catch the light) is called a *catchlight*.

In the forties, Red Barber used so many southern expressions in his broadcasts of Brooklyn Dodgers baseball games that they became his trademark. A *rhubarb* was a fight or heated discussion, a reference to the acidic plant, whose etymological root is from the Latin *barbarum*, a barbarian. To prove that I am also a scholar and not just a jock, the full name of Red Barber is Walter Lanier Barber (1908–92).

From baseball media jargon, success is a *home run* (or "four-bagger"), *triple*, (or "three-bagger"), *extra-base hit, base hit, line drive, no-hitter*, or a *perfect game* (better than a no-hitter, in which no batter reaches first base). Failure (though not for the pitcher) is a *strikeout* or *shutout* (for the scoreless team).

At bat or *come to bat* means taking one's turn, whereas to *go to bat* is to support. *Off the bat* is immediately, as in "right off the bat." To *bat a thousand* is a perfect batting average on and off the baseball field. To *bat five hundred* is great for a batter but only halfway successful for others.

In baseball, *hit-and-run* describes a player who runs from a base while the pitch is thrown and the batter then attempts to hit the ball. It also describes a motor accident in which the offending driver does not stop, or, more generally, something done for specific, quick action or results.

Pitchers warm up (prepare) in an area near the playing field called the *bullpen*, a reference to the fenced enclosure for confining male cattle. The *relief pitchers* (who relieve or replace whoever is currently pitching) as a group also collectively are called the "bullpen." In other sports, such as basketball, the backup players are collectively called the "bench."

A replacement in a contest can be called a *relief pitcher* and the imagery is clear. Similarly, you can participate in such things as *extra innings* (more than the regular time), *fair ball* (proper play), *foul ball* (improper play), *hitting streak* (continuing success), *pinch hitter* (substitute), and *seventh inning stretch* (a pause).

Hardball, the small ball used in professional and other baseball games, has taken on a new meaning in business, politics, and other fields to denote aggressive or ruthless behavior. To *play hardball* is to engage in this type of highly competitive activity. *Softball*, in contrast, is a larger ball that is played with underhand pitchings (instead of overhand) and on a smaller field.

If you are in the *big leagues* (and a "big leaguer"), you are working at the highest level in your field. The *major leagues* (also a symbol of success) in professional baseball are the American League and the National League. You're demoted when you are banished or moved to the *minor leagues*. It's a promotion when you are moved up from a *farm club* in a "farm system" that trains players at a minor-league team affiliated with a major-league team. It's akin to cultivating plants or raising animals.

The *Little League* is an organization of baseball teams with children under the age of twelve, so it's not a compliment if an adult is called a *little leaguer*. A *bush league* is a minor league of baseball or other professional sports. A "bush" is a low shrub with many branches. A *bushleaguer* is an unsophisticated or second-rate person. A "bush-league" advertising campaign or other program is inferior or unprofessional.

Batting average is the average level of competence for a person in any field. Fans know the *lifetime batting average* of hitters and *earned run average* of pitchers.

Well, here we are at the *bottom of the ninth* (last half of the last inning) and I haven't hit the ball *out of the ballpark*. I've had a wonderful run, and I think that what I've written is *in the ballpark* (fairly accurate).

The *home stretch* (not the same as the pause for the *seventh inning stretch* in baseball) is the final part of an undertaking. It's the last chance for the home team to make up for a deficit in the score. To a horseplayer, it's the part of the racetrack between the last turn and the finish line. That's when you know if you've got authoritative information (*from the horse's mouth*) or if you've backed the wrong horse. Hold your horses. I'll stop horsing around.

A *walk-off* hit is bad news for the pitcher. It's a home run or a hit that scores a runner in the bottom of the ninth, or subsequent inning, and causes the pitcher to disgustedly walk off the mound. Ironically, in general use, to "walk-off" is to win easily or unexpectedly. A "walk-off victory" is an easy win. It's also called a "walkaway," though not as successful as a runaway success. In theater, a *walk-on* is a minor part, usually without dialogue.

Baseball is a global sport, played everywhere, while the bat-and-ball game of cricket remains quintessentially British, certainly a favorite in many British Commonwealth countries around the world; ironically, the etymology is from the Old French, *criquet*, a stake or bat.

Americans who are only vaguely familiar with the sport know that cricket connotes "fair play" or "sportsmanship." As the British say, "cricket as it should be played." We tend to use the term "that's not cricket" to mean a thing that's not fair.

At each end of the cricket *pitch* (pitching and batting area) sits a *wicket* (the rhyming is coincidental), which consists of three vertical sticks (stumps). The origin is from the resemblance of the "wicket" to a gate. The small window in a theatrical box office (especially in the United Kingdom) sometimes is called a "wicket."

The cricket field, including the stumps, also is called a "wicket." When it's damp and slow and hard to play, it's called a *sticky wicket*, which has become slang for a difficult or awkward situation.

A beaut of a term, whose origin is from cricket and which has moved beyond athletics, is *hat trick*. A cricket player who made three successive scores (called *wickets*) was rewarded with a new hat, hence a "hat trick." No kidding. In the United States, the term is commonly used by hockey writers and broadcasters, though many sports fans get it wrong. An avid sports fan told me that it means a fabulous feat, akin to pulling a rabbit out of a hat.

"Hat trick" is now used in other sports, such as the winning of three races in a day by a jockey, or the scoring of three goals in a game (not necessarily in succession) by a hockey, lacrosse, or soccer player. Another alleged origin is from the securing of a spectator's seat in the British House of Commons by placing a hat on it, but I'll stick with the cricket origin. The term has come to be a synonym for any remarkable feat, such as to "pull off a hat trick" by writing three successive best-selling books.

The two British-derived games most popular in the United States are golf and soccer. Let's *tee off* (also a synonym for to "start") with some golf words.

Golf is a Scottish verb (originally *gowf)* that means to strike. *Links* sometimes is used as a synonym for a golf course. The word is appropriately from the Old English *hlinc*, or slope. In Scotland, a stretch of rolling, sandy land, particularly along a seashore, is called "links." Thus, "links" is a golf course constructed on land alongside or reclaimed from the sea.

I assume that you are familiar with the small, pointed holder or *tee* on which a golf ball is positioned for a *tee shot*, the first stroke at the start of each section (*hole*) of the course. *Tee* comes from the Scottish *teaz*, for the small mound of sand on which a golf ball was placed.

The "tee" also is the small holder on which a football is placed for a kickoff and a tall adjustable holder to position in front of a ball hitter in the game of T-ball. If you're not familiar with T-ball, ask a child; it's a baseball game played by children in which the ball is not pitched to the batter.

Outside of sports, to *tee off,* in addition to the obvious meaning, to start, also means to make angry or disgusted, the common experience of a *duffer* (a relatively unskilled golfer). Incidentally, a "tee shirt" (or, more commonly, "T-shirt") probably got its name because it's shaped like the letter T when its short sleeves are spread out.

I hope that you are not teed off by all of these *t*'s, and let's move on to another word that is common on and off the golf course. You don't have to be a sports buff to know that *par* is the score (number of strokes) that has been set as standard for each of the eighteen holes of a golf course. If seventy-two strokes is "par for a course," then a golfer with a score of seventy-one is one "under par." By extension, *par for the course* means any outcome that is expected or normal—and, ironically, has come to suggest underachieving, rather than surpassing the norm.

Par, a Latin and French word that means equal, also commonly refers to an accepted or common standard, as in bridge (the card game). In business, *par value* is the amount of a check, note, stock, or bond at the time it is issued (also called the "face value").

A *duffer* is a mediocre golfer or an incompetent, clumsy person. The origin may be from *duff*, which in the eighteenth century was something worthless, and a *duffer* was a peddler, particularly of worthless items.

Putter is a common word on and off the golf course. To a golfer, a "putter" is a club used to lightly hit the ball when it lies on the *putting green*, the closely mowed grassy area surrounding the hole. A "putter" also is a golfer who putts.

Off the course, a *putter* has quite a different meaning, to proceed in an aimless, ineffective way. It is common to *putter around* the house on our days off, tidying up in a leisurely, haphazard manner. A "putterer" is a dawdler. The origin of "putter" is from the Old English *potian*, to push.

Returning to the golf course, the mown area between the tee and the putting green is the *fairway*. It's the longest part of the course and the word sometimes is used in other contexts, such as the middle of a navigable channel in a river or harbor. Bordering the fairway is the *rough*, the area with uncut grass, trees, or other conditions that present a hazard or obstacle to the golfer.

A *chip shot* is a short drive that is lofted (chipped) into the air. Do not call it a *chippy* or *chippie*, slang for a chipmunk or a prostitute. Incidentally, golf articles in newspapers sometimes have an end section of short items, titled *chip shots*.

A *mulligan* is an extra stroke, allowed after a poor

shot and not counted on the scorecard. President Bill Clinton (b. 1946) was known for his use of mulligans. Lexicographers cannot identify the first player, probably named Mulligan, who did this, though the term goes back to about 1949. In a general sense, "mulligan" means an extra chance.

Soccer fans know that their game is not the same as American or Canadian football, though it's called "football" in England, Brazil, and other countries where it's the number one sport. The game *soccer* has become so popular here that our language now includes *soccer mom* (and *dad*), a parent (mostly in suburban towns) who transports and caters to children who play on soccer teams. The *soc* in the name is from the second syllable of Association Football.

In American football, an illegal block, which is hitting from behind an opponent who is not carrying the ball, is called *clipping*. An article that is cut out of a newspaper or other publication also is called a "clipping"; outside of the United States it's called a *cutting*.

A *bureau* is a branch office, such as the media bureaus in Washington D.C. The first clipping services (trained readers of publications) were called *bureaus*. The term persists though the companies (the largest is BurrellesLuce) try to avoid this old-fashioned label.

A "clip" also is a segment of a film or tape. Other *clip* terms that are common in the media are *clip a cue* (to cut in on another performer's line), *clip art* (previously existing drawings that are cut out for use in a publication), *clipboard* (a hard surface with a spring clip that holds paper), and *clipped word* (a shortened word, such as *ad* for advertisement).

A *pit stop* is a pause in a trip for rest or using the toilet. It's from the stop of a racing car in a recessed or adjacent area (a pit) for refueling and repair.

Now that we've covered or *touched all the bases* of sports-related media lingo, let's go on with the show.

THEATER: GEORGE SPELVIN WAS IN THE WINGS

"ALL the world's a stage, And all the men and women merely players," wrote William Shakespeare (1564–1616) in *As You Like It*. These oft-quoted lines should make an apt introduction to a discussion of theatrical language, particularly since many U.S. terms are derived from the British "theatre" (as the Brits spell it). "Theater" sometimes is mispronounced, for comic effect, as thee-AY-ter.

"Theatrical" obviously means having to do with the theater, sometimes referring to a performance that is overly dramatic or histrionic. To "theatricalize" is to make theatrical. *Legitimate theater* relates to serious drama, and not musicals or revues. *Theatricals* are performances of stage plays, particularly by amateurs. "Theatrics" are done or said for dramatic or histrionic effect.

A *thespian* is a performer, from Thespis, a Greek poet, playwright, actor, and an originator of the tragedy form of drama in the sixth century B.C.E. "Thespian" often is used to describe an overly dramatic or pretentious performer.

Theaterland is the theatrical district in a city, such as Broadway in New York, or the world of theatrical people in general. To be "on the stage" is to work in the theatrical field.

To "make it on Broadway" is to be a theatrical success, though, of course, one can be successful in theater elsewhere. *Off-Broadway* refers to theatrical activity, often experimental and low-budget, performed in theaters other than those in the Broadway–Times Square area of Manhattan. *Off-off-Broadway* refers to theater further removed from the mainstream, as with an avant-garde (from the French *vanguard*) production. An older name for a theatrical district is "Rialto," originally an island in Venice,

Italy, which had a major market. In London, the theatrical district is called the "West End," a fashionable residential section in which several theaters are located.

More than one thousand *regional theaters* are located throughout the United States, headed by their own directors, often mounting original plays that are increasingly important to the cultural scene. A *resident theater* has its own staff of performers (a "resident company").

Company, a group of performers, is a common term in theater, as "company crew" (backstage and other nonperforming workers), "company manager" (the business and administrative supervisor), "road company" (a troupe that travels on the road), and "stock company" (a group that regularly works together, as at one theater). The origin of "road show" is from railroad, though today the group usually travels by bus or plane. A "company call" is a gathering or rehearsal.

A *rehearsal* is a practice performance of a play or other work. A work being rehearsed is "in rehearsal." A "dry run," "stagger-through," or "walk-through" is an early rehearsal of a play or other work. An "open rehearsal" is viewed by an audience, especially a concert rehearsal. A "tech rehearsal" coordinates lighting, sound, scenery, and other technical features with the acting.

The *stage*, where the acting takes place, also is another word for the theatrical field in general. *Boards* is an old word for a theater stage. To "tread the boards" is to appear on stage.

Stagecraft is skill in, or the art of, writing or staging plays or theatrical works. A "stage effect" is an effect or impression, created on the stage, as by lighting, scenery, or sound.

Stage directions, generally phrases typed in parentheses, are script notations about movements of the performers. "Stage left" (abbreviated SL) means to a performer's left facing the audience; and "stage right" (SR), to the performer's right. In film, "camera left" and "camera right" mean the opposite, given from the viewpoint of the camera or audience. "Stage center" (C) is the center of the acting area. "Entrance" is a stage direction in a script (E or Ent) indicating the point at which a performer first appears or the place from which the performer enters. EL means "entrance left" and ER, "entrance right." *Entrance cue* is the dialogue line or action that signals a performer to enter (come on stage). The position sometimes is illuminated by an "entrance light." The performer's first words are an "entrance line," sometimes greeted by an "entrance round" of applause.

Performers conduct actions, called *stage business*, supported by *stagehands* who work backstage to set up scenery and props, according to a "staging plan"—a floor plan of the sets and activities to be used in a performance. A "stage whisper" is intended only for the audience, and not to be heard by the other characters. "Stage fright" is nervousness experienced by a speaker or performer. To be "stage-struck" is to have an intense desire to be associated with the theater, particularly as a performer. To "give stage" is for one performer to help the audience focus on another performer.

Stage door is a door on the outside of a theater or other building leading to the backstage area, used by the cast and crew. A "stage-door Johnnie" is a man who waits outside the stage door to greet or court a female performer. The guardian of the stage door is often referred to as "Pop."

Stage fall is a performer's drop to the floor, done in such a way as to appear realistic but avoid injury.

The *stage manager* is a principal assistant to the director of a play or other theatrical production. The "assistant stage manager" assists the stage manager and also may be the prompter.

Stage wait is a period of time in which a performer is onstage, waiting to perform, as when scenery is being changed or there is a planned or unplanned delay.

The front of the stage usually has one or more curtains to conceal it from the audience before the play and to indicate the end of a scene or act (an "act curtain"). Most plays have two or three *acts*, or divisions, each separated by an intermission. You know, of course, that a person who plays a role or performs is an *actor* (man or woman) or *actress* (woman). To "act all over the place" is to overact or exaggerate a role.

Theater curtains include an *asbestos curtain* (also called a "safety curtain"), a flameproof curtain at the front of a stage, now made of materials other than asbestos; and a *scrim*, a gauze curtain used to create various lighting effects, either at the front of the stage at the beginning of a scene or in other places at other times. The stage manager's warning that an act is about to begin is, "Curtain going up!" The command to lower the curtain is, "Curtain down!" A "fast" or "quick curtain" is lowered or closed quickly. To "make the curtain," a performer or stagehand walks behind the curtain to ensure proper closure.

Curtain call is applause or other reaction from an audience that summons performers to return for acknowledgment at the end of the performance, generally to appear in front of the curtain, as well as the return of performers to receive such applause. A *curtain line* is the last line of dialogue before the curtain falls. A dramatic curtain line is called a "strong curtain"; an ineffective one, a "weak curtain." A *curtain raiser* is a short play or other performance presented before a principal production. In the nineteenth and twentieth centuries, "curtain raisers" were presented while latecomers arrived, before the curtain was raised on the major attraction. A *curtain speech* is not part of a performance, given by a performer or other individual associated with the production. *Curtain time* is the time that a performance begins.

A *runner* is a pair of curtains that move (run) horizontally and meet at the center of the stage. It's also a strip of carpet near the stage so that the footsteps of performers are not heard. And, of course, a "runner" is an assistant in theater, film, and other fields who does errands.

House is an ambiguous term. It can be a theater or other building or the audience itself. *House equipment* belongs to the establishment, such as the theater owner, rather than to the troupe or customer. *House lights* illuminate the audience section. Lighting cues include "house to half" (dim house lighting halfway) and "house out" (darkness). The command to the operator of the house lights sometimes is simply, "House!" indicating a change, such as "house up" (turn on the lights) or "house down" (turn off the lights). The staff includes a "house electrician," "house carpenter," and "house doctor."

Front of the house (FOH) denotes the lobby, box office, and manager's office of a theater, though it sometimes refers to the entire theater in front of the stage. "Front-of-the-house calls" are announcements made by the stage manager or FOH staff, such as informing the audience in the lobby when the performance will begin or requesting the audience to turn off their cell phones. In a hotel, the lobby and registration desk ("front desk") is called "front of the house." A common practice was for a desk clerk to summon a luggage carrier by ringing a bell and calling, "Front!" Now you know why the attendant is called a "bellboy" or "bellhop."

A *full house* means that all seats are occupied—preferably as a "sold-out house" (all tickets to a performance were sold), rather than a "papered house" (numerous free tickets, called *paper*, were given out). *House count* is the attendance figure for a specific performance. Related terms include "good house," "poor house," "next house" (the next performance), and "dark house" (unoccupied).

The producer's goal is for a sold-out house with *Standing Room Only* (SRO), meaning additional room only for standees in the rear of the theater. "Wrapping" is slang for successful daily sales. At the other extreme, a struggling or failing show may call for the selling of *twofers*, in which the purchaser buys two tickets and pays for only one—buy one, get one free.

"Two weeks under, one week out" is slang for a clause in a theatrical contract that gives the theater owner or an employer the right to terminate a show that dips below a specified revenue level during a two-week period, by giving one week's notice.

House seats are theater tickets reserved at each performance, for sale or free distribution by the producer or those associated with the producer. The general procedure is that the house seats are held until 6 p.m. of the day preceding the performance. If the holder of the house seats does not call for them by that time, the tickets then are released and for sale.

A *rush ticket* is a general-admission ticket for an unreserved seat, placed on sale on the day of the show or event. The term is used in Canada, the United Kingdom, and elsewhere. An "Annie Oakley" is a pass or free ticket punched with one or more holes to indicate that it cannot be purchased or exchanged for a refund. The term comes from the pseudonym of Phoebe Ann Mozee Butler (1860–1926), a woman renowned for her shooting skills. An "Oakley holder" is a person with a "comp" (complimentary) or free ticket. A *comp list* is a list of people who are "comped."

First night is the official opening night performance, usually preceded by previews. The "first-night list," or "A-list," is a record of the critics, backers, and others invited to attend the opening night, distinguished from the "second-night list" ("B-list") and "third-night list" ("C-list"). A-list critics (on daily newspapers, major weeklies, and TV stations) sometimes attend before opening night, to have a review ready to print or broadcast on opening day or the morning after. An *aisle seat* (the seat adjacent to the aisle) is occupied by an "aisle-sitter," sometimes a critic, who can make a quick exit to write a review.

In conventional theaters, the "apron" of the stage (the part between the front curtain and the orchestra) is called the *proscenium* (pronounced pro-SEE-nee-um, *not* pro-SEN-ee-um), and it juts out into the audience area. In contrast, in an "arena theater," the central stage is surrounded by the audience. In "theater-in-the-round," the audience sits on three sides of, or all around, the stage.

The *parquet*, the main floor of a theater, is generally called the *orchestra*. Sometimes, however, the "parquet" is that portion of the orchestra not overhung by balconies; and the separation between the parquet (the front of the orchestra, also called "orchestra circle") and the "parquet circle" (the rear part, under the balconies) is marked by a "parquet rail." *Parquet* is French for a small enclosed section, and is pronounced par-KAY.

The *orchestra pit*, also called the "pit," is the space in front of and below the stage where the orchestra musicians sit. The orchestra leader is the "conductor." The "orchestra rail" separates the pit from the audience.

The *balcony* is an upper floor in a theater or auditorium. If there is more than one floor, the first upper floor often is called the "mezzanine," the second upper floor, the "first balcony," and the third upper floor, the "second balcony." In British theaters and American opera houses and concert halls, the first upper floor is called the "dress circle," the next tier of seats, the "upper circle," the next tier after that, the balcony, and the final or top tier, the "gallery," sometimes dubbed the "peanut gallery." (The origin is not how the spectators looked from the stage—as small as peanuts—but rather that the audience in the cheapest seats often snacked on peanuts.) To "play to the balcony" (or "gallery") is to overact or seek applause by catering to the audience in the cheaper seats.

The *marquee* (pronounced mar-KEY) is a rooflike structure projecting over an entrance to a theater or other building, with the name of the theater, the title of the play, and other credits prominently displayed on it. A star performer receives "marquee billing" and has "marquee value." The *box office* is a small room where tickets are sold, and also denotes the power of a performer to attract an audience (an actor "has box office").

Dressing rooms are backstage rooms in which performers prepare by putting on costumes (dressing) and makeup. Other "dress" terms include "dress off," a direction to a performer to take a position in relation to a person or object, such as "dress off the chair," meaning to sit on it. "Dress stage" is a direction to a performer to move slightly, perhaps to balance the stage, and should not be confused with "dress a stage," which means to arrange the furnishings and props. "Dressing the house" is seating of a small audience throughout a theater (the house) instead of all in front, to give the impression of a larger number.

A *dress parade* is a lineup of performers for review of their costumes. A *dress rehearsal* is the final rehearsal. A "dresser" is an assistant to the wardrobe chief or a personal assistant to a performer.

Scenery includes "drops" (painted curtains at the rear of a stage) and "flats" (smooth, upright pieces). A "stage flat," or "set flat," is thin, with a two-dimensional (flat) appearance. "Chew the scenery" is to overact. Critics sometimes call an overly dramatic performer a "scenery chewer." *Load in* is the setting up of the scenery and other items on the stage. *Dead* refers to scenery or equipment in storage or not needed, as well as electrical equipment that is inoperative.

[SETS]

Which word has more pages devoted to it than any other in the Oxford English Dictionary? *About two dozen pages are devoted to the word* set *as a verb, noun, and adjective including dozens of common phrases, such as "set about," "set against," "set aside," "set forth," "set off," "set out," "set to," "set up," and "set upon." A "set phrase" is a metaphor or other phrase that is commonly understood in a nonliteral way, such as "raining cats and dogs."*

Set also is a common word in theater, film, photography, printing, television, and other media. Are you set? Let's start with a *set* as a location in a theatrical, film, TV, or other production. A *set designer* or *set decorator* creates the décor of a play, movie, or show; a *set dresser* constructs and decorates it with *set dressing*—props, furnishings, and related items.

Editors refer to interviews or photography made during filming as *on set*. The *set day* is the day scheduled to erect a set in a film or TV studio. It's also called "build day" or "setup day."

Set light is separate illumination of a stage set or studio set as a whole or in part, other than that provided by the lights on the performers. *Set list* is the series of music pieces a band plays during a performance.

Set piece is stage scenery that suggests the environment of the scene, such as a "street set piece" or "garden set piece." In general, a *set piece* refers to something that has been carefully planned or composed, so it has several connotations in various media. It can be a self-contained part of a play, film, novel, or piece of music that is arranged to achieve a specific effect, such as a "comic set piece."

Set the scene is an instruction to provide an introduction or background, particularly to a play. It's also called "set the stage." *Set-and-light* is a director's instruction to a film or TV crew to prepare for shooting.

Setup is a delightful word that has multiple uses. In film and TV, it's a single camera and lighting position, in front of which action takes place. In general, it's a configuration for a presentation, photography, filming, painting, or other work. To *set up* is to arrange the scenery and props or to assemble, as in the erection of a display or exhibit. A *set-up drawing* is the assembly plan to be executed by *set-up personnel*. In show business, a *setup* is dialogue or a plot arranged in anticipation of a climax, such as a "setup situation" or a "setup line" that precedes the "punch line" of a joke.

I hope that I am setting you straight and you are in the right mindset. Politicians and other speakers give *set speeches*, which are carefully prepared and delivered frequently on the same or a similar subject. In music, to "set" is to write or fit, as in "set words to music" or "set music to words."

Let's return to *set a scene*, which is to identify a situation or place in a play, film, or other work, by means of a view, scenery, or other description. To *be set in* is to be in a specific place, time, or situation, as in a novel "set in the Victorian era" or a film "set in Japan."

A common definition of "set" is a collection. In media slang, it's often also used to refer to a group of people with common interests or occupations, such as the *literary set* or the *artsy set*.

A *scène à faire* is an obligatory scene. The French phrase means scene to be made. It is also called a *plot scene*, a scene generally late in a play that is expected by the audience, so that the playwright is obliged to write it. *Scene in one* is a short scene played in the extreme front area ("one") of the stage, in front of a curtain, generally while the scenery behind the curtain is being set.

The *flies* are the areas directly over a stage containing the overhead lights and other equipment, housed or operated on a "fly floor" (above the stage), "fly gallery," or "fly platform." The *catwalk* is a narrow, elevated walkway or platform that is suspended overhead to provide access to the flies. A "catwalk," or "runway," also is a narrow, elevated platform or aisle that is used for fashion shows and other purposes.

A *gobo* means a black flag, screen, piece of cardboard, or other material, generally mounted on a tripod, used to block light or cast shadows. In film, a "gobo" is a hole cut out of a flat or other scenery through which a camera shoots the scene. In the theater, a shape or pattern, called a "gobo pattern," sometimes is inserted in the gate of a spotlight to project an image of the pattern on a curtain, wall, or other surface on the stage. The alleged origins are vaudeville slang for playing a scene in the dark or from "go-between." Another possible origin is from an early era of the film industry when the director of photography would shout, "Go black out!" to indicate that daylight is to be excluded from a set. The plural is *gobos* or *goboes*.

The *wings* are the sides of a stage not visible to the audience. A performer "waits in the wings" before going onstage. To "wing it" is to improvise one's lines, or to improvise in general.

A *cyclorama* is a curved seamless backdrop (painted curtain) to give the illusion of sky or space, common in film and television.

Many of the theatrical job titles are obvious, such as "producer" (assisted by investors, called "angels"), "director," and "writer" (playwright). A "play doctor" revises a play or other work, particularly one that is ailing. (A comparable role is performed in publishing by a "book doctor.") "Actor proof" refers to a script that is extremely likely to be successful, regardless of any ineptness by the performers. "Act well" is a play or show that is relatively easy to perform.

"Author, author!" is a call from the audience on opening night of a play for the playwright to take a curtain call.

In a musical, the *composer* writes the music (the score) and the *librettist*, or *lyricist*, writes the text (the lyrics). "Libretto book," or "libretto," comes from Italian meaning small book.

"Book" also is short for *promptbook*, the text that is held by a "prompter," who is "on the book" (follows the script). In rehearsals, a performer who is "on book" still needs the script to recite his or her lines; a performer who is "off book" no longer needs the script.

A "cattle call" is an audition for minor roles, for which a large number of applicants is likely. "Come back Tuesday" is a polite rejection to an applicant. "Cough and spit" is slang for a brief part. A "bit part" (or "bit role"), played in theater and film by a "bit player," refers to a minor part or a set character type.

Here are a few names that sometimes are listed in theater programs (*playbills*). "George Spelvin" is used to conceal a performer's real name, perhaps because he is appearing in more than one role. If the character in the play dies, "George X. Spelvin" sometimes is used. The female equivalent is "Georgia or Georgiana Spelvin." British programmes (British spelling) use the name "Walter Plinge" for the same purposes. In film, "Alan Smithee" is a fictitious name of a director.

"Macbeth" means a histrionic performance by an actress. Mention of this Shakespeare play by name within a theater is considered bad luck by performers.

"Fifteen minutes!" is a warning call to performers shouted fifteen minutes before the performance is to start. "Five minutes, please!" is the traditional call indicating that five minutes remain until the curtain rises at the start of an act.

An "11 o'clock number" is a rousing finale in a musical show, from the days when Broadway shows started at 8:30 p.m. and ended around 11 p.m. Curtain time now is usually 8 p.m., so shows generally end earlier, but the phrase still is used.

In ancient Greek drama, the "chorus" was a group of performers who commented on the action. Now the *chorus* is a group of dancers and/or singers ("chorus boys" and "chorus girls"), who often perform in a "chorus line." The "chorus" also is the part of a musical composition scored for this group and also the refrain (following the verse, often repeated) of a song.

The *dance director*, who supervises the dancers, may also be a "choreographer" (creator) and "dance arranger." The "dance count" is the tempo, counted out emphatically, such as "one, two, three, FOUR!"

"Pick it up" is a cue or instruction to a performer or musician to speed it up or to start from a specific point in the script or score. To "pick up a light" is to increase the intensity of illumination. To "pick up a cue" is to speak in response to a *cue* (a signal in words or action that initiates action or dialogue). "Exact timing" is on "cue." To "pick up a scene" is to enliven the action. "Exit cue" is the dialogue line or action that signals a performer to begin the "exit line" or "exit action," or to exit without lines. The opposite direction is "enter."

Many theatrical terms come from *vaudeville*, a type of entertainment popular in theaters in the first half of the twentieth century and before, which consisted of singers, dancers, comedians, and other performers ("vaudevillians"). It was also called a "variety show." In vaudeville, a comic sketch often ended with a "blackout"—a sudden, complete darkening—also used in a play, film, or other work to indicate the passage of time or the end of a scene.

Burlesque is any broadly comic or satirical imitation, such as a play or other writing that is a caricature. It's used as a noun, adjective, or verb and originates from the French, which is derived from the Italian *burlesco*, a jest. The slang spelling is "burlesk." In the United States in the first half of the twentieth century, "burlesque" featured low comedy by a "burlesque comedian" and women dancers who undressed, primarily at "burlesque theaters." A "burlesque queen" was a leading stripper, renowned for her striptease act.

Here are a few other colorful theatrical terms. To "blow a line" is to forget a line or speak dialogue incorrectly. To "bury the show" is to put away all scenery, costumes, and other items after the show closes (the final performance). "Save the food" is an instruction to fake an action during a rehearsal, such as not to eat the food. "Save (or kill) the lights" is an instruction to turn off the lights. A "slow clap" is slow, rhythmic applause by an audience, such as to express impatience before a tardy performance. On the other hand (excuse the pun), a "standing ovation" is prolonged applause from an audience that rises from its seats. Sometimes the audience, particularly at an opera, expresses its approval by shouting "Bravo!" The Italian word means bold. A *diva* is a very popular female singer, particularly in opera. An Italian word for goddess, it now also describes an admired or glamorous woman, and, in a negative sense, a haughty one.

A matinee (pronounced mah-tuh-NAY) is an afternoon performance. The French-derived expression "matinee idol" is an old-fashioned term for a handsome stage actor who is popular with women. More women than men attend Wednesday matinees. A typical Broadway show puts on eight performances a week, Tuesday to Saturday evenings, and lower-priced matinees on Wednesday, Saturday, and Sunday afternoons.

Incidentally, a "stock character" is a familiar fictional role, typical of a group or class of people. A "stock performer" plays "stock parts" that are stereotypical or familiar roles.

Deus ex machina is an unconvincing, forced, improbable, or contrived character or event brought into the plot of a play or other literary form to extricate a hero in trouble or provide a trick resolution. Pronounced DAY-us-eks-MAH-kee-nuh, the Latin phrase means "god from a machine." It's based on ancient Greek and Roman plays, in which a deity was lowered onto the stage by a machine.

Another popular foreign term is *commedia dell'arte*, a type of Italian comedy developed in the sixteenth through eighteenth centuries, employing a stereotyped plot, improvised dialogue, and stock characters such as Pantaloon, Harlequin, and Columbine. It's from the Italian for comedy of art. The term is also used to denote professional comedy.

Dramatis personae refers to the characters in a play or a list of characters, usually printed at the beginning of the text, with their relationships or other identification. It's Latin for drama persons.

"Playing weeks" is a measurement of activity of a theatrical show or of an entire theatrical area. It's the total number of weeks that a theater, or group of theaters (such as all Broadway theaters), were in operation (playing) during a season or year.

A *plot* is the outline of the action or story of a drama or narrative. The word is used in books, film, television, and other media. A *scenario* is a synopsis or outline of the plot of a play, film, or other work. It's from the Italian, *scena*, or scene. A "scenarist" is more commonly used in film to indicate a writer of screenplays. "Worst case scenario" is imagining the most terrible thing that can happen in a situation.

A classy word is *dramaturgy*, the art of writing and/or producing plays. Some theatrical professors call themselves "dramaturges" or "dramaturgists," and some theatrical writers also like this word in such forms as "dramaturgic," "dramaturgical," and "dramaturgically."

Time for an *intermission*, an interval between periods of activity, such as between acts of a play or other work. In the United Kingdom, it's called an "interval act wait." The warning to the audience that the intermission is about to end is the "intermission bell." A curtain dropped during the intermission is called the "intermission drop" or "act drop."

An "intermission crasher" is a person who enters a theater without an admission ticket during the intermission of a play or other work. An "intermission dropout" is the opposite: a member of the audience who does not return after a between-the-acts intermission of a show.

Be patient; we almost have reached the final curtain. *Miking* is the setup and arranging of microphones, such as their placement on a stage or on performers. The performers are "miked" when their microphones are attached, but "overmiked" when the amplification is too loud. "Close miking" (or "tight miking") is the placement of a microphone close to the sound source; the opposite is "loose miking" (or "light miking").

Upstage is the rear of a stage, away from the audience. As a verb, to "upstage" means to lessen the effect of another performer by calling attention to oneself, such as by moving to the rear of the stage so that the performer at the front (who is upstaged) may have to turn toward the rear, away from the audience. The opposite area is called *downstage*, the front of the stage or toward the audience.

A *standby* is a performer who is paid to be available to go onstage in place of an ailing or unavailable performer, and is not necessarily an "understudy," a member of the cast who can be a substitute for another performer.

To *chalk off* is to mark (with chalk, or more generally, tape) positions on the stage floor for use as reference by the performers. The term also is used in film and television. "Chalking off" a scene is called "blocking a scene," to indicate areas for the performers or camera to work in.

A *fat part* in a play is desirable and does not require

heaviness in weight or character. A *heavy* is a serious dramatic role, particularly the villain.

A *dutchman* is a device to conceal a defect, gap, or poor workmanship. Remember the Dutch boy with his finger in the hole in the dike? In a theater, a *dutchman* is a strip of muslin or other cloth about five inches wide, glued or affixed to link two pieces of scenery to cover the juncture.

A *straight play* is a drama, not a comedy, musical, or musical comedy, and features straight roles or parts. In recent years, one of the meanings of straight is "heterosexual," but that's not the meaning here. A "straight line" is a feeder line spoken by a "straight man" to a comedian.

To be *in play* is to be in action, as the "fall theatrical season is in play." It's also a sports term (the "ball is in play") or a financial term (a "stock is in play" when there are rumors of a merger or acquisition).

A *pun* is a "play on words." To "play against type" is for a performer to portray a role different from his or her usual character.

Actors' Equity Association (the apostrophe comes after the *s*) is an AFL-CIO union of professional actors and actresses. Members are issued Equity cards and producers hire an Equity cast in accordance with the Equity scale (the Equity pay schedule) and Equity regulations.

Well, here's my exit line. I hope that I have helped you bridge the *fourth wall*, an imaginary barrier between the stage and the audience.

THE WALL STREET JOURNAL:
JOURNALESE

STAFFERS at every publication use the slang terms of printers and journalists, and freelance writers soon become familiar with the favorite abbreviations and jargon of their editors. Since almost everyone is familiar with *The Wall Street Journal* (abbreviated WSJ), one of the most important newspapers in the United States and around the globe, it will be fun to learn about the colorful language used by *Journal* staffers—and helpful, too, since *Journal* jargon now crops up at many other publications.

For example, *pantsfolder* means a how-to-feature, such as, "How to Fold Your Pants in Luggage." *Frisky furniture* is a dull article that was made a bit more sprightly with the addition of anecdotes and pithy quotations.

DBI is the *Journal* description of "dull but important" articles. The term *duck*—to denote a straightforward article or item—was originated by a Detroit bureau reporter who complained that writing routine news was "like being nibbled to death by ducks" (ducks have no teeth, you see, so it would mean a slow, boring death), an expression sometimes heard in other businesses as well.

A *Roche box* is a boxed item within an article that refers the reader to one or more related articles; named after Kevin Roche (b. 1953), a *Journal* editor who devised the computer codes to set up the insert.

Another term originated at the WSJ and now used elsewhere is *curtainraiser* or *walkup*, an article that is published before an anticipated event.

The *to-be-sure graf* is a paragraph in an article that indicates exceptions to the preceding generalizations, sometimes beginning with, "To be sure." To avoid excessive use of this phrase, the paragraph sometimes starts with, "However," "Of course," "Meanwhile," or other transition. Don't confuse it with the *nut graf*, which has the essential information and the theme or core (the nut or kernel) of the article.

Jargon that is limited to the WSJ includes *rando*, an editorial, from the page heading, "Review and Outlook," and *hedcut*, a drawing (or cut) of a person's head. The *Journal* does not use photographs, and, since 1979, "pen-and-ink drawings," or "ink dot art," of people in the news have become the unique signature of the newspaper. No, they are not the dots used by computer printers, nor those created by computer software. A staff of talented artists laboriously create the stippled drawings with pen and ink, usually working from photographs. The original 3 x 5 inch drawings are reduced to the desired size, usually to fit within a single column.

The *restore list* includes pending articles, usually features that previously were downgraded in priority and now are returned to active status. .

A *secondary line* or group of lines in a multiline headline is called a "deck" or "drophead," a standard format used at the *Journal*. Though each "deck" (or headline unit) can be in the same size type, most journalists use the word "deck" for lines that are subsequent to the primary headline. A "deck head" is a heading with two or more groups of type. A "decker" has two or more decks, such as a "double-decker" or "triple-decker."

Now that we've cleared the decks, take a look at the *Journal*'s most popular feature, the article that appears in column four of page one. The subject of this magazine-style article can be just about anything, though it's often on the lighter side. The article usually has an "A-hed," a three-line major headline and a three-line minor headline. Notice that the headlines are surrounded on each side by vertical ruled lines separated by a centered row of three asterisks. Thus, the ruled lines and the asterisks somewhat resemble a square capital A. At *The New York*

Times, the "A-head" means a one-column headline, with large-size type, above major articles on page one.

Have I lost you? *MEGO* is what the *Journal* calls dull or confusing writing—an acronym for, "My eyes glaze over." The phrase would never be used to describe the delightful feature that sometimes appears on page one of the second section of the *Journal*. Since it's an isolated article, it's called an "orphan," and often is whimsical, personal, or offbeat. The unconventional orphan headlines may have periods, parentheses, or other teasing stoppers.

An "orphan" also is an element of type, such as a word or a line, leading into a larger block of type and is intentionally left by itself at the end of a page or column. It's sometimes erroneously called a "widow," which is less than half of a typeset line at the end of a paragraph. Some editors believe that this white space is undesirable, while other editors appreciate it. "Kill the widow" is a proofreader's term meaning to eliminate the line or fill it.

In 2005, the *Journal* added a Saturday edition, which competes with Friday's *USA Today* and Saturday's *New York Times*, and converted its European and Asian editions from broadsheets to tabloids, in emulation of the major daily newspapers in London and elsewhere that converted to tabloids during the last few years.

The Wall Street Journal is headquartered at 200 Liberty Street in lower Manhattan, near Wall Street. The etymology of *journal* is the Old French (before the fifteenth century) *jurnal*, a daily log or book with the times of prayers. At the WSJ, at least, they pray for a bull market.

WHATCHAMACALLIT: GIBBERISH AND THINGAMAJIGS

HOW many times have you gone into Home Depot or Ace Hardware and asked for a *thingamajig*? You probably know, of course, that a "doohickey," "gizmo," "thingamajig," "thingamabob," or "widget" is slang for any device, particularly a gadget, with a name that is not known or perhaps simply forgotten—that is, a *whatchamacallit*. Here are some media whatchamacallits.

The chapter on journalism noted that a full-size newspaper is called a "broadsheet"—sometimes mistakenly called a *broadside*, a large sheet of paper, generally printed on one side and folded to a smaller size, often used as a direct-mail piece or for door-to-door distribution. A "broadside" is often greater in width than height. In fact, a *broadside page* is a page in a publication designed to be read sideways, usually to accommodate wide tables or illustrations. A "broadside" is also a lighting unit that illuminates a large area.

You constantly see in e-mail addresses the symbol @, the letter *a* with a circle around it, called a *commercial a* or an *at sign*, found on your keyboard above the number 2. It was used well before e-mail, especially to mean "each," as in pricing per unit. Also frequently seen in e-mails is the *chevron*, a quotation bracket often used to set off addresses or different parts of an e-mail sent at different times: < and > or << and >>.

Designers and editors often use garbled, meaningless type, called *Greek type*, to fill a space before the actual text is available for insertion. To "Greek" means to produce such bogus lettering. In the United Kingdom, it's called "Latin type." *Jabberwocky* means gibberish type, except that the meaningless syllables may be understood. The term comes from Lewis Carroll (1832–98), the English mathematician who wrote *Through the Looking-Glass* (1871), in which Alice discovers a poem called *Jabberwocky*, the words of which are printed backward so that they must be read in a mirror.

"Gibberish," obscure or meaningless talk, is more often called *mumbo jumbo*, the term probably originating from an eighteenth-century African dialect in which *jumby* was a ghost or an evil spirit.

In a similar vein, the everyday word *bunk* is short for "buncombe" or "bunkum," meaning false, insincere, and nonsensical speech or writing. The origin is from Buncombe County in North Carolina, represented in Congress from 1819 to 1821 by Felix Walker (1753–1828), who made long-winded speeches "for Buncombe."

Gobbledygook means unclear, confusing language, often redundant and pseudotechnical. The word was coined in the thirties by Maury Maverick (1895–1954), a Texas congressman, who was quoted in *The New York Times Magazine* on May 21, 1944: "Perhaps I was thinking of the old bearded turkey gobbler back in Texas who was always gobbledy-gobbling and strutting with ludicrous pomposity. At the end of this gobble there was a sort of gook."

The word *maverick*, though, meaning an unbranded stray animal or independent person, precedes Congressman Maverick and probably comes from his grandfather, rancher Samuel A. Maverick (1803–70).

A *dingbat*, or "flubdub," is decorative type used as a box around an article, to separate portions of text, or for other purposes. It can be a series of long and short dashes, asterisks, and other conventional symbols, and also original art. Asterisks are often used to replace letters within a vulgar word. A "ding letter," however, is a rejection, as from a publisher to an author. Another meaning of *ding* is a blow. The etymology of *dingbat* probably is from *ding*, to strike, and from an English word in the twelfth to sixteenth centuries, *bakke*, or to behave eccentrically.

Here now is a handy collection of "whatchamacallit" words about words. You may know that *onomatopoeia* is a word or words that echo, imitate, or resemble the sounds they describe. My favorites include such words as *bang*, *blast*, *buzz*, *hiss*, *rustle*, *sizzle*, *slush*, *tinkle*, and *whisper*. The word *onomatopoeia*, common in spelling contests, has a Greek origin that means word making.

A *disfluency* is a sound or words that are used by many speakers as bridges or fillers, such as "oh," "uh," "um," and which interrupt the smooth flow (fluency).

A delightful whatchamacallit word is *epenthesis*, meaning a change in the pronunciation of a word, in which a sound or syllable is accidentally or incorrectly inserted. Common examples include "athlete," often mispronounced ATH-a-leet; and "nuclear," now commonly mispronounced NEW-kyuh-luhr.

A *tmesis* is the intentional separation of the syllables of a word and the splicing in of another word, usually an expletive, as in "unbe-damn-lievable." (In popular speech, the often-inserted expletive is the F-word!) Pronounced as tuh-MEE-sus, from the Greek, meaning act of cutting.

A *palindrome* is a word, phrase, sentence, or verse that reads the same backward as forward. An example is "Name no one man." The Greek *palindromus* means running back again.

You undoubtedly have heard or read a *paralipsis*, though you may not know the word. It's a rhetorical device in which the speaker or writer claims to deny or omit a point, while in the process of mentioning it. Examples include, "I won't call my opponent a liar, but…" and, "Far be it for me to bring up the subject, but…"

A *retronym* is a new name used to update an old thing. It was coined by columnist William Safire (b. 1929) of *The New York Times*, to describe such terms as

THE SKINNY ABOUT…MEDIA LINGO

"acoustic guitar" in contrast to the newer invention, "electric guitar." Another Safire coinage is *mondegreen*, words that are heard incorrectly and repeated that way. Many of us do this with the words of popular songs or jingles. The origin is a Scottish folksong, *The Bonny Earl of Murray*, which included the phrase "laid him on the green," misheard and sung as "Lady Mondegreen."

A *heteronym,* or *homograph*, is a word with the same spelling as another word, but with a different meaning and pronunciation. For example, "tear" is a drop of water (pronounced TEER) and, as a verb, "tear" can mean to rip (pronounced TARE).

Reduplicate, to double or repeat, has a special meaning in linguistics—to form a new word by doubling a word or base syllable (a "kernel"). Examples include "boo-boo" and "tom-tom" (kernels repeated without change), "hocus-pocus" (kernel repeated with a change of initial consonant), and "chit-chat" and "mish-mash" (kernel repeated with a change of internal vowel). Reduplicative compounds in the media include "boob tube," "chalk talk," "chiller-diller," "kid-vid," "peewee," and "walkie-talkie." You can invent others.

A *homonym* is a word pronounced in the same way as another word, but with a different meaning and often with a slightly different spelling. Common examples (often confused with one another) include "bare" and "bear"; "here" and "hear"; "its" and "it's"; and "there," "their," and "they're."

It seems appropriate to end this chapter with *page-turner*. Among its meanings are an arrow, a sketch of a hand or index finger, or other notation at the bottom of a page of a magazine or other publication, indicating that the article is continued.

Concertgoers know that a "page-turner" is someone who sits next to a piano soloist, turning the pages of sheet music. Finally, a "page-turner" is a book, script, or other work so interesting the reader cannot put it down, impelled to turn the page and read on.

INDEX